The Revolution Falters
The Left in Philippine Politics after 1986

Patricio N. Abinales, Editor

The Revolution Falters
The Left in Philippine Politics after 1986

SOUTHEAST ASIA PROGRAM PUBLICATIONS
Southeast Asia Program
Cornell University
Ithaca, New York
1996

Cornell Southeast Asia Program Publications
640 Stewart Avenue, Ithaca, NY 14850-3857

Southeast Asia Program Series Number 15

Printed in the United States of America

ISBN 0-87727-132-1

CONTENTS

Preface   7

Contemporary Philippine Leftist Politics in Historical Perspective   9
     Benedict J. Tria Kerkvliet

From Vanguard to Rearguard: The Theoretical Roots of the Crisis of the
Communist Party of the Philippines   28
     Kathleen Weekley

Of Motorcades and Masses: Mobilization and Innovation in Philippine
Protest   60
     Vincent G. Boudreau

Beyond Boycott: The Philippine Left and Electoral Politics After 1986   83
     Eva-Lotta E. Hedman

Popular Support for the Revolutionary Movement CPP-NPA: Experiences in
a Hacienda in Negros Occidental, 1978–1995   110
     Rosanne Rutten

When a Revolution Devours its Children Before Victory:
Operasyon Kampanyang Ahos and the Tragedy of Mindanao Communism   154
     Patricio N. Abinales

Acronyms - Reference   180

PREFACE

This collection is the product of a panel, a fax message, and e-mail. Four of the papers (by Abinales, Boudreau, Hedman, and Weekley) were originally presented at a panel on the Philippine Left organized by Vincent Boudreau and Patricio Abinales for the 1994 Association for Asian Studies General Meeting at Boston. Benedict Kerkvliet's was a written comment sent from Australia on three (Abinales, Boudreau, and Weekley) of the panel's papers, which he later on expanded into the collection's introductory essay. Finally, e-mail acquaintance with Rosanne Rutten eventually led to her contributing her piece on Negros.

The papers represent the first attempt ever to bring together in one collection the works of scholars specializing or interested on the Philippine Left and the Communist Party of the Philippines (CPP). They are notable not only for their particular topics, but also for the diversity of their authorship: two Americans, an Australian, a Filipino, a Dutch, and a Swede. Their background as well as their particular area focus (Filipino Marxist theorizing, peasant politics, elections, urban social movements, and purges and executions) has helped bring about a more nuanced examination of the collection's main topic: understanding the causes behind the current crisis of the Philippine Left. All begin with the 1986 "boycott debacle" of the CPP and proceed to elaborate on the problem based on their specific areas of interest.

The portrait that these papers have drawn shows a Left that has made an enduring mark on Philippine society. Revived mainly by students and intellectuals in the late 1960s, the Left was able to grow despite adverse conditions after Ferdinand Marcos declared martial law. Its forces rapidly spread all over the Philippines, making its presence felt as rural guerrillas, union and community organizers, students and even Church activists. In the last years of martial law, it had become so prominent a political force, that most Filipinos regarded the polarizing politics of the moment as inevitably climaxing in an epic face-to-face confrontation between dictatorship and revolution. This never happened. Instead, "cacique" democracy" supplanted the dictatorship and marginalized the revolution.

Why this scenario never transpired has generated an intense debate within Left circles and spurred renewed scholarly interest on Philippine radical politics outside of the Philippines.[1] The essays in this collection constitute perhaps the second wave

---

[1] Prior to 1986, Filipino activists and academics had already written extensively on the Left. See, Armando S. Malay, "The `Legal' vs. the `Illegal': Problems in CPP-ML Strategy and Tactics", *Asian Studies*, 20 (April-August 1982); Francisco S. Nemenzo, "Rectification Process in the Philippine Communist Movement," in Lim Joo-Jock ed., *Armed Communist Movements in Southeast Asia* (Singapore: Institute for Southeast Asian Studies, 1984); *Marxism in the Philippines: Marx Centennial Lectures* (Quezon City: Third World Studies Center, University of the Philippines, 1984). These continued after 1986, and some of these later works are cited in the essays. Among the post-1986 studies by non-Filipinos, the following are the more important: Gareth Porter, *The Politics of Counterinsurgency in the Philippines: Military and Political Options*, Occasional Paper No. 9 (Honolulu: Center for Philippine Studies, University of Hawaii., 1987); Gareth Porter, "Philippine Communism after Marcos," *Problems of Communism* 36, 5 (1987); *Marxism in the Philippines*, Second Series (Quezon City: Third World Studies Center, University of the Philippines, 1988); Gareth Porter, "Strategic Debates and

of studies that try to probe further on the issues elaborated by earlier works and explore previously unstudied areas of Left-wing politics. The hope of the authors of this collection is that it would bring about more interest to study what may be the last of the left-wing movements in Southeast Asia.

Authors in this volume have used their own discretion in choosing when to capitalize names, such as "the Left," or "the Party," which describe broad-based political organizations.

Each of the authors has thanked individuals and institutions who have helped them in the writing of their respective essays. I wish to thank Benedict Tria Kerkvliet for taking time out of a busy schedule to write a response to the AAS papers, and then expanding this commentary into a full piece for this collection. In this preface, all of us express a collective gratitude to the Cornell Southeast Asia Program, especially its Editorial Board, and to Deborah Homsher, the Program's Publications Editor, for making this anthology possible.

We dedicate this book to Audrey Kahin, Dolina Millar, Roberta Ludgate, Hazel Prentice, and Saya Shiraishi.

Patricio N. Abinales
Ithaca, New York
February 1996

Dilemmas in the Philippine Communist Movement," *Pilipinas* 13 (Fall 1989); Gregg R. Jones, *Red Revolution: Inside the Philippine Guerrilla Movement* (Boulder: Westview Press, 1989); and Walden Bello, Crisis of the Philippine Progressive Movement: A Preliminary Investigation," *Kasarinlan: Philippine Journal of Third World Studies* 8, 1 (1992).

CONTEMPORARY PHILIPPINE LEFTIST POLITICS IN HISTORICAL PERSPECTIVE

Benedict J. Tria Kerkvliet

BACKGROUND

During the late 1970s and much of the 1980s, political winds in the Philippines favored the acceleration of the New People's Army (NPA) and the Communist Party of the Philippines (CPP). Beginning in the late 1960s with a tiny number of members and even fewer rifles, the party and the guerrilla army had grown to become political and military forces in the nation then burdened by the Marcos regime and immense economic and political problems associated with that rule. By the mid 1980s the NPA had between twenty and twenty-four thousand members and controlled an estimated 20 percent of the country's villages and urban neighborhoods.[1]

But by the early 1990s, the underground movement's fortunes had declined sharply. The NPA's "mass base" had diminished to 3 percent of the country's villages and neighborhoods, according to figures cited in Rosanne Rutten's chapter of this book, and the number of armed NPA had dropped to an estimated 10,600. Moreover, serious disagreements within the CPP and NPA sharply divided many members and supporters, while others threw up their hands in disgust over what often seemed to them like petty bickering and name calling. Reverberations of splits within armed movement underground contributed to divisions and splintering within numerous leftist organizations above ground. For instance, two of the nation's largest peasant and labor organizations—the KMP (Kilusang Magbubukid ng Pilipinas) and KMU (Kilusang Mayo Uno)—have broken into pieces for reasons that include deep divisions over each organization's relationship to the CPP and NPA and to the various factions there. CPAR (Congress for People's Agrarian Reform), one of the country's largest and most successful coalitions of organizations pressing for land redistribution and other agrarian changes, was completely dissolved in 1993 due primarily to irresolvable disagreements over strategies, tactics, and other matters provoked to a considerable extent by divisions within the CPP and NPA.

Most of the major disputed matters in the CPP and NPA can be clustered around three issues.[2] The first concerns tactics, strategies, and objectives of leftist politics,

---

[1] See figures in the early pages of Rosanne Rutten's chapter, this book, and in US Senate, 98th Congress, Committee on Foreign Relations. "The Situation in the Philippines" (S.Prt. 98–237) (Washington: Government Printing Office, October 1984), pp. 24–25.

[2] I am distilling these from conversations with several informed people in the Philippines during December 1993 and January 1994, and a number of articles and documents [especially those in *Malalimang Muling Pagsusuri at Pagpapanibagong-siglar* [Profound Re-examination and Revitalization], n.p. (1993 ?). The volume is a collection of documents from within the CPP

particularly those involved in armed struggle. The "reaffirmists," most notably Jose Maria Sison (also known as Amado Guerrero and Armando Liwanag) and other CPP officials close to him, insist on reaffirming the centrality of protracted armed struggle by guerrilla forces. They criticize attempts by some CPP leaders in the 1980s to establish regular armed forces to fight conventional warfare against government troops, and they chastise those who argue that a sudden mass insurrection can be a short cut to capturing state power. The "rejectionists" include people who adopt several positions, not necessarily in agreement with each other except insofar as they assert that conditions in the country now render protracted guerrilla warfare, at least by itself, no longer appropriate. One prominent position here, to which not all "rejectionists" subscribe, is that "parliamentary" and other "legal" struggle should be emphasized as a supplement to underground, armed struggle. Some go further, saying legal methods should now totally replace violent ones. Entwined with this debate over methods are disputes about how the CPP should relate to mass organizations on the left—should it attempt to control them or to cooperate with them, working in partnership with organizations that retain their own autonomy? These issues are often bound up in debates about goals—the kind of politics, economy, and society being fought for—and about how to balance between settling for reforms that are within reach and insisting on revolutionary change, which lies far beyond the horizon.

A second contentious issue has to do with the relative importance of rural versus urban areas as main arenas for mobilizing support for the CPP and NPA, attacking government forces, and struggling for power. The "reaffirmists" argue that the countryside should remain the primary locus of struggle. Critics argue for greater attention to urban areas, not necessarily to the exclusion of the peasantry and other rural people, but give more emphasis to workers, squatters, and other exploited people in the cities. To some extent, these differences are connected to contending analyses of the nature of Philippine society and economy. "Reaffirmists" insist that the Philippines remains primarily a semi-feudal and semi-colonial rural political economy; hence in order for the revolution to win, it must have the support of the peasantry. "Rejectionists" argue that this analysis is far too simplistic because the country has changed significantly during the last half of this century. This matter is also connected to issues of strategy and tactics because, as Eva-Lotta Hedman points out in her chapter in this book, the countryside is associated with protracted armed struggle, while the urban areas are associated with parliamentary, legal forms of struggle.

The third issue concerns governance and decision making within the CPP and NPA. Broadly speaking, the "reaffirmist" position stresses the principles of "democratic centralism," with emphasis on "centralism" and top-down discipline. Critics, again holding diverse views, generally put more emphasis on "democracy"; they favor fuller discussion and debate, and would reserve more room for input from local cadre in NPA and CPP policy making. This area of contention often includes criticisms and counter-criticisms about how policies were made and implemented in the past, about leadership styles and personalities, and about hundreds of details

[Communist Party of the Philippines] and NPA [New People's Army]. Colloquially it is referred to as the "red book" and is said to be a publication of a group of CPP members. See also Joel Rocamora, *Breaking Through: The Struggle within the Communist Party of the Philippines* (Metro Manila: Anvil Publishers, 1994) and chapters in this book.

concerning who did what, when, and to whom, debates that have become extremely cantankerous.

In this chapter, I want to argue, first, that these are not new issues. Aspects of all three have been lurking within the CPP and NPA for some time. Moreover, they are reminiscent of debates in earlier eras of communist party and underground leftist struggles in the Philippines. Next, I will outline several reasons for the debates and divisions, again drawing parallels between the recent and earlier ones. I will end by pondering the future of the "left," suggesting that it is brighter than many think.

CURRENT DEBATES COMPARED TO PAST ONES: THE 1970S TO EARLY 1980S WITHIN THE CPP AND NPA

Numerous CPP documents, personal accounts by party members, and academic analyses have been published about present disputes within the underground left, much of it footnoted in the next five chapters, which are themselves substantial contributions to our understanding of the splits and issues. Disputes became apparent after the 1986 presidential election, which the central leadership of the CPP and NPA instructed all followers to boycott. Many party members, guerrillas, and sympathizers with the armed struggle, however, ignored that directive, throwing themselves into the campaign against Ferdinand Marcos and/or for Corazon Aquino. From then into the 1990s, divisions became more vociferous and increasingly public, to the point that charges and counter-charges among contending sides were regularly exchanged in Manila's daily newspapers. Meanwhile, communist party-dominated states in Eastern Europe and the Soviet Union were collapsing, giving Filipino leftists even more reason to reconsider their positions and the future of their movement. In this context we are inclined to think, understandably, that the disagreements within the CPP and NPA are new, particularly since primary materials and analyses about what was happening within the CPP and NPA prior to the 1986 election are scarce. There are, certainly, unique features to the debates and reasons for them. At the same time, what is happening now in the underground left is not unprecedented.

One earlier revealing event about which we do have some knowledge is the 1978 election for the interim Batasang Pambansa (National Assembly). Again, the official position of CPP was boycott on the grounds that the election was a total sham, the Marcos government (which still ruled as a martial law regime) would make sure that only its candidates would win, and parliamentary struggle in general was a waste, sapping scarce resources needed for the armed struggle. But in Metro Manila, leaders and members of the CPP's Manila-Rizal committee had already plunged into the electoral campaign, helping groups opposed to the Marcos regime to forge alliances and support opposition candidates, among them Benigno Aquino who campaigned from prison, where he had been under military arrest since 1972. Even after being instructed by the CPP national leadership to desist, cadres in Metro Manila continued to campaign for these candidates.

Analysts disagree about the significance of the 1978 election event for CPP internal politics. In her chapter of this book, Kathleen Weekley says those disagreements were over tactics, not over the strategy of protracted guerrilla warfare. Other analysts, though, argue that the local Manila-Rizal committee of the CPP took exception to the central leaders' overriding emphasis on rural resistance and their dismissal of urban struggle, and also took exception when the central leaders dismissed the committee's argument for coalescing with others who opposed Marcos and martial law.[3] An account about Manila-Rizal committee members in the thick of the debate is unclear on this matter but does suggest that they believed the party's central leaders were too dogmatic in their insistence on armed struggle as the only legitimate political activity to advance the leftist movement.[4] Also at issue was how decisions should be made within the party. Manila-Rizal committee leaders argued that they were in a better position than were the central leaders to judge local circumstances and decide how best to respond.

One can only speculate about what might have popped out of these disputes had some of those 1978 candidates supported by Manila-Rizal cadres actually won the count or had there been a more sustained public demonstration against the fraudulent results than actually occurred, forcing the regime to make concessions. Quite likely the internal debate would have become more heated and focused more clearly on tactics and strategy as well as governance. That is, the difference between 1978 and 1986 may not be determined by measuring how far activists were prepared to take the debate in each case, but may instead have to do with the circumstances in which the debate occurred.

Weekley's larger main argument is that, apart from that 1978 event, debate did not occur within the CPP and NPA. The structure and political culture of the CPP "discouraged any substantial exchange of ideas beyond the core leadership and encouraged a . . . deference to the wisdom of the leadership."[5] One can readily imagine that those conditions did indeed stifle much discussion and debate, especially between low level cadres and highly ranked ones. Another likely contributing condition was fear of running afoul of top party authorities who could impose stiff punishments, including death. Nevertheless, might there have been more ferment and discord than Weekley allows? Granted, outright confrontational disagreements were unlikely to come to the surface. But that does not preclude the possibility, even likelihood, of considerable dissent beneath it.

Hierarchical organizations and other social situations characterized by considerable power differences do discourage questioning and dissent. Subordinate people typically do hold their tongues and avoid crossing the powers that be. But they might still do things discreetly that are at odds with their superiors, as research in the Philippines and elsewhere shows.[6] In hierarchical institutions, such behavior need not necessarily be aimed at trying to subvert the entire enterprise; the purpose could instead be to alter it. Either way, often the result is a considerable difference between what "leaders" say and what "followers" do.

The splits that have recently surfaced probably have longer histories and are far more complicated than is yet known. We are now seeing contested truths, lessons,

---

[3] Armando Malay, Jr., "The Dialectics of *Kaluwagan*: Echoes of a 1978 Debate," *Marxism in the Philippines: Second Series* (Diliman: Third World Studies Center, University of the Philippines, 1988), pp. 10–14. Also P. N. Abinales, "The Left and Other Forces: The Nature and Dynamics of Pre-1986 Coalition Politics," *Marxism in the Philippines: Second Series* (Diliman: Third World Studies Center, University of the Philippines, 1988), pp. 26–49.

[4] Benjamin Pimentel, Jr., *Edjop: The Unusual Journey of Edgar Jopson* (Quezon City: KEN Inc., 1989).

[5] Kathleen Weekley, following in this book, pp. 36, 58.

[6] Benedict J. Kerkvliet, *Everyday Politics in the Philippines: Class and Status Relations in a Central Luzon Village* (Berkeley: University of California Press, 1990), and James C. Scott, *Domination and the Arts of Resistance* (New Haven: Yale University Press, 1990).

and theories among Communist party leaders. Still to be heard from are the underground movement's average participants and supporters. Some evidence now available does indicate that much was being done and voiced locally that did not square with official policies and programs. A party organizer's account reveals that cadres in Mindanao frequently discussed and weighed alternative tactics and strategies—for example, strategies that determined how much emphasis to give urban, as opposed to rural, issues and organizing—and other fundamental issues.[7] In the early 1980s, the CPP top leadership instructed local activists to survey rural conditions in their areas. The results showed what many activists knew from experience: that class relations, modes of production, and other conditions were far more complicated than the party's official view of the country's political economy. For fear, however, of being openly at odds with official doctrine—especially since Jose Maria Sison and other party officials at the highest level had recently restated that the Philippines remained a semi-feudal society—subordinate party officials did not release the results of their studies.[8]

Passages in Weekley's chapter also suggest that CPP and NPA activists had long disagreed with important aspects of the party's official stance. Describing reactions of regional and sectoral cadres to the 1991 "Reaffirm" statement by Armando Liwanag [Sison], Weekley writes,

> . . . as [they] saw it, the author [Sison] had certainly not made any attempt to adjust the original strategic framework in light of lessons learned on the ground. . . . A common (and strongly made) criticism of the document (from those 'second-tier' cadres) was that it was simply unacceptable—and unrealistic—to 'reaffirm' the same 'basic principles' as had inspired Party leaders more than twenty years ago. Much readjusting, improvising, and filling in of detail had occurred since 1968, as movement activists responded to varied and changing political, economic, and cultural conditions."[9]

This suggests that lower level cadres were upset *precisely because* they had held for a considerable time contrary conclusions about the movement, what it should be doing, and how it should act. That they showed their dissent only when top leaders were disagreeing among themselves is not surprising. Subordinate people generally refrain from revealing their thoughts on delicate matters until they think the system is in disarray or their superiors are weakened and vulnerable.

Several studies have indicated that organizers in and around the country experimented with various methods and ideas as they worked to expand the movement. To an extent, this was in keeping with the "principle of self-reliance" that Sison told the dispersed guerrilla bands to follow.[10] But diversity grew to the point that the party's central leadership was unable to maintain sufficient control. A Communist Party document assessing the movement during the 1980s complains of ". . . widespread practice among leading Party committees in the regions and

---

[7] Anonymous, "Comments on the Current Polemics Within the Party," in *Malalimang Muling Pagsusuri*, pp. 155–57.

[8] Discussions in the Philippines with acquaintances close to the CPP and NPA, January 1994.

[9] Weekley, following in this book, p. 36.

[10] Amado Guerrero, "Specific Characteristics of People's War in the Philippines" (Oakland: International Association of Filipino Patriots, 1979), pp. 9–11.

territories" during the first half of the decade to exercise ". . . autonomy in 'particularizing' revolutionary strategy and tactics . . . without central guidance." At the same time, outside the CPP, there flourished "all sorts of theories and lines opposed to Marxism-Leninism and the line of protracted people's war—such as . . . Eurocommunist theories, social-democracy, and various types of insurrectionist lines or urban terrorism." These "were allowed to gain influence and sow confusion even within the Party." Moreover, many draft documents on strategies, policies and orientations that had not been finalized were, nevertheless, "going around in various forms" within the CPP, creating more disorder. In addition, the number of party members quadrupled between 1980-1985, yet training, education, and orientation for the new recruits were largely neglected, contributing to growing problems of discipline and diversity in thinking and action within the party.[11]

Party leaders in Mindanao were so encouraged by their successes with unorthodox forms of struggle, especially in *urban* areas, that they worked up enough confidence to actually propose to the top leaders in the early 1980s that the orthodox strategy be changed. Leaders from Mindanao, argues Patricio Abinales in his chapter of this book, "began lobbying for a modified *ruse de guerre* which would emphasize what they called a 'politico-military framework'" that would combine "'all forms of struggle' with the final confrontation not to be decided by just the rural guerrilla army's tempo of development." They wanted the CPP to do away with its "stubborn partiality to countryside resistance over urban political and armed mobilization."[12] Tensions grew between these Mindanao leaders and their superiors, particularly as the former continued to proceed with their own plans, foreshadowing the open splits that were to come later in the 1980s.

EARLIER MANIFESTATIONS OF SIMILAR DISAGREEMENTS

The underground left's situation in the late 1980s–early 1990s resonates with communist party and armed rebellion situations from earlier in this century. The closest parallel is what happened to the Huk rebellion in central Luzon and the country's first communist party, the PKP (Partido Komunista ng Pilipinas), during the 1950s.[13] The Huk rebellion, more formally known as the *Hukbong Mapagpalaya ng Bayan* or People's Liberation Army, which was in a sense the predecessor of the New People's Army (Bagong Hukbo ng Bayan), was at its peak strength in the 1949–1951 period, when it included 11,000–15,000 armed guerrillas. From 1952 to the mid-1950s, its armed strength and popular support dropped significantly. As with the CPP and NPA, an important precipitating reason for its decline was an election, or to be more precise, two elections—1951 for Congress and 1953 for both Congress and the Presidency. Like the CPP's central leadership in 1985-1986, the majority in the PKP's political bureau ordered all party and Huk members and supporters to boycott both elections, using much the same argument that the CPP leaders would use in 1985—

---

[11] Central Committee, CPP [Communist Party of the Philippines], "General Review of Significant Events and Decisions (1980–1991)," *Debate: Philippine Left Review* 7 (August 1993): 47, 59–60, 73. The document was originally dated July 1992.

[12] Patricio N. Abinales, following in this book, p. 169.

[13] Much of my discussion of the Huk rebellion and PKP [Partido Komunista ng Pilipinas] in the following paragraphs and later in this chapter is drawn from Benedict J. Kerkvliet, *The Huk Rebellion: A Study of Peasant Revolt in the Philippines* (Berkeley: University of California Press, 1977).

the elections would be frauds, parliamentary politics were useless, participation would sap resources better spent on the armed struggle, armed struggle was the only meaningful political activity, etc. But, as in 1985-1986, many Huk guerrillas and party members and their supporters ignored the party's official position. They saw possibilities for making the 1951 and 1953 elections more meaningful, honest, and democratic exercises than had been possible since 1946, when the country became independent of the United States. Elections in 1947 and 1949 still stand out as among the most fraudulent, vicious, and violent in Philippine history. Indeed, the horrors people saw and experienced during those occasions induced many witnesses to join or support the Huk rebellion.

The 1951 and 1953 elections turned out to be much more respectable than the boycotters had predicted, in large part because groups of citizens all around the country, including central Luzon, vigilantly monitored the campaigning, balloting, and the tallying and reporting of votes. The largest coalition for this purpose was NAMFREL, the same acronym as that famous 1986 watchdog organization, though with a slightly different name.[14] As in 1986, a major concern for millions of citizens in the 1951 and 1953 elections had to do with the integrity of the elections themselves. Another similarity to 1986 is that in 1953 a popular, unconventional (for that time) presidential candidate, Ramon Magsaysay, challenged a corrupt incumbent, Elipidio Quirino. And Magsaysay won. His victory was also a victory for "people power"— especially for those tens of thousands of citizens who had thrown themselves into the struggle to make the electoral process legitimate. In central Luzon, both outcomes— the relatively honest election and Magsaysay's significant victory—also raised the hopes of many rebels, PKP members, and their supporters that peaceful, unarmed struggle for tenancy reform, the right of workers and peasants to organize, and other objectives might be possible now. For many of these people, such reformist objectives, rather than radically revolutionary ones, had been central to their struggle anyway.

This whole situation plus other factors (discussed below) heightened discussion and debates that had been building since late 1951 within the underground Huk and PKP. Members argued whether to press ahead with armed struggle or attempt parliamentary struggle, and discussed how decisions on these matters ought to be made. Should the movement insist on overthrowing the system or settle for more tangible reforms that now, more than at any time since the rebellion began in 1946, seemed within reach? By 1953, debates around principles, strategies, and tactics had deteriorated into bickering and squabbling over petty matters, personality clashes, name calling, and attacks by innuendo, not unlike some of the feuds within the CPP and NPA in the 1990s. Huge numbers of members and supporters quit the rebellion; morale plummeted among those who remained.

Broadly speaking, two factions were apparent by 1954. The official position of the PKP—the one pressed by the party's Secretary-General, Jesus Lava—was to continue armed struggle as the principle means for waging a protracted revolution in the countryside, though possibly combined with some "legal tactics." This position rejected surrender and opposed negotiation with the Magsaysay government. The second, a minority position within the top PKP leadership, but probably the majority position among provincial and sub-provincial guerrilla and party leaders, favored

---

[14] The NAMFREL of the 1950s was the National Movement for Free Elections; the NAMFREL of the mid-1980s was the National Citizens Movement for Free Elections.

negotiation and endorsed peaceful, unarmed methods to achieve reforms meaningful for villagers. This cleavage between those who advocated protracted armed revolution, on the one side, and those who recommended parliamentary struggle and reform politics, on the other, obviously has parallels in the debates of the early 1990s. Gradually a third position emerged during the second half of the 1950s and into the 1960s—one which might be repeated in the second half of the 1990s and beyond the year 2000. Scattered armed groups dotted the landscape, still calling themselves or called by others "Huk," but not really intent on revolution or even rebellion. Some stole from the rich and gave to the poor; others stole and pillaged from rich and poor alike; some became involved in gambling, prostitution, and other racketeering. Some did all these. A few of the younger recruits into such "Huk" groups were among the first to join the New People's Army formed in 1969, including Commander Dante (Bernabe Buscayno).

Looking further back, one finds additional debates in and around the PKP which echo those heard in the 1990s. The official position of the party in the 1930s and 1940s on several issues was opposite its official position in the 1950s and the CPP's in the 1990s for reasons which there is no time to examine here. In other words, since the early years of the country's communist parties, leaders have frequently disagreed on several key issues and majority positions have flip-flopped on numerous occasions. From this history one can readily imagine the flip-flopping will continue.

The PKP, founded in November 1930, advocated legal, nonviolent methods for pursuing its radical, anti-imperialist objectives. At the first opportunity, in 1931, the PKP ran a slate of candidates for public office. Despite discrimination and harassment during that campaign and, in 1932, the outlawing of the party and banishment, by the government, of its principal spokesperson, Crisanto Evangelista, and other leaders to distant provinces, the official PKP position continued to favor parliamentary struggle. After being legalized again in 1938, the party resumed involvement in electoral politics. Evangelista, for instance, though he foresaw the day when the party might need to take up arms to defend itself and the proletariat it claimed to speak for, argued that such a time had not yet come by the dawn of the 1940. For this and other reasons, the PKP opposed uprisings that occurred in the countryside during the 1930s—Tayug, Tanggulan, Sakdalista, Theodoro Asedilo's revolt—and condemned the rebels as "anarchists," "revolutionary adventurers," and even claimed they were attempting to undermine the PKP. The party's leaders also opposed peasant groups that burned and destroyed the property of landlords and plantation owners who abused their tenants and workers. This stance favoring legal methods and opposing violence and armed rebellion was not, however, unanimously supported. The position was frequently debated, with some high-ranking leaders arguing against it.[15]

During the Japanese occupation (1942–45), the PKP endorsed guerrilla resistance. Afterward, however, from 1946 to 1948, it opposed and denounced the peasant-based Huk rebellion, then raging in central Luzon. But a minority of the members in the Central Committee and Political Bureau disagreed; some even defied the party's

---

[15] This paragraph is based in part on Crisanto Evangelista, *Communism and Capitalism: Before the P.I. Supreme Court* (Manila: n.p., 1932), pp. 10–14, 19, 23; Crisanto Evangelista, *Patnubay sa Kalayaan at Kapayapaan* (Manila: Kalayaan Publications, 1941), p. 2, part 1 and p. 127, part 2; Gregorio Santayana "Milestones in the History of the Philippine Communist Party," typescript, 1950, pp. 17–18, 21. Santayana is a pen name for Jose Lava. I wish to thank Melinda Tria Kerkvliet for her notes on Evangelista's *Patnubay sa Kalayaan at Kapayapaan*.

policy by joining the rebellion. By mid-1948, the minority position became the majority position, and the PKP officially endorsed armed struggle for the first time. By 1950, the party's top leaders went even further, concluding that conditions were such that "Rather than a long period of military struggle in which the enemy would be slowly bested through superior tactics and maneuver, our military strategic offensive must be relatively short and speedily victorious. It must, in other words, have an insurrectionary character." Seizure of the state would come by a combination of guerrilla, insurrectionary and even "regular warfare. . . ."[16] This policy is the precursor of the insurrectionary stance held by some CPP and NPA in the early and mid-1980s but opposed and severely criticized by Sison and other top CPP leaders, probably in part because Sison is on record for having denounced the PKP leadership's 1950 analysis and endorsement of insurrection.[17] By the late 1950s, leaders of a PKP which by that time had grown tiny and emaciated reverted to legal, parliamentary struggle, even cooperating in the 1970s with Marcos and his martial law rule. Meanwhile, Sison and others who had broken away from the PKP denounced their old party's position and its leaders and embraced instead protracted, guerrilla, rural-based armed struggle—the course which is now vigorously debated and sharply criticized by many inside and outside CPP.

Another contested issue among communist party leaders and others working with them has been the relative importance of workers and urban areas compared to peasants and the countryside. The priority for most PKP leaders in 1930s was the urban proletariat, not rural peasants, although some within the party's ruling councils strongly disagreed. This emphasis continued through much of the 1940s. Only in the face of the growing rural-based Huk rebellion did the PKP's official emphasis switch to the countryside, where it remained for years.

Little material is available pertaining to governance concerns or disagreements within the PKP. Whether lower ranking leaders and members criticized the decision-making process cannot be determined, although we know that significant policy positions set by the top leadership of the PKP were ignored, even defied, by other members. Besides those cited earlier, other examples of leadership policies which provoked some defiance were the PKP's "retreat for defense" policy during the guerrilla war against the Japanese occupation, the party's call in 1950 for the conversion of guerrilla units into regular army units, and the official position in 1953–54 against surrender and negotiation with the government. In each instance, numerous PKP members, including prominent leaders, disagreed and acted in ways at odds with the national pronouncements. Disciplinary measures against party members who disobeyed could not be made in many cases, especially when the defiance involved numerous members, but could involve demotion, suspension, expulsion, and sometimes death. It is impossible to estimate with much confidence how often rebellious party members were punished, but punishment appears to have been meted out more frequently in 1952–54 and in the early 1970s—periods when the PKP leaders were sharply divided over issues of strategies and tactics.[18]

---

[16] PKP Politburo, "Additional Political-Military Strategic Conceptions: Clarifications of the Enlarged PB Conference Resolution," circa 1950; PKP, "Military Strategy and Tactics," circa 1950.

[17] Guerrero, "Specific Characteristics of People's War in the Philippines," p. 70.

[18] Here I'm drawing mainly on Luis Taruc, *He Who Rides the Tiger* (London: Geoffrey Chapman, 1967), chapter 9, and Francisco Nemenzo, seminar on the "Decline and Resurgence

WHY THE SPLITS?

The central leadership's decision to boycott the 1986 presidential election is frequently cited as the prime reason for subsequent splits within and on the fringes of the CPP. The implication is that had the CPP leadership decided to encourage participation in the election campaign, the party would have avoided its present predicament.

While it is impossible to know what would have happened if the official policy had been different, I would guess that debates within the CPP and NPA today would not be significantly less divisive than they are now. Disagreements over rural versus urban organizing, over questions about governance within the CPP and NPA, and over questions involving strategic and tactical matters and reforms which may conflict with revolutionary objectives could be even more vexing than they are now because the party would have been divided over the extent to which it should collaborate with the Aquino government. It is possible to glimpse this scenario in conflicts which actually occurred as groups on the left, including some closely associated with the CPP and NPA, argued over how to relate to the Fidel Ramos government following the 1992 election.

In any event, as we know, the official CPP position was to boycott the 1986 election. Weekley, in her chapter of this book, summarizes several reasons for that decision. She contends that the party's history, culture, and commitment to protracted armed struggle significantly constrained the leaders, making it extremely unlikely for them to come to any other position on the matter, an argument also made by another scholar.[19] She is probably right as far as some leaders are concerned, including a majority of members in the key decision making body at the time, the Executive Committee of the CPP's Central Committee. But as Weekley documents, the vote within the Executive Committee was close—three for boycott, two against. Thus, not all leaders even at the top level were equally constrained by the party's past nor did they analyze events the same way. Similarly, many regional and sub-regional leaders debated the matter and came to opposite conclusions; subsequently some defied official policy set by the Executive Committee majority while others abided by it. Such differences in analysis and action regarding elections and other questions on strategies and tactics has long featured in the history of Philippine communist parties.[20]

---

of the Philippine Communist Movement," Department of Political and Social Change, Research School of Pacific Studies, Australian National University, November 13, 1984.

[19] Olle Tornquist, "Democracy and the Philippine Left," *Kasarinlan* 6, 1 and 2 (1990): 27.

[20] To elaborate briefly on one such split, in 1946 the majority in the PKP's ruling circle decided to get involved in the election that year, but insisted that the Democratic Alliance [DA]—the coalition party of the "left" at that time—also run a full slate of candidates, including candidates for president and vice-president. A minority within the PKP leadership disagreed with the decision to enact this requirement. So did a majority of the DA's leaders. Rejecting the PKP majority position, the DA leadership decided to endorse the Nacionalista Party's presidential and vice-presidential nominees, for they were convinced that this was a better way to prevent Manuel Roxas, the Liberal Party nominee, whom they regarded as a fascist and former collaborator with the Japanese occupation, from becoming president. Significantly, the PKP majority did not withdraw from the DA even though its position had been rejected. Kerkvliet, *The Huk Rebellion*, pp. 140–41.

Returning to the question of cause, no doubt the official boycott stance of the CPP contributed significantly to the blossoming of divisive debates. The majority of party national leaders and numerous leaders at lower levels fundamentally missed the importance of the 1986 election for a huge proportion of the population, including people in areas that the CPP and NPA claimed to control or greatly influence. That mistake coupled with the electoral defeat and consequent collapse of the Marcos regime and the success of a popular uprising in which the CPP, as an organization, exercised no leadership, greatly marginalized the party at a crucial juncture in the country's history. And all that, in turn, helped to empower many CPP and NPA members to voice doubts they had long harbored about the wisdom of the CPP's official position on a range of issues.

But there are other reasons for the splits besides the 1986 election miscalculations. Some are specific to the NPA and CPP armed struggle. Abinales's chapter in this book makes a compelling argument that the CPP and NPA campaign in 1985 in Mindanao against alleged "deep penetrating agents" from the Philippine armed forces divided and injured the party. That crusade quickly got out of hand. Within a few months nearly a thousand party members, NPA guerrillas, and supporters were killed by fellow revolutionaries. Only a few of the dead had been agents. Scared for their lives, thousands of other Mindanao activists quit the movement, reducing the number of party members and NPA guerrillas to a tiny fraction of what it had been before. On a smaller but nevertheless chilling scale, CPP and NPA members were also killing each other in southern and central Luzon.[21] After-the-fact recriminations and counter-recriminations about these sordid killings certainly contributed to the splintering of the party and NPA.

Additional reasons for the splintering are more general. One discovers them by examining a number of underground, armed guerrilla movements confronted by conditions similar to those experienced by the CPP and NPA from 1986 to the early 1990s. In this century, the Philippines has been home to numerous other rural guerrilla movements that have each lasted for several years: the anti-American ones at the 1900s–1910s, several Muslim-based ones for autonomy and independence, the anti-Japanese guerrilla movements in 1942–1945, and the Huk rebellion from 1946 to the early 1950s. All have eventually ended or disintegrated into small bands of armed men posing no serious threat to the state. Specific reasons vary and certainly are important. But one common to all is instructive for the CPP and NPA today: significant changes occurred in the political environment that had been crucial for their growth in the first place. This does not mean the system changed to become totally acceptable to the rebels. In most cases it changed only enough to make rebellion no longer sensible for significant number of guerrillas and their supporters. Let me elaborate by describing the Hukbalahap guerrilla movement and the Huk rebellion, cases closest to the NPA and CPP situations chronologically and in other respects.

The Hukbalahap guerrilla movement arose in large measure because of the Japanese military regime's repressive and rapacious political and economic system. That regime ended when the Hukbalahap, other guerrilla organizations, and the

---

[21] Accounts in 1987–1989 of NPA members in Nueva Ecija killing civilians and fellow members who were suspected, but not proven, to be military informers contributed to growing disillusionment with and anger against the guerrilla movement among villagers I know.

returning United States armed forces drove the Japanese military out of the Philippines. Subsequently, most Hukbalahap guerrillas disbanded, believing they had no more reason to continue fighting.

The Huk rebellion also grew and spread to a considerable extent because another political system—this time a Filipino one backed by the United States—was creating havoc for thousands of people in central Luzon. Government troops and police, mayors and governors, and many private armies employed by large landowners and other wealthy families were hounding, beating, arresting, and killing villagers. They targeted villagers who were or were thought to be Hukbalahap veterans, members of peasant organizations pressing for reforms in tenancy conditions and other matters, activists in the Democratic Alliance political party, or others perceived as "communists," "revolutionaries," or some other brand of rebel threatening to the political system which had an extremely low tolerance for criticism and opposition. In this oppressive political environment, which was exacerbated by worsening economic conditions that hurt many rural people in the region, peasant leaders, former Hukbalahap rebels, and many PKP members and leaders (initially, as mentioned earlier, in defiance of official PKP policy) organized the Huk rebellion.

This environment, however, did not last much beyond the early 1950s. Between 1952 and 1955, repression lessened as the military became more disciplined, considerably more discriminating in its use of force and violence, and better able to target actual guerrillas rather than abusing numerous civilians. The military also reined in the private armies. Meanwhile, the government offered amnesty programs to rebels, made serious overtures to engage in peace negotiations with Huk leaders, and began, especially following Magsaysay's election to the presidency in late 1953, to consider reforms in land tenure arrangements and other social-economic arrangements that had been central to many villagers' grievances. All this contributed to a political situation that provided much greater scope than had existed since the 1930s for peasants, workers, and other sectors to organize legally, press for reforms, and have reason to hope that change was possible and could bring immediate relief. The more peaceful and legitimate elections of 1951 and 1953 also contributed to the improved political climate. These circumstances, coupled with growing weariness among rebels and their supporters—many of whom had been involved in underground, armed struggle since the formation of the Hukbalahap in 1942—persuaded more and more Huk and PKP guerrillas to quit.

The NPA and CPP flourished from the mid-1970s to mid-1980s. The why's and how's are more complicated than for the Huk rebellion. The latter was confined primarily to central Luzon, where underlying economic, political, and social conditions were fairly similar and were made even more so by repression and other adversities that the state and local landed elites inflicted on people in the region. Huk leaders tried to export the rebellion to other parts of the country, but without much success, largely because political, social, and economic conditions elsewhere were not nearly as volatile and because of weaknesses within the Huk and PKP organizations.

The NPA and CPP armed struggle has been far more widespread. At its peak in the mid-1980s, it was prominent on Negros and Samar islands in the Visayas, many areas in the Bicol region, and some parts of southern Luzon. Its strongest areas were northern Luzon and central and eastern Mindanao.[22] Conditions in these principal

---

[22] Based on *Ang Bayan* (the CPP Central Committee's monthly publications) for the early and mid-1980s and on *The Bulletin Today* and *Business Day* (prominent Manila newspapers) in the mid-1980s. A joint study by Philippine and US government officials prepared in December

areas, though sharing similarities, were also different in important respects. One gets a sense of this from the analyses in this book by Rutten and Abinales. In Negros, according to Rutten, the underground movement grew primarily due to skillful organizational methods that took advantage of political opportunities. Crucial to the latter was the ability of local and outside NPA and CPP organizers to "re-frame" local grievances and ways of seeing the world in order to inspire and motivate people to act collectively so that, through collective action, they might gain some tangible social and economic improvements, and ultimately support and join the armed struggle.[23] In Mindanao, the underground movement's rapid growth, Abinales argues, came " . . . not from its cadre's organizing skills but from the social context of Mindanao itself. The CPP's lack of experience was more than made up by a readily available mass of 'warm bodies' stirred up by the turbulence of the land frontier. The tragic human and social consequences of Mindanao's transformation and militarization ultimately profited the CPP when it came time to recruit new members. . . ."[24]

One major condition common to all areas of NPA and CPP was the Marcos regime's policies, which were more adverse in areas beyond central and southern Luzon.[25] Another was deteriorating economic circumstances, which were especially severe in the sugar, coconut, and other agribusiness areas of Mindanao, several Visayas islands (particularly Negros), Bicol, and areas of southern Luzon, in part because of the volatile international markets and in part because of domestic politics within the Philippines.[26] Also prevalent in many NPA and CPP strongholds were militarization, extensive repression, and arbitrary violence by military forces, constabulary, police, and private armies (which officials often tolerated, even endorsed). The relationship between repression and rebellion is complicated, as Rutten's analysis of Negros indicates. Under certain conditions that existed in many parts of the country, military abuses and related repression were, according to some studies, " . . . a key factor, if not the most important consideration, for . . . the degree of support people give to the NPA."[27] Bernabe Buscayno, one of the most prominent guerrilla leaders, said after leaving the movement that repression was a "principal recruiter for the NPA."[28]

Toward the late part of the 1980s and into the 1990s, several of these adverse conditions eased noticeably for large numbers of people in CPP and NPA areas. Repression initially worsened under the Corazon Aquino government but, as Hedman's chapter indicates, had dropped significantly by the 1992 election. The military become more effective in countering insurgency rather than aggravating it.

1984 reported that one-third of NPA forces and 44 percent of NPA/CPP "penetrated" villages were in Mindanao. *Business Day*, June 18, 1985, p. 23. This would suggest that Mindanao's importance to the NPA and CPP was significantly greater than the 15 percent figure assumed in Table 1 of Abinales's chapter, this book.

[23] See essay by Rosanne Rutten, following in this book, pp. 126,152.

[24] Abinales, following in this book, p. 176.

[25] Benedict J. Kerkvliet, "Possible Demise of the Marcos Regime," *Crossroads: Journal of Southeast Asian Studies* 1 (October 1983): 67–83.

[26] Dante B. Canlas et al. "An Analysis of the Philippine Economic Crisis: A Workshop Report" (Quezon City: School of Economics, University of the Philippines, 1984).

[27] US Senate, "The Situation in the Philippines."

[28] "Panayam kay Dante Hinggil sa Estratehiya at Taktika," *Diliman Review* 35, 3 (1987): 22.

Rutten's revealing analysis of the situation in Negros after 1987 indicates that the government military actions made the NPA and CPP organizers' work considerably more difficult and dangerous, costing many lives. At the same time, government forces apparently avoided excessive and indiscriminate use of force. Indeed, she found that the military won over to its side some of the most respected local NPA and CPP organizers. Meanwhile, amnesty programs and widening possibilities in the post-Marcos political years for reforms through peaceful methods and the retaining of advances already won through violent means reduced the hardships which underground rebels and their supporters suffered. Adding to their growing doubts about the viability of armed struggle and possibility of victory and also to their demoralization were the splits and bitter disputes among NPA and CPP leaders locally, regionally, and nationally. In the context of these and other factors, many people quit the underground struggle, often turning to other avenues of political involvement instead. This is the "demobilization" examined in Vincent Boudreau's chapter of this book.

One can draw reasonable generalizations from the Hukbalahap, the Huk rebellion, and the NPA and CPP cases about how changes in the political environment affect the viability of continued rebellion for a significant proportion of rebels and supporters. These general changes take place: the enemy that was previously rather clear becomes hazy or disappears altogether; reforms which can be won through nonviolent tactics and strategies become more possible and attractive; violent repression by agencies of the state and local elites diminishes drastically; costs of enduring the hardships of underground life remain high while actual achievements decline and the likelihood of attaining more through underground work and rebellion diminishes sharply. In the Huk and the NPA and CPP cases, these new conditions aroused doubt, debate, and infighting, which in turn aggravated demoralization and other internal problems. In sum, the conjuncture of conditions that directly contributed to the movements' rise in the first place changed sufficiently so that it became impossible for the movements to continue as before. Fundamental shifts, reorientation, and rethinking resulted. For the NPA and CPP, the 1986 election was an important part of those altered conditions, not the entirety.

Another factor that helps to explain current problems within the underground left and the left more broadly is "communism" itself—at least as it has been advocated and represented by the country's communist parties thus far, both the PKP and CPP. The long term viability of an underground movement led by or claimed to be led by the CPP (or the PKP before it) is highly questionable, I think, except under the most extreme conditions, conditions which assure that the party provides the only palatable alternative or hope. I have in mind two kinds of reasons which help explain flaws in "communism" itself.

The first involves the CPP's goals and projects—as articulated or intimated in its official statements and documents—for remaking the Philippines, especially by establishing a command economy, collectivizing the means of production and distribution, creating a single-party political system which has little tolerance for opposition groups and dissent, running the CPP in an authoritarian way, and being hostile to religious practices and teachings. Few Filipinos, including those on the left end of the country's political spectrum, can embrace such plans. Indeed, probably few within the underground do. Certainly in the past, during the 1940s and 1950s, there was a wide gap between the PKP top leadership's long term goals and the objectives for which many lower ranking party members and Huk guerrillas were fighting. I suspect much the same has been true in the NPA and CPP experience.

Rutten's chapter notes that NPA organizers in Negros did not talk about the guerrilla army's connection to CPP because, as one former NPA member told her, "'the masses are against communism.'" Elderly people, for example, "' . . . fear they will be killed under communism and made into food seasoning.'"[29] The reason suggested in Rutten's chapter for such fears is decades of anti-communist propaganda. Yes, but that propaganda includes some truth as well. I know villagers in central Luzon, including former Huk members and supporters, who are aware of Stalin's terror against peasants in the Soviet Union and the Khmer Rouge's slaughter of rural people tales that any Philippine communist party will have immense difficulties overcoming. Another obstacle is that most of "the masses" object to the future that the party has planned for them. Among the reasons for the sharp decline in Negros of support for the NPA during the late 1980s–early 1990s, Rutten finds, is the negative experience hacienda workers had with collectivized production organized by the local NPA. In effect, this experiment with collectivization added another negative connotation to communism as far as those workers were concerned. They were happy with the NPA's help to get land for their families but objected to making the land communal property and farming it collectively. I can well imagine that most rural Filipinos have similar views. The same can be said regarding democratic processes. Democracy as a practice that at least encourages discussion and the expression of alternative views by members of whatever rank and educational background, a practice which opposes rule by a few who are out of touch with the many, certainly appeals to those within the party who criticize the CPP's past practice. The general Philippine population, I am quite certain, has even less tolerance for the rigid, top-down political organization to which leaders of the CPP, and the PKP before it, aspired.

My second critique of communist parties concerns the leaders most closely identified with both the PKP and the CPP. In the 1940s and 1950s, those leaders were the Lava brothers, Jose and Jesus. In the 1970s to the present, the principal figure is Sison. These men sacrificed a great deal, devoting the best years of their lives to the movement and championing causes they sincerely believed would bring better lives to the majority of Filipinos. Intelligent, dedicated, and daring, these men inspired others also to give much of themselves for a better country. Despite their significant contributions, however, these leaders and others like them have created notable problems for their organizations.

Their shared personality characteristics include aloofness and arrogance, especially about their theoretical sophistication and intelligence—traits also found among several top PKP leaders in the late 1930s.[30] The few former Huk guerrillas

---

[29] Rutten, following in this book, p. 125.

[30] Guillermo Capadocia, a member of the PKP in the 1930s from a working class background who in the 1940s rose to higher leadership positions, complained that several PKP leaders in the late 1930s who had studied Marxist-Leninism in Moscow were "'theoretical,' 'bookish,' and 'bureaucratic.'" "Why was it," he wondered, "that while they mentioned plenty about Marxism-Leninism, they could not even supervise a small cell? They were given work to organize the mass[es] and they could not do it and what they wanted was to be given work in the Party's office as directors only." When one was made "supervisor of the mass and party

and PKP members whom I have met over the years who had some image or knowledge of Jesus or Jose Lava typically saw each as self-centered, removed from the common people, and cold. According to one story about Jesus Lava, for instance, when meat was scarce in the underground, Lava ate what he wanted before others in his group were given a chance because, being a leader and theoretician, he claimed that he needed the protein for his brain power. In contrast to Lava were leaders like Luis Taruc, widely regarded among villagers involved in the Huk rebellion as down-to-earth, affable, and concerned about the welfare of others. Although Taruc in the 1940s through the early 1950s moved in the PKP's central governing circles, people rarely saw him as a communist. To them, he was a Huk leader, a peasant leader, not a communist. Though people never stated explicitly why they perceived him this way, an underlying message seemed to be that Taruc could not really be a communist because he did not live, talk, and act like one—he was not like Jose or Jesus Lava.

The image Sison conveys resembles more closely that of the Lavas than of Taruc. Sison comes across as stern, distant, and egocentric, not a man of the people nor readily able to communicate with them. He writes and speaks almost entirely in English, not Tagalog or any other Philippine language. He does not use idioms and vocabulary readily accessible or translatable to most Filipino peasants and workers. He claims to be the authoritative voice on Marxist-Leninist-Mao Zedong thought as well as "the leader" of "the Philippine revolution."[31] That egotistical view of the struggle contrasts sharply, for instance, to how Communist revolutionary leaders in neighboring Viet Nam projected themselves during their revolution and wars for independence. Ho Chi Minh, Sison's Vietnamese counterpart, was noted for his modesty, consensual and collaborative leadership style, and ability to bridge differences among activists. He also projected a sense of humor, ease with people from all walks of life, and pleasure in communicating in Vietnamese. Even if some of these characteristics are not entirely real, the point remains that they were the ones Ho Chi Minh and others emphasized and wanted people to see, and they are starkly different from how Sison and those close to him portray themselves. The CPP has leaders, even at high levels, whose personalities and styles are much more appealing to a broader range of Filipinos. But Sison and others like him are the ones most conspicuously linked to the party. And that, in my view, has been a handicap for its long term viability.

In the 1990s, the leadership styles and actions of Sison and those close to him figure prominently in criticisms from within and outside the NPA and CPP. Regional and sub-regional guerrilla and party leaders object to the "feudal" and "autocratic" ways of those central leaders. They criticize Sison's desire for a "one-man monopoly" over party policy, as well as the "insults and despicable treatment" that Sison has heaped on those with whom he disagrees, and other objectionable characteristics of

schools, his students said that it was only he who could understand what he was talking about." Guillermo Capadocia, "Notes Which May be Used in the 'Milestone in the History of the CCPI,'" typescript, n.d., circa 1949, p. 17.

[31] See Jose Maria Sison, with Rainer Werning, *The Philippine Revolution: The Leader's View* (New York: Crane Russak, 1989). For a critical analysis of Sison and his leadership, see P. N. Abinales, "Jose Maria Sison and the Philippine Revolution: A Critique of an Interface," *Kasarinlan* 8 (Third Quarter, 1992): 6–81.

national leaders' behavior.[32] Officials in the party's Visayas Commission wrote that the way Sison regards lower level members is like the "Contemptuousness of *hacenderos* looking down their noses at poor peasants."[33] This attitude together with other features of their leadership and their view of the party greatly impedes their ability to learn from the experiences of those who fought on the ground in the thick of the armed struggle. Instead, as Metro Manila-Rizal regional committee members wrote, Sison "relies only on his storehouse of knowledge that has been eclipsed by time."[34] When Sison and his close associates claim to be the CPP's principal leaders while living in the Netherlands they become even more suspect in the eyes of many CPP cadre and officials. Upset by Sison's accusations that the NPA and CPP in some regions have been "lazy and cowardly," an NPA commander in Samar wrote, "these insults and humiliation are too much to bear. . . ." After illustrating the hardships NPA guerrillas have endured, the commander asks rhetorically, "Who are the cowards, the leaders who do not want to return to their country because they are afraid they will die, or we who are on the frontline, in the face of battles where we are wounded and killed?"[35] Critics who grant that Sison once was brilliant in the history of the CPP nevertheless conclude that " . . . our future is dim if we are to be under his leadership. . . . Because of his absolutist and conspiratorial leadership style, it is not excessive to say that he is now the party's principal problem."[36]

THE LEFT'S FUTURE

A popular view these days is that human civilization has reached the "end of history" because no serious debate remains about how societies should organize their polities and economies. Capitalism, bourgeois democracy, and individualism have triumphed, according to this analysis. The "left"—which generated fundamental challenges to those values—has been pronounced dead or dying not only in eastern Europe and the former Soviet Union, but around the globe. Leftist parties and organizations in most of the world, including Asia, are said to have shifted so far "right" as to be scarcely recognizable.[37]

---

[32] The quotations come from Tagalog and English documents from within the CPP and NPA printed in *Malalimang Muling Pagsusuri*, 1993(?), pp. 19, 41, 77.

[33] The Tagalog reads, "Panghahamak ng matapobreng asendero sa mahirap na magsasaka." Standing Group-Visayas Commission,' CPP, "Magpunyagi sa Wastong Paglalagom Punahin ang Makaisang-panig ng 'Reaffirm,'" in *Malalimang Muling Pagsusuri*, 1993(?), p. 19.

[34] Komiteng Rehiyon ng Metro Manila-Rizal, "Tumindig sa Tama at Totoo, Pawalang Bisa ang Bogus na Plenum!" October 10, 1992, in *Malalimang Muling Pagsusuri*, 1993(?), p. 85.

[35] The Tagalog original reads, "Sino ba ang duwag, ang namumunong ayaw umuwi sa bansa dahil takot mamatay? O kami na nasa frontline na humaharap sa matinding labanan na minsan nasusugatan at namamatay?" Punong Kumander VMAC, "Igiit ang Batalyon at mga Kumpanya!" October 1992, in *Malalimang Muling Pagsusuri*, 1993(?), p. 58.

[36] " . . . madilim ang ating kinabukasan kung tayo'y papailalim ngayon sa kanyang liderato. . . . Dahil sa kanyang absolutista at konspiratoryal na istilo ng liderato, hindi kalabisan na sabihing siya ang prinsipal na problema ngayon ng Partido." Komiteng Rehiyon ng Metro Manila-Rizal, "Tumindig sa Tama at Totoo, Pawalang Bisa ang Bogus na Plenum!" October 10, 1992, in *Malalimang Muling Pagsusuri*, 1993(?), p. 87.

[37] Seymour Martin Lipset, "No Third Way: A Comparative Perspective on the Left," in Daniel Chirot, ed., *The Crisis of Leninism and the Decline of the Left: The Revolutions of 1989* (Seattle: University of Washington Press, 1991), pp. 183–232.

In the Philippines, however, and I imagine in many other countries as well, the left, broadly understood, is neither dead nor dying. Indeed, the Philippine left is in better health now than perhaps at any other time in the twentieth century. Though the CPP and NPA have been breaking down, the "unfinished revolution," which Reynaldo Ileto has highlighted as a prominent theme in twentieth-century Philippine political discourse, continues to energize people on the leftist portion of Philippine political curve. [38]

This chapter has been discussing the extreme left. It is "extreme" in both methods—armed guerrilla warfare—and goals, although not all those engaged in armed struggle agree on the extreme goals. At the moment, this portion of the left is, indeed, in considerable disarray. The acrimonious struggle between "reaffirmists" and "rejectionists" might lead one to think that this extreme left is about to disappear. As the joke in the Philippines says, "reaffirmists" and "rejectionists" have given rise to the "rejoice-ists"—those who are delighted that the CPP is doing itself in.

But, as this chapter has indicated, the extreme left has been in similar straits before and come back with even more vigor and vitality. The same can happen again. Much depends on those conditions discussed earlier that initially engender underground guerrilla movements based on the country's poor, exploited, desperate, and angry people. Whether those circumstances return depends to a considerable extent, though of course not entirely, on what the elites, the government, and other powerful interests in the Philippines do. Does the future hold more Manuel Roxases, Elipidio Quirinos, Ferdinand and Imelda Marcoses, Danding Cojuangcos, Juan Ponce Enriles, and short-sighted IMF and World Bank "experts"? I hope not. If it does, there will likely be leftist armed rebellion again—a new*er* people's army.

Meanwhile, the rest of the left has been active. It is difficult to identify with much precision what characteristics define "left."[39] I see at least three main elements. First, those on the left are critical of capitalism. They do not necessarily believe it must be replaced with socialized ownership of production and distribution, though some do hold those goals. The broad agreement on the left is that unmodified, unfettered capitalism is inappropriate for Philippine society and too costly to values which guide the distribution of resources. Some people come to this critical stance through academic learning. Others come from religious orientations. For still others, such criticisms derive from social values concerning just claims to basic needs, which the capitalist market sphere does not recognize, let alone address.[40] Second, people and organizations on the left are particularly concerned with the interests, concerns, and problems of the poor and oppressed in Philippine society. They themselves may be individuals and groups from these sectors of society; or they may instead be from more privileged sectors, yet they want to work with the poor. Third, the broad left presses for a fuller, more genuine democracy than has often been practiced or tolerated by powerful, often anti-democratic interests in the country.

---

[38] Reynaldo C. Ileto, "The 'Unfinished Revolution' in Philippine Political Discourse," *Tonan Aija Kenkyu* [Southeast Asian Studies] 31 (June 1993): 62–82.

[39] For a helpful attempt, see Rocamora, *Breaking Through*, pp. 215–17.

[40] For an analysis of social values which contend with capitalist values, see Benedict J. Kerkvliet, *Everyday Politics in the Philippines: Class and Status Relations in a Central Luzon Village* (Berkeley: University of California Press, 1990), pp. 248–59.

Earlier in the twentieth century, the Philippine left in this broad sense included numerous organizations involving peasants, workers, lawyers, teachers, students, women, minority groups, urban poor, and others. Today these organizations would be called NGOs and POs (people's organizations). The left lobbied local and national governments, marched, paraded, occupied public buildings, defied police, were arrested, shot at, killed, formed political parties, ran candidates for elected office, and supported sympathetic candidates of other parties.

Since the early 1980s, organizations spanning a range of interests and social sectors have sprouted and blossomed after a decade of near dormancy during the worst of the Marcos martial law regime. Many emerged in the wake of the protest movement sparked by the assassination of Benigno Aquino. They sank deeper roots in the 1985–86 presidential campaign and, as Boudreau argues in this book, they have flourished in the more liberated political climate of the 1990s. Many individuals and organizations in this broad left, Hedman demonstrates, have jumped into election campaigns even while often continuing to debate among themselves the efficacy of electoral politics. Some on the left are primarily concerned with addressing immediate material needs of poor Filipinos; others have more long term objectives. New coalitions among organizations have been created, based on certain shared understandings and objectives, even while groups and individuals involved adopt different stances towards tactics, strategies, and expectations. The broad left in the Philippines is by no means a unified political movement, untroubled or unopposed. But neither is it dead. It is vibrant and will likely remain so for a long time.

FROM VANGUARD TO REARGUARD: THE THEORETICAL ROOTS OF THE CRISIS OF THE COMMUNIST PARTY OF THE PHILIPPINES

Kathleen Weekley

INTRODUCTION

Over the past eight years, the Communist Party of the Philippines (CPP) has gone from being the most significant threat to the stability of the Philippine state and the hegemonic force on the Left, to a splintered party in danger of eventually becoming merely a thorn in the side of the administration and, perhaps worse, one of the obstacles to new forms of radical political organizing in the Philippines. Since the end of 1991, a "Rectification" process has been carried out in the CPP. The theoretical orthodoxy (the set of "basic principles" laid down at the founding Party congress in 1968) has been "reaffirmed" on paper; key cadres have been purged; many people have resigned or simply drifted out of the Party; some regional and sub-regional Party units—including the one covering Metro Manila—have declared their "autonomy" from the Party; and some of the Party's legal organizations, including the national peasant and trade union federations, have split into two camps. In one sense, the orthodox tendency in the CPP has succeeded in "saving" the Party from its dissidents; it has maintained control of the Communist Party organizations (including the New People's Army) in most regions of the country and thereby retained the greater part of the "mass base" of the revolutionary movement (which is still substantial). However, in the process of purging those dissidents, the Party has lost a significant proportion of its intellectuals and of the cadres most capable of forging united front links with other progressive forces, especially in Metro Manila. On the other side, the dissidents have failed, so far, to harness their various forces to a clear alternative radical project; those who were somewhat misleadingly collectively identified as "rejectionists" during the rectification campaign now constitute at least two distinct non-Party groupings.[1] The story told in

---

[1] The "Rejectionists" were so called because they rejected the CPP leadership's directive to "Reaffirm Our Basic Principles." The orthodox tendency was referred to in this dispute as the "Reaffirmists."

the following pages will, hopefully, help to explain why the CPP's 1992–93 dispute has resulted (so far) in a splintered Party and an opposition without a coherent or united theoretical and strategic agenda.

The crisis of the Communist movement in the Philippines emerged out of the troubles that began in earnest with the February 1986 "People Power" revolution. At no earlier moment had political events so resoundingly contradicted the CPP's predictions. The dictatorship collapsed and civilian rule was installed, thanks to a combination of military mutiny, a popular and determined presidential candidate, and a mass uprising. While the Communists could neither have instigated nor prevented the 1986 revolt even if they had wanted, internal and external critics of the CPP agree that the national democratic movement would have suffered less from this change in political regime had they been participants in the process. If they had not opted for boycott, but instead joined with the broad opposition to defeat Marcos first at the ballot and then on the streets, then the revolutionary movement would have been in a better position to influence the course of events that followed.

In contrast, this essay will argue that such an alternative—indeed any substantially different approach to the 1986 presidential elections—was never an easy possibility for the Party. The Party's history and its strategic situation prior to the surprise election announcement militated against a different decision, not regarding the election itself (whether to boycott or participate), but regarding the strategy that would underpin such a choice. That is, it was difficult to resolve questions about how the Party would behave towards a post-Marcos government should it ascend, for example, or about the deployment of cadres between countryside and city during the anti-Marcos campaign. Like any institution, the Party's own history and culture have always been strong determinants in its decision-making—they shape the way in which the Party sees the "objective, structural facts" of the world around it and in general, tend to slow down the process of adapting to exogenous change. At that particular moment in the political history of the Philippines and the revolutionary movement, key people in the CPP leadership could not read the changes outside the tried-and-true protracted people's war framework. Over the years, the explanatory powers of the CPP's revolutionary lexicon have been increasingly stretched in order to explain the vagaries of political "realities," and they were bound to snap at some stage; but that could not happen easily or quickly.

Underlying the argument in this essay is the notion that central aspects of CPP theory and practice that have contributed to its success have also been obstacles to its further development, or, crucial elements in its decline into the present crisis. Specifically, this refers to the simplicity and clarity of the Party's ideology and its set of tight, disciplined organizational structures. At different moments, the Party's emphasis on revolutionary "correctness" and organizational unity have been either assets or liabilities. Contrary to the views of some other observers, however, the story of strategy debates within the CPP has not been a simple one in which those with new ideas always ran up against a dogmatic and recalcitrant central leadership bent on imposing the official "line."[2] The arguments rarely have been simply dichotomous, and "self-censorship" has always been an important brake on conflicts over substantial matters of policy. The culture of the Party—its history, structures,

---

[2] This kind of explanation is implied, for example, by Gareth Porter, "Strategic Debates and Dilemmas in the Philippine Communist Movement," *Pilipinas* 13 (Fall 1989): 19–40.

symbols—created, over the years, a tendency towards unity and away from discord, which resulted at times in a lack of initiative (especially in theoretical matters) and a kind of institutional inertia. The present review of some Party debates which took place prior to this current crisis will illustrate the point.[3] Before the CPP could have led its legal mass movement forces act effectively in the events from December 1985 to February 1986 and after, a fairly sudden but thorough review of strategy and tactics would have had to occur. Such a review necessarily would have involved changes to the ways individuals and Party units viewed their own roles within the movement, and a fundamental reassessment of some long-held assumptions about the nature of the state and society. As it was, the CPP was unprepared for the relatively peaceful transition to a civilian regime and Cory Aquino's ascendancy to the Presidency.

The People Power revolution was indeed a watershed for the Communist Party and the national democratic movement as a whole because it revealed key problems in the Party's analysis and strategy more starkly than they had been revealed before. It was therefore a catalyst for the articulation of open dissent within the Party and outside it. The self-criticism at the highest levels of the Party which followed the boycott "error" provided an opening, albeit very narrow at the time, for the expression of longer held doubts, questions, and disagreements that had not been strongly expressed before then. However, the Party's failure satisfactorily to debate the questions that arose, and especially its later attempts to deal with the challenges to Party theory and leadership by administrative fiat, led to more serious antagonisms. These antagonisms finally could not be contained within the Party's discursive and organizational boundaries, and a crisis ensued.

THE CRISIS

The earliest signs that a crisis threatened the CPP loomed with the release of a document on December 26, 1991, entitled "Reaffirm Our Basic Principles and Rectify Errors," signed "Armando Liwanag, Central Committee, CPP."[4] The historical reference is recognizable immediately to those who are familiar with the document prepared by Jose Maria Sison for the old Partido Komunista ng Pilipinas (PKP) in the late 1960s, in an attempt to get the Party to criticize its past mistakes and prepare itself for future revolutionary tasks. The analysis and proposals for strategy were rejected by the old leadership, and the paper ended up as the key document for the "Congress of Re-establishment" in 1968 which founded the Communist Party of the Philippines (Marxist-Leninist Mao Tse-Tung Thought). The very title of the 1991 document signified that the leadership of the CPP regarded the state of the Party as critical. The echoes of the 1968 rectification campaign suggested that the Party needed once again to take serious stock of the movement's strengths and weaknesses and make crucial decisions about its future. All the signals said that the situation was so grave that extraordinary measures would be required to rectify it.

---

[3] Due to the difficulties of researching the relatively recent goings-on of a revolutionary party that is still, for all practical purposes, an underground organization, the arguments and conclusions presented here are intended only to be preliminary notes on the subject.

[4] Since reprinted in *Kasarinlan* 8, 1 (Third Quarter 1992): 82–133. By now, it is well known (but not admitted by Sison himself) that "Armando Liwanag," the Chairman of the CPP, is Jose Maria Sison.

Accordingly, "Reaffirm" is a quite extraordinary document; it makes some sweeping statements about wrong directions taken by various elements in the revolutionary movement and states in categorical terms the correctness of sticking to the "basic principles" laid down at the 1968 CPP Congress. These include: 1) the repudiation of modern revisionism and adherence to . . . 2) the theory of Marxism-Leninism, 3) a class analysis of Philippine society as semi-colonial and semi-feudal, 4) a general line of a new democratic revolution, 5) the leading role of the working class through the Party, 6) the theory of people's war and the strategic line of encircling the cities from the countryside, 7) the concept of a united front along the revolutionary class line, 8) democratic centralism, 9) a socialist perspective and proletarian internationalism.[5]

While declaring that the movement is "still far stronger in several respects than [it was] in 1968, 1977, or 1980," Liwanag states that the Party must now confront "certain long-running problems" and "an unprecedented loss of mass base."[6] The last section, headed "The Rectification Movement," begins by announcing that it is

a matter of life and death for the entire Party to reaffirm its basic principles, assert its correct line, and criticize, repudiate, and rectify those major deviations and errors which have run for so long (*overlapping with half of the existence of the Party and armed revolution*) and which have brought about unprecedented setbacks to the Party, the New People's Army and the entire revolutionary movement.[7]

In a deliberate effort to draw a line of historical continuity from the first "rectification," in 1968, to the present, Liwanag/Sison argues that all the errors of the last few years constitute one fundamental problem: the latest form of "modern revisionism." Very briefly, this involves "adulat[ing] Gorbachev on a simplistic notion of anti-Stalinism" and seeing him as "the ideologist of socialist renewal and democracy," whereas, his

glib advertising job . . . has turned out to be a cover for the total negation of Marxism-Leninism and the entire course of Bolshevik history; for capitalist restructuring; for the rise of the bourgeois class dictatorship; for unleashing nationalism, ethnic conflicts, and civil war; and for the emergence of all kinds of monsters, including racism, fascism, and rampant criminality.[8]

Growing demands within the Party for a repudiation of "Stalinism"—especially strong after the revelations of the extent of the anti-infiltration campaigns (discussed by P. N. Abinales elsewhere in this volume)—were of great concern to Sison. They represented (for him and his followers) not only a weakening of the line against the

---

[5] Ibid., p. 84.

[6] Ibid., pp. 83–85, passim. Two years later, the CPP stated that the loss of the mass base was even higher than 1991 estimates showed; around 60 percent overall, up to 85 percent in some regions, and in one area, as high as 97 percent. "Assessment of the Rectification Movement and the Struggle Against the Anti-Party Campaign (August 1992 –December 1993)," by the Political Bureau of the Central Committee of the Communist Party of the Philippines, reprinted in *Rebolusyon* 3, English Edition (July–September 1994): 6.

[7] Ibid., pp. 131–132. Emphasis added.

[8] Ibid., p. 93.

conservative, bureaucratic form of socialism practiced in the Soviet Union and the Eastern bloc, but perhaps more importantly, a call for "ultrademocracy" within the Party and a weakening of traditional Marxist-Leninist democratic centralism. The extent to which party members actually advocated these revisions to Party doctrine will be discussed later; suffice to say here that it seems from most available evidence that, in this and other matters of contention, Sison was closing off sources of potential trouble rather than responding to explicit demands for specific, fundamental changes to Party policies.

So, while the "Reaffirm" document was presented as an authoritative "summing-up" of the Party's successes and failures since 1968, it is, more importantly, a political document, identifying the trends in thinking which led to certain "errors" so that those responsible for the errors would be pressured into admitting their own mistakes and affirming the correctness of the author's view. Those who had been in error but who refused to admit it and restate adherence to the original "principles" were either to leave the Party voluntarily or be thrown out. The document states:

> The rectification movement should raise the Party's level of theoretical knowledge, political consciousness, and practical activity. The Party membership should be mobilized to join and support this movement. Only those who oppose this movement and who are incorrigible should come under disciplinary action and be removed from the Party . . . It is a fair estimate to make that only a few will be removed from the Party . . . In this regard, the slogan of the Party is "A bit fewer but a lot better, to paraphrase Lenin and Mao."[9]

By the end of 1993, it is true that relatively few people had been "removed from the Party," but some of those who might have been expelled announced their split from the Party before that could occur, taking with them whole groups of Party members and other cadres.[10] Adding to the volatile atmosphere was the fact that some of those who were expelled or who left "voluntarily" also were publicly charged with "criminal offenses" under CPP rules.[11]

The appearance of the "Reaffirm" document was bound to anger many people within the Party simply because its range of fire was so broad, but there were other problems as well. First, it seemed that the paper had been released without being approved by the Central Committee, the Politburo, or even the Executive Committee of the Central Committee (KT-KS), yet it was released under the pseudonym usually reserved for the Chairman of the Party. (Indeed, it was not officially approved by the Central Committee until around six months later.) Even many people not usually given to criticism of the leadership were concerned that it had not been clearly identified as merely a discussion paper before being distributed. Second, the summary assessments of various aspects of the CPP/NPA/NDF's (NPA—New

---

[9] Ibid., pp. 132–133.

[10] "Declaration of Autonomy by the Manila-Rizal Regional Committee of the Communist Party of the Philippines," July 10, 1993; photocopy of original press release. See report on the split in the *Manila Chronicle*, July 16, 1993. Not long after Manila-Rizal's declaration, sub-regional units in the Visayas and Mindanao made similar declarations.

[11] "Press Statement of Jose Maria Sison On Bloody Scheme of US-Ramos Clique," December 21, 1993. Photocopy of original fax.

People's Army; NDF—National Democratic Front) history did not fit with participants' own views, and many felt strongly that such a comprehensive assessment should not have been made without a more involved process of collecting and integrating "summings up" from the various regional and organizational units of the Party. Third, there were many questions of substance, not only about the Party's history but about the nature of the post-Marcos political situation, the state of international communism, the assessment of Stalinism, and so on, which many Party members thought required a more thorough investigation and theorizing than is represented by the call to "Reaffirm Basic Principles."

In the months following its publication, a number of papers were written in response to the document by both individuals and Party units. Some of them called for the Party to hold its second Congress,[12] following a period of proper discussion and debate, in order to settle important questions of past practical experiences, and future strategy and tactics. Some criticized the assessments of "errors"; some criticized the lack of consultation before the document was released. Tensions increased, as did the number of Party members identified as "Rejectionists," when the Central Committee met to hold its Tenth Plenum in mid-1992 and approved the "Reaffirm" document presented by the KT-KS, with minor amendments. As far as the leadership and those loyal to them are concerned, this document and the "Rectification movement" were now official Party policy.

However, a number of CPP members, including some top-level cadres recently released from prison, rejected the Tenth Plenum as invalid. According to many reports, the number of Central Committee members who attended was very low; intelligence reports and sources quoted by the *Philippine Daily Inquirer* and other newspapers put the figure at eight. (Some of those former Central Committee members whose status had not been resolved since their release from prison were not invited.) Critics of the Tenth Plenum asserted that eight members does not constitute a quorum; so, during the second half of 1992, heated discussions continued. The critics continued to argue for further discussion and consultation, asking that the Plenum be reconvened (with expanded attendance) to initiate plans for a subsequent "Unity Congress." However, the leadership responded with further memos, one of which instructed members to keep discussion of the "Reaffirm" document within their immediate Party units; there should be no "horizontal" discussion of the issues—all discussion beyond the immediate Party unit should follow a vertical line upwards through the Party hierarchy, from the lower unit to the next "higher-up" unit.[13]

It was a time of confusion, disappointment, and disillusionment for many long-time Party members; but at the same time, many lower-ranking members had little idea of the arguments occurring at the higher levels. Of course, there were many who had not even seen the document in question. Then, in an extraordinary move by "Joma" Sison, the internal problems became a matter of very public curiosity. On December 10, 1992, he sent a fax from his base in Utrecht, Netherlands, to the *Philippine Daily Inquirer*, denouncing three former CPP leaders as "renegades":

---

[12] None has been held since the first, in December 1968.

[13] Author's interview with "Art," former national-level cadre member, Quezon City, December 11, 1992.

Three of those recently released [Ricardo Reyes, Benjamin de Vera, and Romulo Kintanar] are now prominently active in a psy-war campaign to discredit the CPP central leadership in a futile attempt to decapitate and destroy the movement and the CPP.

In the same article, the *Inquirer* quoted a press statement received from Sison two days earlier, in which he said that he had information from the Philippines that,

those who oppose the rectification movement most bitterly are those who have been responsible for the militarist viewpoint, the gross reduction of mass base, witch-hunts of monstrous proportions . . . and degeneration into gangsterism.[14]

The three "renegades" held a press conference to deny the charges and to express their hope that the issues being debated within the revolutionary movement could be studied and discussed in a "rigorous and scientific" way, and one which would "preserve the integrity of the national democratic movement."[15]

While Sison's "fax war" seemed to harden the opposition of many members to the Rectification campaign, as mentioned earlier, the camp of the so-called "Rejectionists" was not a homogenous one; the only basis of unity was some measure of dissatisfaction with the "Reaffirm" document and the process by which it was approved and its recommendations set in motion. That is, while some wanted further discussion about how to shape strategy and tactics for the 1990s, many others rejected the leadership's decisions only on the basis of "organizational questions." The criticisms coincided only at the point where the leadership's methods were regarded as inappropriate for resolving the dispute. Consequently, while tension was mounting, little headway was being made on the organizational front by the "Rejectionists." This happened partly because many members were genuinely disinclined to make any move that would jeopardize Party unity or leave them open to charges of creating a faction, but also because no strong consensus developed around an alternative vision from the one presented in the "Reaffirm" document. The core group of oppositionists was at that time committed to "exhausting all administrative channels" to resolve matters; this precluded the possibility of producing, for example, written material explaining their views on how the movement's strategy and tactics must change. In fact, even those seen to be the key antagonists in the dispute did not then have a shared set of clear ideas about how things should be changed. During the first few months of 1992, they were holding meetings among themselves in order to discuss their ideas. The topics included the general question of "strategy," tactics for the peace talks, internal democracy, the future of socialism and the nature of the NDF program.[16]

---

[14] *Philippine Daily Inquirer*, December 10, 1992, pp. 1, 11.
[15] *Philippine Daily Inquirer*, December 12, 1992, pp. 1, 10.
[16] Author's interview with "MM," ex-Central Committee member, Quezon City, December 12, 1992.

CAGES OF PARTY CULTURE

If the way in which the Communist Party of the Philippines "behaves" is strongly affected by both its revolutionary rhetoric and its organizational structure, the two aspects are in many ways inseparable. Very briefly, the CPP was founded on an analysis of Philippine society that mirrored Mao Zedong's analysis of pre-revolutionary China.[17] The Philippines, Guerrero said, is a "semi-colonial, semi-feudal" society requiring a "national-democratic revolution . . . seeking the liberation of the Filipino people from foreign and feudal oppression."[18] Because "the peasant problem" is the main problem of Philippine society, the revolution must be an armed struggle fought mainly by the peasants, and "the principal stress should be put on revolutionary struggle in the countryside and the secondary stress on revolutionary struggle in the cities."[19] These were adopted as the "basic facts" of the revolution. For various reasons (only some of which are raised in this essay), this founding framework was not subjected to serious review before 1992.

An important reason why this reassessment did not take place earlier had to do with the past successes of the Party; for more than a decade, the national democratic movement was the most highly organized, consistent, and daring opposition to the Marcos regime.[20] With no serious contender for the position of chief active moral and political critic of the dictatorship, the national democratic revolution inspired a deep commitment and faith in its cadres and its rank and file members. They were inducted into a movement that occupied virtually the whole of "Left stage," that sustained a significant challenge to the militarized state, and was winning increasing support from the various "basic sectors" of urban and rural populations. Sison's vision and plans for the revolution seemed to be affirmed. Where was any credible critique or alternative to come from?

A second reason had to do with a scarcity of leftist alternatives. The absence of significant challenge to the CPP's ideological hegemony from other progressives within the country has been compounded by the parochial nature of Philippine communism. Probably largely because of the circumstances of the CPP's founding (as a Maoist split from the old communist party), Philippine communists have had relatively little access to ongoing debates within other, broader, Marxist circles in the world. One critic argues that this isolation from international communism has been an obstacle, for instance, to CPP appreciation of a dialectical view of reform and revolution.[21] It certainly seems to have contributed to the CPP's narrow view that a revolution in a "Third World"/post-colonial setting must follow the particular Maoist strategy of a protracted people's war wherein the cities are eventually encircled from the countryside.

---

[17] See the revolutionary "bible" written in 1970 by Amado Guerrero (Jose Maria Sison), *Philippine Society and Revolution*, reprinted (Oakland, CA: International Association of Filipino Patriots, 1979).

[18] Ibid., p. 129.

[19] Ibid., p. 158–159. The metaphor used most frequently is that of "the sword and the shield," where the NPA is the sword and the legal mass movement is the shield. The Party is the head directing these two components.

[20] There are many accounts of the significance of the underground movement both in the lives of its individual activists and supporters and in national political life; they were confirmed by the interviews with CPP cadre members carried out for my PhD project.

[21] R. Ciria Cruz, "Why the Philippine Left Must Take the Parliamentary Road," *Debate* 2 (March 1992): 9.

The relationship between the CPP's theory/analysis and its structure requires deeper consideration than is possible here. However, it can be noted that the democratic-centralist principles around which the CPP is organized have discouraged any substantial exchange of ideas beyond the core leadership and encouraged a voluntary, or internalized, deference to the wisdom of the leadership. Even when leading cadres have criticized or questioned prevailing views, debate has been stultified by a self-imposed need to speak within the protracted people's war framework.[22] One former member of the Executive Committee of the Central Committee of the CPP told of his difficulty in pushing hard for any new ideas he had about tactics:

> [One] always operate[s] with a theory and in my theory, there was always [the] possibility of mistake. I even doubted my own proposals. So, I would not die fighting for my case, knowing that I myself was not sure where it is going. And against somebody who is arguing on the basis of certain time-honored principles that are in "the books," it is hard to win . . . I was caught within the same mold, trying to propose something that I believed is still within the same [principles] . . . [I was] not arguing out of a different framework, so, if [confronted] with some basics, [I] lost the battle easily.[23]

This aspect of Party culture has discouraged not only individual dissent but also the theorizing of regional, local, and sectoral practical experiences that could have had an impact on the traditional strategic discourse. Thus, it has been a key weakness in the CPP's ideological and theoretical development, or lack of development.

The widely held view among students and supporters of the national democratic movement that one of its strong features has been its "dogmatism in theory but flexibility in practice" overlooks a significant problem. That is, the flexible interpretations of central leadership policies by regional and sectoral cadres, which so often produced imaginative, successful local action, rarely worked their way "upwards" as ideas that prompted a re-thinking of the central tenets of Party thought. This became rather shockingly clear when the "Reaffirm" document began to make its way around the upper levels of the Party: its "summing-up" of the past few years of the movement's experiences often did not match the regional and sectoral cadres' own understandings of those experiences. And, as the latter saw it, the author had certainly not made any attempt to adjust the original strategic framework in the light of lessons learned on the ground by the movement's chief policy implementors. A common (and strongly made) criticism of the document (from those "second-tier" cadres) was that it was simply unacceptable—and unrealistic—to "reaffirm" the same "basic principles" as had inspired Party leaders more than twenty years ago. Much readjusting, improvising and filling in of detail had occurred since 1968, as movement activists responded to varied and changing political, economic, and cultural conditions.

---

[22] As far as this writer knows, the only critiques of CPP policy (before 1992) by a contemporary Party member that go so far as to say that the strategy itself is wrong have been those by "Marty Villalobos" (pseudonym) former national-level cadre. See, for example, "For a Politico-Military Framework," unpublished paper, February 23, 1987.

[23] Author's interview with Isagani Serrano, Quezon City, December 18, 1992.

So, both the "world view" of CPP communism and the culture of the revolutionary movement, especially that of the Party proper, have acted to circumscribe critical thinking about the prevailing strategic analysis. Also, and not surprisingly, it has only been when the movement's practices seem lacking that any challenges have been made. This is why fundamental challenges to party thought did not commence until after February 1986. Even then very few members articulated their doubts in any thorough-going fashion until the powerful core of the central leadership moved deliberately to divide the critics from the unsure and/or dedicated at the end of 1992. Critics kept quiet not simply because they were acting diplomatically, for the sake of Party unity, but also because they had not yet understood how far beyond the traditional framework their thinking would take them. Until pushed to argue their points of criticism more thoroughly, many had not admitted to themselves that their thoughts might be "heretical." In the last two years, it was the central leadership's attempts to resolve those ideological differences by organizational means that prompted the articulation of some clear disagreements over strategy and tactics.

The next five sections of this essay comprise a brief review of some discussions about electoral and other legal politics within the Party which took place beginning in the early seventies up until the decision to boycott the Presidential elections of 1986. These debates raised questions about, among other things, the nature of the state, the balance between struggles in the countryside and urban areas, united front work, and regional versus central control of party activities. Investigation of the two situations shows that the "strategy debate" was never simply polarized and that the challenges were not necessarily as directly threatening to official analysis and strategy as they might have appeared.

ASSERTING THE PRIMACY OF THE SWORD

Between the time of his re-election to the presidency in 1969 and the 1978 elections for an "interim" parliament, Ferdinand Marcos allowed only two electoral exercises. In 1970, there were elections for the delegates to the Constitutional Convention. There seems to be little existing documentation about this, but in Manila, the national democrats (NDs) supported the candidacy of a progressive, Voltaire Garcia. In the rest of the country, the NDs boycotted the election.[24] The so-called "moderate" youth and student movement led by Edgar Jopson was active in the campaign and was criticized by the "radicals" (the NDs) for "making people expect much from the Con-Con when you know that they have nothing to expect from such a body."[25] This view was confirmed later, of course, by the Con-Con's inability to withstand the pressures from Marcos to produce a Constitution designed to enable his plans for dictatorial powers.[26]

---

[24] Author's interview with "Marty Villalobos" (Nathan Quimpo), Utrecht, August 11, 1992.

[25] The remark was made to Jopson by Antonio Zumel (then president of the National Press Club, future leader of the National Democratic Front), and quoted in Benjamin Pimentel, *Edjop: The Unusual Journey of Edgar Jopson* (Quezon City: Ken Inc., 1989). "Edjop," as Jopson was known, later became one of the leading lights of the underground national democratic forces. He was killed by the military in 1982; it was considered by most leaders of the revolutionary movement to be one of its greatest cadre losses.

[26] D. Wurfel, *Filipino Politics, Development and Decay* (Quezon City: Ateneo de Manila University Press, 1988), pp. 115–117.

In 1971, there were elections both for local governments and for the Senate, which the CPP-led forces appear to have boycotted. Six of the eight seats in the Senate were won by the opposition Liberal party candidates.[27] If Gregg Jones's assertions are true that some CPP leaders planned and executed the infamous Plaza Miranda bombing, then the attitude of at least part of the CPP leadership to the electoral exercise was a great deal more than merely condemnatory.[28]

Between the declaration of martial law in September of 1972 and the 1978 elections, Marcos tried to sustain the legitimacy of his regime by holding referenda via the notorious "Citizens' Assemblies" in which voting was conducted sometimes by "secret" ballot and sometimes by the raising of voices/hands in open public meetings in the barrios. For the first few years of martial law, there was little organized opposition to these machinations of Marcos. Many of the non-revolutionary, Social Democratic forces had been badly shaken by their sudden "illegal" status and the repression that followed Marcos's decree, and the Communist Party was concentrating on building the New People's Army:

> Those who can no longer conduct legal work or underground work in the cities and towns should be dispatched to the people's army through the various regional Party committees. The people's army is the Party's principal form of organization and should be built up as such.[29]

Even if it had been capable of doing so, the Party was thus not inclined to organize mass opposition to Marcos's "legal" maneuvering in those years.[30]

---

[27] Ibid., p. 18.

[28] On August 21, 1971, grenades were thrown at the Liberal Party's pre-election rally in Plaza Miranda, Manila, leaving nine dead and at least one hundred injured, including Liberal Party senatorial candidates. Marcos claimed that it was the work of the Communists and immediately suspended the writ of habeus corpus. His legitimacy was at such a low point at this time that his accusations were believed by almost no one. It has been widely assumed that the bombing was the work of Marcos loyalists, if not by order of Marcos himself. See Raymond Bonner, *Waltzing With a Dictator: The Marcoses and the Making of American Policy* (New York: Times Books, 1987), pp. 79–80. Years later, Gregg Jones created something of a scandal with his accusations that the Communist Party had carried out the bombing in order to provoke greater repression by Marcos. His charges remain controversial both within and outside the CPP. See Gregg Jones, *Red Revolution* (Boulder, CO: Westview Press, 1989), pp. 59–69. Parenthetically, I asked a number of CPP members whether or not they believed Jones's claim. Most replied that they were not sure, that they distrusted Jones and his motives in "revealing" the story, but also that, whether or not the story is true, they believed it could be so. That is, they believed it possible that Sison could have taken such a decision.

[29] "Tasks of the Communist Party of the Philippines in the New Situation," *Ang Bayan*, Special Release (English Edition), October 1, 1972, p. 11.

[30] In the early 1970s, the Communists had been instrumental in organizing some local demonstrations by urban poor people in Manila (around the Tondo foreshore), over the issue of demolition of their houses. But these were not what are described as "mass actions." As one long-time CPP united front cadre member described it, "the earlier forms of mass actions were the stations of the cross, undertaken by the church groups during Lent. They started in 1976, 1977; they mobilized people for prayer . . . mov[ing] from one church to another, gathering people in the process, and projecting mainly human rights issues." Author's interview with "CN," Quezon City, December 14, 1992.

However in 1975 an urban communist committee proposed to challenge the dictatorship on legal grounds in the urban center.[31] The Manila-Rizal Regional Party Committee (MR-KR) proposed that a campaign be launched to demand an end to martial law and for democratic elections. Such elections would be, MR-KR argued, " . . . the last alternative for a "peaceful revolution," before the majority of the masses understand and support the only true alternative . . . the armed revolution for national democracy."[32] As Malay notes, the Executive Committee of the Central Committee did not agree, and the Manila regional leadership was later criticized for errors of "Right Opportunism."[33]

One of the supporters of the proposal at the time claimed that the Manila cadres saw it as merely a "freeing move" for the mass movement in the national capital.

> The situation was: [from] '66 to '72 [there] was an upsurge; then '72 to '74 was a real ebb, [there was] no movement . . . We were trying to break the bind [so] we said . . . "what is the form [of struggle] and slogan that can enliven again the mass movement in the cities . . . that can unite as many sectors of the population [as possible] and make an assault on the legal hold of Marcos?" . . . At that time . . . the fettered elements of the Marcos regime were trying to [conduct a] campaign [to amend the martial law constitution] and our idea was to come up with a parallel campaign whereby, eventually, we [would] link up with them in a broader front, an anti-fascist, legal front . . . [34]

Fortuna insisted that this did not constitute a questioning of the Party's basic strategic framework because:

> [our] overriding [understanding] at that time was that we could only win power through a people's war; that premise was never challenged by the proposal of ['75].

Hence, he, for one, claimed to have been dissuaded from supporting the proposal quite easily when it did not meet with central approval.

At that time, "the Metro Manila committee had no allies in the Central Committee," and the head of the Party at that time, Jose Maria Sison, "was really a figure of such prestige" that the only reason Fortuna personally could debate with

---

[31] There seems to be little knowledge within the Party of this proposal, outside the individuals directly involved at the time. When asked about his thoughts on it, another CPP national level cadre member declared that he could not remember hearing anything of the "debate." Author's interview with Serrano. Serrano was in prison at the time, but top ranking cadre members in jail were usually privy to information about significant discussions taking place in Party circles. Other cadre members interviewed had also heard nothing of the proposal. By the author's own account, deliberations over it were neither long nor broad.

[32] Executive Committee of the Manila-Rizal Regional Party Committee, "Ang Ating Taktikal na Islogan sa Kasalukuyang Yugto ng Rebolusyon" [Our Tactical Slogan for the Present Stage of the Revolution], translated by and quoted in Armundo Malay, *The Dialectics of Kaluwagan: Echoes of a 1978 Debate*, in *Marxism in the Philippines*, Second Series (Quezon City: Third World Studies Center, University of the Philippines, 1988), p. 11.

[33] Ibid.

[34] Author's interview with Julius Fortuna, former CPP cadre member, Quezon City, August 12, 1992.

him at all was that their relationship had already been a long one. The leadership argued that the mass movement must be rebuilt at a time and in a manner suitable to the protracted people's war strategy; they did not want to revive it "for the wrong reasons." MR-KR's proposal, they said would be

> giving the initiative to the bourgeois reformers . . . After about four exchanges [between M-R and the Central Committee] . . . we were prevailed upon not to continue with [the idea] . . . [However], the essence of that campaign was revived in '78.[35]

A few years later, the leader of the MR-KR of the party was willing to go further than this in arguing for participation in broader front work in the legal arena in the national capital. 1978 saw the CPP's first serious internal dispute, when the Manila-Rizal Committee refused to obey a KT-KS directive to abandon its project of supporting an opposition election campaign.

A CHALLENGE FROM THE URBAN CENTER?

Supposedly as a key element in the process of "normalization" of national politics, and under pressure from the US administration, Marcos called an election for an "Interim Batasang Pambansa" (national parliament—IBP), to be held on April 7, 1978. Martial law was still in place and the chief opposition figure, Benigno ("Ninoy") Aquino, was still in prison. Although the US suggested that Marcos release Aquino at least for the duration of the election, he refused, so Aquino ran his campaign from jail.[36] Aquino was the head of the Lakas ng Bayan (People's Power) ticket, known as Laban ("fight," in Tagalog), which included some personalities much more radical than himself. Alex Boncayao and Trinidad Herrera, for example, were both national democrats, well known organizers among Manila's working class.[37] Most felt that the Laban ticket, no matter how well-received by the Manila citizens, had little hope of being "allowed" to win seats. On the day before voting, the US Embassy reported to its government that, "Marcos will likely resort to major fraud and manipulation to assure KBL (Kilusang Bagong Lipunan. New Society Movement) sweep in Metro Manila."[38] That is exactly what happened. Election results were manipulated so that every Laban candidate in Metro Manila "lost" the contest, even "Ninoy" Aquino.

The KT-KS of the Communist Party had declared that the IBP was a "gimmick of the US-Marcos fascist dictatorship to deceive the Filipino people and the world at large that . . . Marcos is finally yielding some of the powers he has usurped." Quite correctly, they pointed out that the IBP would be "powerless to repeal or even just amend any of the 2,000 anti-national, anti-democratic 'laws' promulgated . . . since 1972 [because] Marcos can veto and completely disregard any 'laws' that the IBP may pass." The Executive Committee's memo went on to state that:

---

[35] Ibid.
[36] Bonner, *Waltzing with a Dictator*, pp. 232–233.
[37] Pimentel, *Edjop*, p. 208; and author's interview with Serrano. Later, the CPP named its armed city partisan group in Metro Manila after the late Alex Boncayao.
[38] Bonner, *Waltzing with a Dictator*, p. 236.

A massive boycott of the polls on "election" day itself, combined with the most militant protests of the people during the "election campaign" is the most effective and strongest means of frustrating the regime's deceptive scheme. We must all do our best to achieve this.

Perhaps as a remark specifically aimed at the pro-participation elements in the MR-KR, the memo pointed out that the non-revolutionary Civil Liberties Union had already "correctly exposed the hand of US imperialism" in the IBP election and taken a "principled stand" in favor of a boycott.[39]

However, the leaders of the Manila-Rizal Party unit had different ideas. They had already decided to participate in the election by helping to set up the Laban ticket and including national democrat activists on the ticket. Claiming not to hold "too many illusions about winning," the Secretary of the MR-KR at that time argued that the Committee was "more concerned about maximizing the opportunity to propagate the national democratic line and expand to other areas."[40] Edgar Jopson, former leader of the moderate National Union of Students of the Philippines, who had become head of the Manila-Rizal United Front Committee, was among those in favor of participation. His role as a liaison between the Party and the personalities of the "traditional opposition" was undoubtedly very important in convincing some of the latter to work with the Manila Party cadres as "tactical allies."[41] (When the KT-KS decided to remove the leader of the MR-KR for acting against its directive to abandon the participation campaign, Jopson replaced him.)

It seems that the Manila protagonists did not intend their position to be taken as a critique of the basic strategic framework, but rather as an interpretation of what was the most effective way for the revolutionary forces to work, within that broad strategy, in the national capital. The central leadership, however, recognized that MR-KR's tactics may have caused cracks to appear in the basic project, especially in relation to the Party's uncompromising attitude towards the bourgeois opposition. As Malay says, the 1978 election was the first opportunity since the declaration of martial law for the "anti-Marcos, anti-communist 'third alternative'" to become a real political force. The Central Committee also pointed out that, if the revolutionary movement helped anti-Marcos "reactionaries" to topple the martial law regime, it would then have had great trouble further advancing the armed struggle, the goal of which was seizure of state power.[42] The oppressive aspects of martial law were proving conducive to the growth of the armed struggle in the countryside, if not to the mass movements in the urban centers. At such an important moment in the revolution's development, the Party leadership did not want to lose those conditions to a regime of anti-Marcos but conservative, traditional politicians.[43]

What happened between the KT-KS and the MR-KR is well known in general outline, if not in detail. Briefly, when the Central Committee released its memo (dated March 3, 1978) calling for Party-led forces to boycott the elections, the Manila committee was already involved in the Laban campaign. The national leadership insisted that the boycott policy be adhered to, but the MR-KR voted to disregard the

---

[39] "Our Stand on the 'Interim Batasang Pambansa' and the 'Election' of April 7, 1978," *Ang Bayan*, Special Issue (English Edition), March 3, 1978.

[40] Quoted in Pimentel, *Edjop*, p. 207.

[41] Ibid.; also, author's interviews with CN and Serrano.

[42] Malay, "The Dialectics," p. 14.

[43] Ibid.

KT-KS directive, claiming that abandonment of the campaign at that stage would mean "chaos and confusion in our ranks, not to mention among our allies." [44] Faced with its first serious case of insubordination, the KT-KS was determined to act decisively, but not without at least a show of democracy. After a special conference lasting weeks, in which the two sides debated the matter but resolved nothing of any substance, the central leadership charged the MR-KR head and other members of the committee of "factionalism." "Disciplinary actions" were meted out. [45]

The entire process created a lot of bitterness within the Manila ranks and organizing work in the region suffered for some time. [46] However, the fallout, so to speak, was related not to ideological difference, but to the central leadership's method of dealing with dissidence. The most significant issue seems to have been that of regional control over tactics. None of the Party members interviewed in 1992 (including ex-MR-KR members) considered the dispute to have been about strategy. One former "united front cadre" said:

> the theoretical arguments of MR were not really deviating from [the] protracted people's war [line] . . . Even if participation [had been] the correct tactical approach, it would not necessarily mean that the MR analysis was correct. And perhaps because of the incorrectness, in a manner of speaking, of the MR position (i.e. the analysis), a lot of the key cadres were not convinced and therefore, adopted the position taken by the center.

He went on to say that, at that time however, a substantial deviation from the strategy could not have come from inside the Party anyway:

> One becomes a member of the CPP because of [a] belief . . . in the primacy of the armed struggle, to achieve power. The CPP was founded on armed struggle; that was the cutting edge. . . . In '78, the CPP was just in its ninth year, and not mature enough to detach itself from the original sin, as it were. No-one in the CPP, not even the most avant-garde . . . could have seen things in a qualitatively different way. [47]

In the light of this reality, Gregg Jones's conclusion that in 1978, "an opportunity to carefully redefine CPP policies toward the prickly question of participation in elections and alliances . . . was allowed to pass," [48] is overstated. At that early stage, it was difficult for cadres even to think outside the protracted people's war framework. Any articulate bid to challenge that theory would have failed, perhaps less spectacularly but just as finally as the Manila-Rizal group's attempted "adjustment."

---

[44] MR-KR cadre member quoted in Pimentel, *Edjop*, p. 209.

[45] Pimentel, *Edjop*, pp. 210–217. For another, fairly detailed discussion of the "debate" and the way in which it was resolved, see Jones, *Red Revolution*, pp. 113–122.

[46] See Malay, "The Dialectics"; see also A. Guerrero, "Our Urgent Tasks," (1975) reprinted in *Philippine Society and Revolution*; and Jose Maria Sison with Rainer Werning, *The Philippine Revolution: The Leader's View* (New York & London: Crane Russak, 1989), pp. 105 & 114.

[47] Author's interview with "NT," united front cadre member (who worked directly underneath MR–KR in 1978), Quezon City, December 21, 1992.

[48] Jones, *Red Revolution*, p. 122.

SHAPING THE "SHIELD"—DISCUSSIONS ABOUT UNITED FRONT WORK

The controversial 1991 "Reaffirm" document states that the "1978 boycott had more damaging consequences [for the Party] than the 1986 boycott error," but it is difficult to find any CPP cadre member who agrees with that assessment.[49] The 1986 boycott policy and the consequent marginalization of the national democratic movement is generally seen as having been "disastrous."[50] But the period between the 1978 dispute and the beginnings of the serious splits in the broad "anti-fascist" fronts in 1984 is described by Party cadres now as a time of relative harmony and unity for the Party, despite the severe shock of the 1978 clash.[51] Although there was certainly a great deal of debate, especially about the question of the balance between armed struggle in the countryside and urban mass movements, it seems that we cannot characterize the debate about strategy simply in terms of growing tensions that eventually "blew up."

Some months after (but not simply as a result of) the 1978 dispute between MR-KR and the central leadership, the Party restructured its work in the national capital. The armed struggle in the countryside was forging ahead and the leadership wanted to ensure the effective development of the urban, legal movement.[52] From 1979 to 1982, a relatively rancor-free series of discussions about the legal mass movement, especially united front work, seem to have been conducted, involving both the "basic sectors" and the "middle forces." One of those centrally placed in the mass movement work circles at the time recalled that:

> there were some key issues raised. One was the role of the middle forces in the Philippines, the students and intellectuals, the petit-bourgeoisie. If you compare the size of this class [in the Philippines] at that time with, say, the Chinese or Vietnamese revolutions, the [latter] were much smaller. We [were] in a situation where we have a bigger intelligentsia, and it became obvious that they [were] playing a very important role in the movement. So, [we thought], maybe we should review this dimension.[53]

What came out of this "review" was a number of proposals for mass movement work based on a more realistic view of the "hegemonial [sic] influence of bourgeois democracy in Philippines."[54]

Limited space makes it impossible to explain in detail all the debates and proposals, but, briefly, in 1979 a group of top Party cadres ran some discussion groups to thrash out new ideas for the non-military aspects of the revolution and to draft plans to be taken to the eighth plenum of the Central Committee. There were two special groups to deal with the two different "blocs" within united front work: the first, headed by Isagani Serrano, covered the trade unions, peasants, urban poor—the "basic forces." At the 1980 plenum, this group was formalized as the

---

[49] "Reaffirm," p. 109. I asked a number of high-ranking CPP members whether they agreed with the statement. None did.

[50] Author's interview with "MM," ex-Central Committee member, Quezon City, December 12, 1992.

[51] Author's interviews with Serrano and CN; also with Rudy Salas, former Chairman of the CPP, Quezon City, December 8, 1992.

[52] Porter, "Strategic Debates," p. 21.

[53] Author's interview with CN.

[54] Porter, "Strategic Debates," p. 21.

National Commission for Mass Movements. (It later became the National Urban Commission.)[55] One of the most important proposals to come out of the original group was for a national trade union center; the Kilusang Mayo Uno (KMU) was set up in 1980. There was also a proposal to build up a national federation of legal peasant organizations. However, it took a few more years for some cadres to convince a majority of the leaders that such an organization was necessary, that it was not merely a "reformist" move liable to weaken the peasants' commitment to the revolutionary armed struggle. The Kilusang Magbubukid ng Pilipinas (KMP, Peasant Movement of the Philippines) was not established until mid-1985.[56]

The second of the 1979 special groups, headed by Horacio "Boy" Morales, dealt with the "special forces"—the nationalist opposition, the anti-Marcos opposition, the "bourgeois liberals," and "the various wings of the social democrats."[57] Out of this group's discussions, among other things, came a proposal for a very broad united front formation within which the National Democratic Front (of Party-led groups) would be only one force. The original proposal was not adopted, but later the Party developed some plans for a National Revolutionary Council which, in the long-term, would form the basis of a national coalition government. Other elements of the proposals for this kind of united front work also appeared later, with the institution of the Nationalist Alliance for Justice, Freedom, and Democracy (NAJFD) which had its own specific plan for a national democratic coalition government.[58] It should perhaps be noted here that these legal organizations did not function simply as "fronts" for the CPP over the following ten or more years. Even tightly organized but at least nominally independent institutions will acquire some autonomy and can be very difficult to control completely. However, the closeness of the relationships between the Communist Party and both the KMU and the KMP, for example, is evidenced by the impact of the 1992–93 CPP disputes on those organizations: both the KMP and the KMU suffered splits along ideological and organizational fault lines very similar to those that occurred between Party members and units.[59]

The innovations arising out of these special united front groups were based, as Porter notes, on some novel ideas about the Party's legal work.[60] However, it is not clear that Serrano, Morales, et al. were "argu[ing] for a strategy that would put primary emphasis on a combination of . . . urban mass movements and united fronts with liberal democrats and reformists."[61] They did not see their ideas for this new work as a direct challenge to the strategy of a protracted people's war, but rather as a vehicle for incorporating a greater emphasis on both legal and underground urban

---

[55] Author's interviews with Serrano and Salas.

[56] Author's interview with Serrano; also with two other "national level cadres": "Steve," national level cadre member in the peasant sector, Manila, December 9, 1992, and "MM," ex-head, National Commission for Mass Movements and Trade Union Department of the CPP, Quezon City, January 28, 1992.

[57] Author's interview with Serrano.

[58] Author's interview with CN.

[59] See the reports in the *Philippine Daily Inquirer*, on the splits within KMU (November 8, 1993) and KMP (November 9 and 10, 1993).

[60] Porter, "Strategic Debates," p. 21. The importance accorded to the work can be gauged by the standing of some of the people involved in it: Isagani Serrano, Horacio Morales, Ed de la Torre, and Edgar Jopson were all top-ranking cadres. The then chairman of the CPP, Rudy Salas, was involved in his official capactiy and took part in the constant discussions.

[61] Porter, "Strategic Debates," p. 21. Emphasis added.

struggles within the existing strategic framework. Such ideas very likely sowed some seeds of doubt about the adequacy of that framework, but they were not to be articulated fully or clearly until some years later. The current central Party leadership has criticized the turn taken by the leadership at the beginning of the 1980s towards "city-centered alliance work and political movement."[62] However, it is important to remember that the decisions made then were not being somehow forced or manipulated by a disenchanted fraction of the Party, but were made and acted upon by the leadership as a whole. Serrano, at least, insists that it was not a time of great frustration and conflict:

> I consider '79 to '82 as really a time of creation and imagination about all these possibilities in the united front arrangements. I have been checking with people about how they look at those times—we were all happy. [There were] some little organizational dynamics between some guys [which] we were able to manage at the time, some hard feelings about who's [heading] what [but] that's very normal.[63]

Something was certainly going right for the revolutionary movement in the national capital at that time. When Marcos called a presidential election in 1981, the national democrats were able to convince all the Marcos oppositionists, including Salvador "Doy" Laurel, to join a boycott campaign. It was a highly successful campaign. The coalition for this campaign, known as the "People's MIND" (Movement for Independent National Democracy) was the brain-child of the ND united front cadres. There was not to be another such campaign that would unite almost all the "traditional opposition" politicians and revolutionary activists against the dictatorship. By the time of the next election, the political environment was changing and the NDs' united front work was suffering from lack of that creative, experienced leadership.[64]

Unfortunately almost the whole core group of cadres working on re-shaping the revolutionary movement in Manila was arrested in 1982 and not released until 1986, after Cory Aquino came to power. This was a very heavy blow to the Party's united front work. The chairman of the Party was not among those captured, so he was able to provide the continuity of ideas required to keep the projects going. However, there was a severe lack of personnel just at a time when more was needed. The top people were in prison and others had been sent to Mindanao, because the Party's project of advancing the revolution on that island was also considered of great strategic importance. Edgar Jopson, for instance, had been assigned to help the movement develop there, as had Serrano's deputy in the National Commission for Mass Movements, Ric Reyes.[65]

---

[62] Central Committee, CPP, "General Review of Important Events and Decisions from 1980 to 1991," reprinted in *Rebolusyon*, Special Issue 2 (April 1993): 13.

[63] Author's interview with Serrano.

[64] See Wurfel, *Filipino Politics*, pp. 251–253; for another brief discussion of the 1981 election, see Emmanuel S. De Dios, "The Erosion of the Dictatorship," in Aurora Javate de Dios, Petronilo Bn. Daroy, and Lorna Kalaw-Tirol, eds. *Dictatorship and Revolution: Roots of People's Power* (Quezon City: Conspectus, 1988). For detailed discussion of anti-Marcos united front activities between August 1983 and the 1986 election, see Ma. Serena I. Diokno, "Unity and Struggle," also in this edited volume.

[65] Author's interview with Serrano; and see Pimentel, *Edjop*, pp. 247–249.

THE "UPSURGE" AGAINST MARCOS BEGINS AND THE CPP'S ISOLATION LOOMS

According to plan, the Party and the New People's Army (NPA) had made great headway on many fronts. The revolutionary movement had become truly national, with around sixty guerrilla fronts in place throughout the archipelago. The NPA consisted of at least ten thousand regulars and thousands more part-time "red fighters," and the "mass base" of supporters numbered hundreds of thousands.[66] At its eighth plenum, in September–October 1980, the Central Committee had decided that the revolution was moving out of the "early sub-stage of the strategic defensive."[67] The Party would launch the "strategic counter-offensive" (SCO) "to develop further the intensity of the people's war" and move into the "advanced sub-stage."[68] Then came the assassination of Marcos's old rival, former senator Benigno Aquino, on August 21, 1983.

As is well known by now, Aquino's assassination sparked off, among other things, a flight of capital from Manila and the beginnings of active protest against the Marcos regime by the middle classes. Protest rallies and marches grew in frequency and size, providing the spirit and experience for what eventually culminated in the huge gatherings on Epifanio de los Santos Avenue (EDSA) in February 1986. For the national democratic movement, however, the period between the Aquino assassination and the "People Power" revolution at EDSA was not one of a smooth strategic or even tactical integration with other anti-dictatorship forces.

From the end of 1983 until February 1985, national-democratic mass organizations of students, workers, and peasants, along with the previously largely acquiescent middle classes, took to the streets under the banners of a number of loose alliances, to demand political changes. First came "JAJA" (Justice for Aquino, Justice for All). Although ND forces were centrally involved in organizing this formation, it was not considered a priority by the CPP leadership. A top cadre member in urban mass movement work at the time states that, at first, this kind of coalition work was officially left to the national youth and student wing. However, the Party's united front people in Manila at the time decided to involve themselves anyway,[69] and, as the protest movement grew bigger, the CPP leadership took it more seriously. Along with that serious interest, however, came the desire to shape or keep the protests in line with the revolutionary agenda. At the same time, the non-revolutionary groups were concerned to keep the anti-dictatorship movement out of the hands of the communists. As one former CPP cadre put it, while

---

[66] See Philippine military and CPP estimates cited in Mediansky, "The New People's Army: A Nation-wide Insurgency in the Philippines," *Contemporary Southeast Asia* 8, 1 (June 1986): 2–4.

[67] The CPP formulation of the "stages" of the revolution is the same as Mao Zedong's: 1) strategic defensive; 2) strategic stalemate; 3) strategic offensive. For a critical discussion of the concept, see Omar Tupaz [pseudonym for Nathan Quimpo], "Towards a Revolutionary Strategy of the '90s," *Debate* 1 (September 1991).

[68] Author's interview with Frank Fernandez, General Secretary, NDF [National Democratic Front]; Southern Tagalog region, December 30, 1992; (Frank Fernandez has since resigned from the General Secretary position).

[69] Author's interview with MM.

the Party is very protective of its own integrity, its own position and line; the others are also guarding their own agenda and are very jealous or suspicious of the Party and Party elements.[70]

Large parts of the social democratic movement in the Philippines have long been strongly anti-communist.[71] It was a difficult battle, particularly since the national democratic organizations provided so much of the "critical mass" in the street demonstrations.

None of these coalitions lasted long, so great were the strains of alliance work involving representatives from an ideological spectrum ranging from revolutionary communists to "anti-fascist" Makati business people. While the national-democrats' penchant for sectarianism was not the only obstacle to a tighter, more effective anti-dictatorship front, it was, by all accounts, an important contributor. The hard-line positions taken by some of the legal organizations closely associated with the CPP in the run-up to and during the 1986 election have been criticized since by major Party figures. Debilitating arguments about, for example, whether the slogan for the marches and rallies should be "Marcos Resign!" or "Overthrow the US-Marcos Dictatorship!" reflected not only ideological and political differences, but also a deep-seated resistance on the part of the national-democratic forces to participate in what they saw as "non-revolutionary" politics.

Tensions between the different political forces came to a head at the founding congress of the national-democrat-initiated BAYAN (Bagong Alyansang Makabayan. New Nationalist Alliance) in September 1985, shortly before Marcos called the "snap" presidential election. BAYAN was to be the most advanced "anti-fascist" alliance ever established in the Philippines, but it ended up as another coalition of national-democratic mass organizations after the Independent Caucus (of socialists, which later became BISIG [Bakluran sa Ikauunlad ng Sosyalistang Isip at Gawa]), social-democrats, and most of the liberal-democrats walked out of the founding congress. They charged the national-democrats with reneging on agreements about how the leadership of BAYAN would be constituted and of "stacking" the congress with their supporters in order to push through the changes. Later, when BAYAN followed the CPP line of "boycott" of the "snap" presidential election, remaining united front ties between the national democrats and other progressive anti-Marcos activists were all but severed. The mistrust generated within the Philippine progressive ranks by the BAYAN affair lasted for years and some degree of suspicion still lingers.

As the protest movement against him grew in both numbers and determination, and as the economy worsened, Marcos came under increasing pressure from the Reagan administration to find a way to silence his critics. With an overconfidence that was to prove disastrous, on November 3, 1985, Marcos announced (on a US current affairs television program) that he was calling an early presidential election for February 1986.[72] Like the US State Department at the time, the Executive

---

[70] Ibid.

[71] Author's interview with (left-wing) social democrat activist, Karen Tanada, Quezon City, November 19, 1992.

[72] Bonner, *Waltzing with a Dictator*, pp. 386–87. Bonner explains that the State Department was not in favor of an election at that time, because they believed that the opposition was not sufficiently prepared for the contest. In this situation, they thought, the only winners would be

Committee of the CPP assumed that Marcos could not (would not) lose the election. The Committee decided on a boycott policy, thereby relegating the CPP-led legal organizations to the sidelines as the movement to replace the dictator with the widow of his long-time political rival grew. Believing that Marcos would cheat his way to victory yet again while still retaining the support of the US, the Executive Committee declared that,

> the February election is . . . meaningless to the broad masses of our people. No candidate of consequence is upholding their fundamental interests. If at all, there is the mere possibility that exploitation and oppression may not be as intense under a new regime. In exchange for this are the illusions which aim to delay the attainment of genuine national freedom and democracy . . . The Party vigorously exposes and firmly opposes the snap election as a blatant swindle and evil scheme of the US-Marcos clique. And the Party's stand is that a boycott is the correct response of the people to an election that avails them nothing . . . As long as we are creative, patient and resolute in carrying the boycott campaign forward through our persuasive arguments, whatever negative effects some comrades and friends think would emerge will be temporary in nature.[73]

This was not to be, unfortunately. Friends would be alienated and many comrades deeply disheartened by the decision, despite the "self-criticism" made by the Party in 1986.

To date, it is not clear why the Executive Committee's decision to proceed with a boycott decision was sustained despite the opposition of two out of the five KT-KS members and, it appears, opposition from so many other ranking cadres in the Party. At least one person who was a Central Committee member at the time is convinced that, had a Central Committee meeting been held, the decision would have been different. And he believes that the likelihood of such an outcome was probably "one of the considerations for the staunch pro-boycott people [in] the KT-KS" when they chose not to call a meeting of a wider body to make such an important decision. He explained that the KT-KS decision can be understood in the context of the imperatives of the "strategic counter-offensive":

> If you believe that the situation is going fast, [that it is] a revolutionary situation, rapidly developing towards an insurrectionary moment . . . you believe it is combustible, [then] you know that this parliamentary intervention has to be counteracted. [But] not by participation, because the momentum is for the people to fight the regime, outside of [those parliamentary processes] . . . It would be contradictory to your reading of the situation and your big plan, to participate.[74]

When the Politburo later assessed the boycott policy, it criticized the way in which the decision was arrived at as well as the policy itself.

---

the Communists. See the discussion of the US policy chaos at the time in chapter 15, *Waltzing With A Dictator*.

[73] *Ang Bayan*, December 1985.

[74] Author's interview with MM.

At its 1985 plenum, the Central Committee had declared that the major task was the overthrow of the US-Marcos dictatorship, which could catapult the revolution into a strategic shift, to the "stalemate" stage.[75] This prospect was, of course, interrupted by the snap election call. The Party leadership was unprepared to make the decisions necessary to position itself in the front ranks of the anti-dictatorship forces. Although the CPP-led legal organizations' united front work with anti-Marcos allies had been foundering for the last twelve months at least, the continuing growth of the armed struggle and the masses on the streets encouraged the CPP leadership's perception of the Strategic Counter Offensive rolling inexorably on towards "strategic shift." As in 1978, but unlike events in 1981, the leadership refused to compromise its revolutionary principles for the sake of a broad united front. The difference was that, this time, they were completely on their own. And the historical events would leave the revolutionary movement on the political sidelines—a new and debilitating experience for the national democrats.

DIFFERENCES EMERGE FROM THE CRACKS

Among CPP cadres and rank and file, the boycott policy was the most controversial position taken by the Party leadership to that date; debates on the policy were contentious from the start. Those former united front cadre members in prison during this period were, no doubt, very disappointed with how the coalition tasks were being managed. And they certainly made their views known to the Party leadership about the boycott vs. participation question. Serrano says,

> they [the central leadership] consulted individuals on what position to take
> . . . They consulted all around the prisons; all the top guys, the key guys were
> [incarcerated] in Metro Manila, so they were accessible. I don't remember
> anyone agreeing to the boycott decision. We wrote notes, to follow up our
> positions. . . . We were not simply observers inside prison.[76]

Other high-ranking cadres also remember that there were many voices raised against the boycott decision. Those voices, Joma Sison claims, included his own. (He had been in prison since 1977). Sison states firmly that the question of whether or not to boycott the election should never have divided the revolutionary movement because the Communist Party will necessarily boycott such a bourgeois farce anyway, since aside from anything else, the Party declares itself to be outside that bourgeois system. But, the CPP-led legal movements should play whatever role is most appropriate to their "arena of struggle" and in this case, some kind of "critical participation" was most appropriate.[77]

Given its own historical conditions of theoretical and cultural rigidity, as well as a political environment in which "moderate" anti-Marcos forces were dominant for the first time in years, it is not clear to what extent the CPP could have affected or influenced the events during and following the People Power revolution had they decided to participate in the election process. Probably, the Party would need to have been much better prepared, theoretically and organizationally, to keep its

---

[75] Author's interviews with MM and "Steve."
[76] Author's interview with Serrano.
[77] Sison and Werning, *The Philippine Revolution*, p. 115.

momentum more or less intact after the EDSA revolution. That is, even if the national democratic forces had participated in the campaign to have Cory Aquino elected and thereby won some right to greater input into decision-making after her inauguration, they probably would not have gained much more as a revolutionary force (in the way that the Party defines "revolution," at least). On the other hand, they might, at least, have begun a reconsideration of the Party's role earlier and with less bitterness and confusion:

> [Participation] wouldn't have catapulted the movement into power, or into a position near power. The benefit of an anti-boycott position mainly would have been to trigger a process of re-thinking strategy and tactics. In turn, this would have minimized the political losses between 1986 and the present.[78]

In documents criticizing the boycott policy, leading cadres—especially in Manila—had pointed out that the mistaken decision reflected a deeper malaise in the Party's analysis and program. The National Youth and Student Department of the Party wrote:

> As a final word, we submit that our questions go far beyond the boycott policy. Behind the boycott tactics lurk the deep-rooted problems concerning the antifascist struggle, the parliamentary struggle, the united front, the urban mass movement and generally speaking, the whole strategy and tactics of the Philippine revolution. It goes without saying that the ideological roots of the multifarious problems [should] be submitted to a rigorous examination.[79]

The editorial board of Praktika (leaders in the National Urban Commission) went further, but still couched the critique in terms that avoided calling into explicit question the protracted people's war strategy:

> In retrospect, the boycott tactic [was] just the latest, and perhaps, the costliest manifestation of a tendency to . . . give undue importance to the comprehensiveness of national democratic politics in formulating tactics in the open mass movement and legal democratic alliances.[80]

Both of these critiques were concerned mostly with the failures in the field of united front work, for obvious reasons. The revolutionary movement's experience (or lack of it) in the election campaign and the popular uprising which followed

---

[78] Author's interview with "NT," author of the CPP's National Youth and Student Department's "Against the Snap Election Boycott," *Praktika*, a "Theoretical Journal of the Party in the National Capital," 1, 1 (May 14, 1986).
[79] "Against the Snap Election Boycott."
[80] Editorial, *Praktika*, May 14, 1986, p. 21. "Comprehensiveness" here refers to the view of CPP cadres that the revolutionary national-democratic agenda of the Party (and its legal organizations) is the only one among opposition groups that offers a comprehensive analysis of Philippine social ills and a corresponding strategy for overcoming them. In alliance work, this belief manifests itself in the general Party position that, in any activity in which the CPP is involved, the national-democratic agenda should be central, whether it appears in its "minimum" or "maximum" program versions.

prompted many Party members to raise questions about their working relations with other political forces, questions about the vanguard role of the CPP, the problem of sectarianism, and whether the Party has a monopoly on "correct" interpretations of Philippine politics. However, it was not until later, after some experience of the behavior of a non-dictatorial state, that the Party's intellectuals began openly to question the notion of "total military victory." The nature of the Party's own critique of the boycott policy slowed this process.

Several weeks after the EDSA "People Power" revolution, and, no doubt, following some intense discussions among the Party's central leadership, the Politburo vindicated the many critics of the KT-KS. It declared that the boycott policy had been a "tactical error" and a "major political blunder," arrived at through a hasty decision-making process and a flawed political assessment. The political assessment had:

1. Overestimated US capacity to impose its subjective will on local politics.
2. Underestimated the bourgeois reformists' capabilities and determination to engage the Marcos regime in a decisive contest for state power.
3. Ignored the fact that the Marcos clique had become extremely isolated and its capacity to rule was fast eroding.
4. Misread the people's deep anti-fascist sentiments and readiness to go beyond the confines of the electoral process in their determination to end the fascist dictatorship.

To help the Party revive itself after the demoralization which resulted from its failure to assist in the ousting of Marcos, the Politburo further declared that:

the Party leadership is now encouraging leading Party organs . . . to sum up their experiences regarding the boycott policy. . . . Steps are being taken to encourage and develop the democratic spirit and democratic way of doing things in the Party.[81]

The terms of the Politburo's judgment portended what would be the limitations of this new democratic debate; it suggested the error was merely tactical, rather than strategic. An ex-united front cadre member, now involved in legal movement work, believes that this assessment "resulted in a lot of damage" because it was not critical enough.

It would have been different if the center [had] acknowledged that the boycott led to strategic problems, and [that] therefore, we had to address those strategic problems. That would have provided a larger framework for rethinking. [Instead], it was reduced to a simple tactical error, [so] it was but logical that the policies would be more of the same.[82]

Gareth Porter states that, after the events of February 1986, "dissident cadres campaigned openly for an alternative to the people's war strategy" and goes on to cite Marty Villalobos' papers outlining the "insurrectionary" line and where the

---

[81] *Ang Bayan*, May 1986.
[82] Author's interview with NT.

Party had gone wrong.[83] But this is an overstatement of the situation. Indeed, Villalobos wrote what were then very radical critiques; however, he was the only one to do so, and they were not greatly admired within the party, even among the most critical cadres. Villalobos himself says that virtually nobody got to read them,[84] and those who did were less than comfortable with the strength of his critique. The following view was typical among leading dissident cadres (and ex-cadres) in Manila at the end of 1992:

> Marty articulated his position[s] [but] it had no immediate result of provoking debate and convincing people to his side. . . . It is quite possible that his style turned off some people. . . . He made some definitive statements and he openly challenged Joma. Well, maybe what he did contributed to the whole process of rethinking, but in the immediate term, he was not able to get the support. . . . What I'm saying is that, the style of your debate, the rhetoric, should also be calibrated; at that time, it would have been better if the approach was more polite, more diplomatic. The situation now is different; Joma is accusing people [in public], so they have a right to defend themselves.[85]

The reality of the situation was that, although many people had many questions about the tactics pursued over the last couple of years, especially in the urban areas, even those who had been the most critical were shy of stating explicitly that the Party's basic strategy should be abandoned or of formulating alternative policies. Some did, of course, assert that the protracted people's war strategy was no longer appropriate now that an elected civilian government was in place. But the ways in which they explained their criticisms or their breaks from the movement undermined any potential for their actions or words to have a larger effect on Party policy.

THE PARTY SPLITS

In 1987, in Negros, one of the best-known guerrilla leaders (and a former Secretary of the Negros south-east sub-regional Party Committee), Nemesio Dimafiles, led a break away from the CPP of fifteen to twenty members/guerrilla fighters. Among other things, Dimafiles was opposed to the Party's policy of "waging full-scale war against the Aquino government."[86] After he had left the CPP, he explained in interviews run by the Negros newsmagazine *Viewpoints* (published by the brother of one of Dimafiles's fellow resignees) that he no longer believed the armed struggle was appropriate: "Where the light of peace, no matter how dim, shines through, the argument for war is lost."[87] Dimafiles had doubts about Communist Party policies often during his many years in the movement (and as a member of the Party),[88] but they did not amount to a coherent critique of strategy,

---

83 Porter, "Strategic Debates," p. 24.
84 Author's interview with "Villalobos."
85 Author's interview with NT.
86 B. Pimentel, "The Outlaws of Negros," Part I, *Midweek*, July 27, 1988, p. 4.
87 Ibid., p. 2.
88 Ibid., pp. 3–9 passim; also see Pimentel, "The Making of Nemesio Dimafiles," *Midweek* January 11, 1989, pp. 3–5 passim.

and certainly do not seem ever to have been presented to the Party as such. He was in no sense an intellectual of the movement, which made it easier for the Party to dismiss his actions as those of a renegade and a traitor. The fact that the Dimafiles group itself later split, amid stories of financial and other corruption, only confirmed this characterization in the eyes of CPP members.[89]

A more dramatic departure from the people's war project in the Aquino era was that of the founding head of the NPA, "Ka Dante." He too believed that the moment for armed struggle against the government had passed, at least for now, and that the Party should turn its attention to legal political struggles in order to further the cause of improving life for impoverished Filipinos. He was particularly critical of the urban guerrilla campaigns involving the assassination of police officers and military men, etc., claiming that this kind of action provoked rebel right-wing military men to murder a certain number of legal left personalities. Dante, too, was no intellectual who could methodically present his arguments in coherent form so that the ideas could be disseminated and discussed in detail. Even if he had been, however, his public criticism of those choosing to continue with the armed struggle—rather than merely saying, for example, that it was no longer his chosen way—ensured that the national democrats would dismiss him as a traitor to the cause, as someone no longer qualified to speak about the revolutionary struggle. Dante had further undermined his continued right to speak as a revolutionary by accepting government funding in order to set up agricultural cooperatives—he was seen to have been co-opted by the regime.[90]

Other critiques of the strategy in the post-Marcos era were implied rather than stated. For example, the "pop-dems" ("popular-democrats") were a small group of formerly high-ranking CPP intellectuals who, while critical of the Party leadership's lack of imagination, still believed to change the way the national-democratic movement approached its political tasks by encouraging the party to put more emphasis on the "democratic" aspect of the national-democratic struggle.[91] They knew, however, that to question the basic strategy would be to render their critique illegitimate; the suggestions had to be presented as tactical, or as adjustments to the traditional national democratic strategy. But while their ideas were not condemned outright by the CPP, neither were they tackled seriously. The "pop-dem" organizations gradually established a quite distant (though non-antagonistic) relationship to CPP forces, and failed to have any real impact on the national-democratic discourse.[92]

While these more or less overt, albeit rather ineffective, challenges were troubling the CPP, more disturbing during the Aquino years were other internal problems and altered political conditions. The Politburo's self-criticism policy had opened a period of debate in the CPP, but by mid-1987 the Party leadership had closed off that opening and denounced the Aquino regime as "fascist with a liberal

---

[89] Author's interview with Frank Fernandez.

[90] Author's interview with Loretta Rosales, President, Partido ng Bayan, Quezon City, November 13, 1992.

[91] The main figures in this movement were and are Fr. Ed de la Torre, Horacio "Boy" Morales, and Isagani Serrano—all former key united front activists in the revolutionary movement.

[92] Author's interview with "AS," former CPP united front cadre who eventually grew frustrated with the pop-dem's reluctance to engage in a direct and substantial critique of the CPP's theory and policies. Interview in Quezon City, February 24, 1993.

facade." While it was deemed by many to be a premature and ill-considered decision, it should be noted that serious government provocation played a part in the situation. Influential sections of the Armed Forces of the Philippines, including the Reform the Armed Forces Movement (RAM) were already dismayed by the progressive tint of Aquino's first cabinet and were fighting hard to have all vestiges of left influence removed from the administrative apparatuses.[93] Some of the most audacious assassinations of left-wing figures took place during Aquino's term, mostly apparently carried out by the rebel military elements bent on destabilizing her regime. Those murdered included KMU leader, Rolando Olalia, and young BAYAN leader Leandro Alejandro. Nor were the assassinations restricted to known radical figures. Amnesty International reported that human rights abuses overall increased under the Aquino regime. Killings included one of the worst state massacres in contemporary Philippine history, when twenty-one peasants were shot dead while demonstrating for land reform on Mendiola bridge next to Malacanang Palace, in January 1987.[94]

What became known as the "Mendiola massacre" was the last straw for the failing peace talks then taking place between the NDF and the government of the Republic. Although the cease-fire of December 1986–January 1987 had been reasonably well observed by both sides, negotiations on the substantive issues—for the NDF, the "root causes" of the civil war—never really started. The government insisted on using the newly ratified Constitution as the framework, but the NDF had already declared the 1986 Constitution "pro-imperialist and anti-people." Just a few months earlier, the CPP had called for a boycott of the plebiscite to ratify the new Constitution. Despite this call, and reflecting the confusion and lack of order among the national-democratic ranks at the time, many CPP-led organizations went instead for a "critical 'yes' vote." The boycott failed and the "Yes" vote won convincingly.

The NDF withdrew from the peace negotiations, accusing the government of being insincere about tackling the "unjust socio-economic and political structures causing the widespread poverty and oppression of our people." Aquino then dropped all pretense of forging a negotiated settlement with the rebels and instead, declared that she would unsheathe her "sword of war"; she then embarked upon the "total war" against the revolutionary forces.[95] The next few years were difficult ones for the NPA. The "total war" policy, involving a "low-intensity conflict" strategy (whereby the military tried to deprive the NPA of their mass base support) took a great toll on the guerrilla forces in many regions. One of its nastiest components was the use of fanatical anti-communist "vigilante squads" such as the Alsa Masa (Masses Arise).[96] The savage exploits of these Filipino death squads are well documented by now, as is the Aquino government's complicity in their activities. Sometimes trained and usually manipulated by the armed forces, the vigilante squads helped to destroy many formerly strong bases of support for the NPA.[97]

The collapse of the peace talks and the renewed intense fighting between the NPA and the AFP (Armed Forces of the Philippines) did not mean the end of the CPP-led legal organizations' participation in the "democratic space" of the early

---

[93] Wurfel, *Filipino Politics*, p. 315.
[94] Jones, *Red Revolution*, p. 173.
[95] Communist Party of the Philippines, "General Review of Important Events," p. 34.
[96] Wurfel, *Filipino Politics*, pp. 316–317.
[97] Author's interview with Frank Fernandez.

Aquino years, however. In the 1987 Congressional elections, the new national democratic political party, the Partido ng Bayan (PnB), ran a number of candidates for the House of Representatives and the Senate. Among them were well-known personalities of the revolutionary movement, including Bernabe Buscayno ("Ka Dante") and "Boy" Morales. Despite the visibility of the left candidates, only two of them won their seats. It was a demoralizing experience for the legal left, but was partly explained by the lack of unity surrounding the very idea of participating in "bourgeois" elections. Some argue that such a political party should not have been so clearly associated with the Communists (Jose Maria Sison, released from prison under Aquino's early move to release all political prisoners, was the first President of PnB), but others did not support the idea of a parliamentary party at all.[98] PnB all but collapsed after its losses in 1987 and was only revived again in 1992—too late to be of much impact in the 1992 synchronized national elections.

In many respects then, the CPP's fortunes went from bad to worse by the end of the 1980s. The CPP had suffered from the military losses sustained under the total war assault. It was also hurt by "self-inflicted" wounds, for the party lost legitimacy in the eyes of the "middle forces" following the election and constitutional referendum boycotts, and later, the CPP's equivocal stand in relation to the right-wing coup attempts by "rebel" soldiers of the AFP. The greatest blow to CPP members' morale and legitimacy resulted from the revelations concerning the disastrous "anti-DPA" (deep penetration agent) campaigns carried out in 1985 in Mindanao and 1988 in the Southern Tagalog region, which includes Metro Manila. The "hysteria" of the campaigns to rid the movement of its real and imagined enemy agents is the saddest story in the CPP's history.[99]

The period of rapid expansion in the early 1980s left the revolutionary movement, particularly the NPA, open to infiltration by military saboteurs and informers. This was first recognized by the Mindanao Commission in mid-1985, so they instigated a campaign to investigate and solve the problem. The campaign got out of hand as it moved down and across the Party's organizational ranks; after learning of how rampant the "investigations" had become, the regional leadership attempted to stem the flow of accusations and "punishments" but it had taken on a momentum of its own. Possibly more than five hundred party members or "red fighters" died in Mindanao alone during the "DPA" purge. More shocking is the fact that a second campaign was started in Southern Tagalog three years later, after the Mindanao Commission leadership had reported their own devastating experience. Perhaps more than one hundred died during the 1988 campaign before the national leadership demanded that it be called off.[100] These campaigns were reported in the Philippines and internationally, provoking accusations from some quarters that the CPP/NPA was indeed the "new Khmer Rouge."[101] While this is a comparison wildly off the mark in so many ways, the revelations of comrades executing comrades, often with little evidence of wrong-doing, had a lasting demoralizing effect on the movement.

---

[98] Author's interviews with "Villalobos" and Loretta Rosales.

[99] W. Bello, "The Philippine Progressive Movement Today: A Preliminary Report on the State of the Left," *Philippine Alternatives* 1, 2, p. 5.

[100] Bello, "The Philippine Progressive Movement," and author's interviews with ex-Mindanao Commission officers, "Villalobos" and "Art."

[101] This charge was first made by Ross Munro in his article, "The New Khmer Rouge," *Commentary* 80, 6 (December 1985).

The CPP criticized itself for the mistakes, announced its adherence to the principles of international human rights laws (including Protocol 2 of the Geneva Convention) and is still in the process of making reparations to the victims' families.[102] However, for many Party members the "anti-DPA" purges raised serious questions not only about the way in which the revolutionary movement conducts itself during the struggle, but also about how the CPP would manage matters of justice if and when it ever holds the reins of state power.[103] One experienced cadre member said:

> What happened with these campaigns was a system of investigation, adjudication and punishment far worse than the bourgeoisie has put in place. It's equally as condemnable as the Inquisitions. In certain cases, [it was] far worse than what happened [then] in some areas of Europe . . . I heard a lot of stories [about the purges]; many ordinary commanders, guerrillas, Party level cadres, were unwilling to participate but were ordered to do so. You see the Party training here—you obey; the cult of obedience is very high, it's treasured, it's cherished, it's inviolate, it's stronger than that practice inside the Catholic Church![104]

Subsequently, people began to question some long-held tenets of Party dogma, especially the concept of "revolutionary class justice," and the influence of Stalin on the CPP's world-view.[105]

Those who did were greatly dismayed by the 1992 paper by "Armando Liwanag" defending the "merits" of Stalin against his detractors, the revisionists Kruschev, Brezhnev and Gorbachev.[106] The question of the CPP finally repudiating Stalinist-type methods was one of the elements of the controversy in the Party during the 1992 "rectification" campaign. But again, among those critical of standing CPP policy, there was no clear or agreed alternative put forward during the "debate." They demanded, simply, that the matter be studied carefully and discussed widely, along with the other substantial issues facing the revolutionary movement at that time. To do otherwise, they believed, would be impossible and or ill-advised for at least two reasons. First, no one felt certain enough about their own views to present

---

[102] Author's interview with Frank Fernandez.

[103] This concern was expressed to me by a number of CPP members interviewed in 1992. For most of them, the original questioning had eventually turned into a demoralizing fear that the CPP in power would be just as repressive as, if not more repressive than, an autocratic regime.

[104] Author's interview with MM.

[105] A CPP cadre member explained it thus: "There is a tendency [in the CPP] to equate class struggle with the physical elimination of the class enemy. This . . . can be traced to the tradition of the communist parties since the Third International, because it is based on the Stalinist concept of intensified class struggle during socialist construction, which brought about the great purge. . . . [The CPP] was set up on the basis of the Great Cultural Revolution. . . . Mao wanted to revive that principle of intensified class struggle and his Great Cultural Revolution was a campaign against [Stalin's later] revisionism. . . . The Great Cultural Revolution brought about [many] killings. . . . That is the immediate historical root of our Party." Author's interview with "Art." For more discussion of the problems of "revolutionary justice," see Bello, "The Philippine Progressive Movement," p. 6.

[106] Armando Liwanag, Chairman, Central Committee, CPP, January 15, 1992, "Stand for Socialism and Against Modern Revisionism," *Rebolusyon* 2 (April–June 1992).

a complete alternative blueprint; the dissidents claimed sincerely to want a process of debate from which coherent positions could emerge. Second, they feared that presenting already formed alternative policies, counterpoised against existing Party ones, would mean to court charges of "factionalism" from the leadership and appear, to the rank and file membership, to be deliberately creating disharmony.[107]

In the light of these remarks and as mentioned earlier at that time, the criticisms in the "Reaffirm" document relating to "petty-bourgeois" challenges to the notion of democratic centralism seem to have been overstated. In relation to other charges made in "Reaffirm," Sison was seen to be overstating the "crime" in order to keep the Party on the theoretical and strategic straight-and-narrow path. In many of these cases, however, he may have been reading the implications of certain questions and criticisms more clearly than the critics themselves. While for so long leading cadres with doubts about aspects of the traditional strategic framework had been thinking and speaking about their new ideas in terms of "adjustments" and "improvements," Sison's attacks on them and their actions forced them into seeing, at least to some extent, how challenging their critiques might be. One former Central Committee member who was one of the core group of early "rejectionists" and who wrote critical commentaries on the Reaffirm document said:

> I was going through that [traditional strategic] framework in the first commentary. I tried to situate the comments within the frame and principles [of protracted people's war], but in the process, I realized it was going beyond that. . . . It would be dishonest on our part to claim that we are still [adhering to it] when a more theoretical study will show that we have to go beyond it to relinquish past mistakes.[108]

Once he had decided to think clearly beyond the traditional framework, or the set of "basic principles," however, this ex-CPP leader was willing to subject all the Party's items of faith to critical study, even if that might mean rejecting "some of the thinking of Marx in the process, and of Lenin." The problem at that time, as he saw it, was that such a step was unacceptable to many of those who were critical only of the way in which the Rectification campaign was being conducted by the Party leadership. It is worth quoting at length how this cadre member thought the process must proceed if the movement is to advance:

> The problem with our forces . . . is that they have been brought up to follow what has been said by the duly constituted authority; they have not been trained to be critical [because] of the low level of theoretical development, especially in the armed forces [i.e., the NPA]. . . . We have to study in small groups and expand gradually; this moment is the testing moment. There is already a big portion of the movement that is going on towards the new thinking, although many . . . are still [thinking] within the narrow framework . . . . So, within the opposition, we have to conduct more theoretical discussion, to show them that [this dispute] is not only about the misuse of

---

[107] Author's interviews with "Art," MM, "Steve," "Villalobos," and AS. Also author's interview with "KS," former NDF activist, Quezon City, October 28, 1992, and with "TD," former Central Committee member, Utrecht, August 18, 1992.

[108] Author's interview with "Art."

authority, it is an ideological conflict. . . . Some people in the middle ground are critical of both JMS [Sison] and the opposition. But that is an illusion . . . the line has been defined, the line has been drawn. . . . I was telling them, you must study the basic issues, because if you are criticizing the opposition because it is going beyond the usual parameters, you should understand it in the context of an intense ideological debate. If they follow the [usual] parameters, they will not win, because they will have to follow the framework of Reaffirm. . . . It has its own logic, it's very logical. . . . The problem is, it doesn't correspond to what really happened [or] to the theoretical advancements worldwide. . . .

Unfortunately, for those "rejectionists" who most wanted to see change in the Party, this (none-too-loud) call for participation in an ideological debate came too late to have any direct positive effect on the CPP during the testing time. The dominant tendency within the leadership was able, through various means, to purge and discredit key dissident figures, and to dissolve or reorganize troublesome Party units and organizations.

CONCLUSION

There is a general view among its intellectual commentators and political supporters that the Communist Party of the Philippines is dogmatic in its theory and flexible in its practice. That is true up to a point, but it gives an overly static picture of the two elements. The relationship between words and deeds has been closer than that observation implies, but in a way that has been damaging for both. While there have been some divergences from or liberal interpretations of national Party scripture, these practices have rarely been conceived as seriously subverting the basic analysis and strategy. They have almost always been thought of and offered as "adjustments" or complements. So, local or sectoral experiences of revolutionary work have not been theorized and incorporated into, or allowed to affect in any fundamental way, the basic strategic doctrine. There was no perceived need for these alternative theories to be formulated while the original theory was assumed still to be correct (and universal) and capable of accommodating the practical adjustments that led to the revolution's successes. It was only when the revolutionary movement's fortunes waned sharply that the cracks widened in the Party and positions become polarized.

The history of the "debates" about strategy and tactics in the CPP shows that it has been impossible to be considered a committed revolutionary except while speaking inside the protracted people's war discourse. The correctness of that framework has been practically an article of faith for Party members. It was not a matter for critique or review. Commitment to the revolution, or even commitment to the Party, demands commitment to the established strategy; there cannot be one without the other. If you are a Communist, a revolutionary, then you speak inside the established framework, what the Party's founder calls the "basic principles" of the revolution. Once you begin to think outside that framework, you are beginning to think outside being a true Communist, a true revolutionary. This "rule" functioned in the CPP almost from the beginning, up until 1992. It was maintained by a combination of authority exercised by the leadership through hierarchical structures and a culture of "self-censorship." Only when the Party went into a crisis could Party members finally begin to think, at one and the same time, that they were committed revolutionaries who considered the established strategy inadequate to the revolutionary task. Such thinking became possible only when the orthodox tendency in the top leadership itself launched stinging attacks on those who had been doing the most successful "adjusting," and when the founder of the Party, Jose Maria Sison, had drastically undermined his own legitimacy (as leader and as chief theorist for the struggle) among other Party intellectuals. Only then did some of the latter began to think and articulate their criticisms distinctly outside the traditional strategic framework. By that time, however, they were too late to convince a sufficient number of people in the Party that their ideas had merit, too late to avoid the debilitating splits and purges that have occurred since.

OF MOTORCADES AND MASSES: MOBILIZATION AND INNOVATION IN PHILIPPINE PROTEST

Vincent G. Boudreau

INTRODUCTION

The fifth and, at that time, bloodiest coup attempt against Corazon Aquino's Philippine presidency occurred in August of 1987. Government troops needed three days to root out the pockets of rebellious soldiers scattered throughout the metropolis, at the end of which time Manila radio stations made an announcement: a segment of the popular movement had called a peculiar sort of demonstration, to commence within hours, in Aquino's defense. Participants were instructed to drive their cars to the parking lot of a major shopping center, from which point a motorcade would embark to tour the city and signal popular support for Aquino.

The demonstration calls attention to itself in two respects. First, because it occurred *after* that particular military challenge had been defeated, it celebrated— rather than contributed to—the government's victory. Second, and perhaps more obviously, a motorcade is a strange form of collective action in a developing setting because it cannot help but exclude those with the most material basis for social activism. The 1987 motorcade seems significant because, at precisely the moment the popular movement chose to commemorate, rather than recreate, its popular intervention of 1986, it adopted a form of praxis which excluded the working classes.

I wish in this piece to regard that August 1987 demonstration as a singular moment in a waning protest wave which had peaked a year and a half earlier. This coincidence of the popular movement's spectatorship, on the one hand, and its exclusionary mode of praxis (separating, in this case, those who drove cars from those who walked) is emblematic of larger changes afoot in Philippine politics, and particularly in Philippine protest. I will also elaborate my understanding of demobilization as a process wherein changing external conditions (i.e. state form, the posture and availability of movement allies) alter the interrelationships between the constituencies allied within the movement. Accordingly, I will view demobilization not as a mere cessation of activity, but as the product of conflicts which arose between movement sub-groups as they attempted to advance—or define—collective goals, and as a product of the dilemma that these disagreements created for cadres.

PEOPLE POWER II: PROTEST AS COMMEMORATION

Scant months after the February 1986 popular uprising, glossy coffee table books recounting the four day adventure were already in the nation's bookstores. On gallery quality pages, rich photographs and heroic prose described Corazon Aquino's presidential campaign leading to the extended mass action in Manila's streets and the dictatorship's eventual flight.[1] These volumes quickly replaced similarly packaged New Society mythologies as the valorized objects of perusal in marble-floored Philippine salas. In a more popular vein, the *Philippine Star* newspaper ran an extended series of articles in which the participants related their individual experience of "people power," in what was supposed to be a many-voiced history of the event. These different commemorations placed a certain punctuation mark on the activism that brought down strongman Ferdinand Marcos; the story's major movements having been completed by mid-1986, little remained but to celebrate the event.

The post-Marcos scenario brought a new texture to Philippine protest, mainly due to realignments within the ranks of the broad anti-dictatorship movement.[2] The national democratic (ND) network's boycott of the 1986 presidential elections marginalized the NDs under the subsequent dispensation.[3] That the national democrats at the time maintained the largest organized constituency and had fought

---

[1] Perhaps the proto-typical book of this sort was Nick Joaquin's hyperbolically titled volume, published under his pen name: Quijano de Manila, *Quartet of the Tiger Moon: Scenes from the People Power Apocalypse* (Manila: Book Stop, 1986). Interestingly, the bibliographic reference of this text lists not only its date and place of publication, but also the information that it is "exclusively distributed by Gift Gate Center Corporation . . . " Others of the same genre include: Cynthia Sta. Maria Baron and Melba Morales Suarez, *Nine Letters: The Story of the 1986 Filipino Revolution* (Quezon City: G. B. Baron, 1986); Monica Allary Mercado, *People Power: The Philippine Revolution of 1986: An Eyewitness History* (Manila: James B. Reuter, S.J., Foundation, 1986); Patricio Mamot, *Profile of Filipino Heroism* (Quezon City: New Day Publishers, 1986).

[2] In what follows, I shall use the term "movement" in a manner consistent with the social movements literature, and particularly follow usage laid down in the resource mobilization and collective behaviors literature. Accordingly, the term "movement" shall signify a broader and more amorphous social phenomenon than social movement organization [SMO]. The broad anti-dictatorship (or progressive) movement includes the range of formal organizations, looser networks, and individual participants first assembled against Marcos. Within this broad assembly existed more discrete and politically homogenous organizations or SMOs--terms I will use in contrast to *movement* or to *broad movement*. This usage allows two helpful distinctions. First (inasmuch as organizations seldom act alone in national Philippine politics) a multi-organizational conception of political movements more exactly depicts the assemblies which actually gather at demonstrations. Second, conceiving of a single and broad pool of movement participants which goes beyond any single organization's constituency allows one to envision cadres (those activists most firmly allied to specific organizations) in their relations with this larger and looser assembly--to conceive the broad movement as both an *agent* and an important *object* of organizational politics.

[3] Regarding their marginalization, the Communist Party of the Philippines' [CPP's] official organ, *Ang Bayan*, called the boycott policy "a major error." It went on to state that, "The revolutionaries were not able to position themselves, and instead were sidelined from the leading current of the people's political struggles during and after the elections. The revolutionary forces were in an almost passive position due to the limitation of the political maneuver of the boycott movement." ["Hindi nakapuwesto ang mga rebolusyonaryo so ubod, at sa halip ay naibukod pa nga sa pangunahing agos ng mga pampulitikang pakikibaka ng mamamayan noong eleksyon at matapos ito. Halos nasa pasibong pusisyon ang mga rebolusyonaryong pwersa dahil sa mga hangganan ng kanilang pampulitikang maniobra na itinakda ng kilusang boykot."] *Ang Bayan*, May 1986.

the dictatorship since 1972 proved inconsequential when post-election protests produced the 250,000-strong demonstration that finally overthrew Marcos. Since virtually everyone regarded these demonstrations as an extension of that electoral process, the NDs' boycott placed them outside of the Aquino popular juggernaut. Indeed, following its boycott, the national democratic movement staged almost no demonstrations until Kilusang Mayo Uno (KMU) labor leader, Rolando Olalia, was murdered in October of 1986.[4] In the vacuum, other political forces—mainly those committed to Aquino's presidency from the movement's moderate flank—sought to consolidate their gains by seeking access to and participation in the emerging Philippine state.[5]

Two discontinuities between movement form and substance, signaling this realignment, surfaced in protest activity during this time. On the one hand, a radical patina persistently overlay demonstrations which, at their core, represented the most moderate and state-supporting activities. On the other hand, this radicalism found its clearest outward expression in the consumption and conspicuous display of technologies so expensive as to be available only to social strata more or less consistently opposed to any radical social transformation.

Anyone sifting through patterns of political mobilization in the immediate post-Marcos period would perhaps conclude that their participants risked great personal danger. At a demonstration which launched the campaign to ratify the constitutional plebiscite, for example, marchers broke intermittently into the link-armed trot of a rally closing ranks. Observing the drizzle that fell that day, one organizer remarked that to start a march in the rain indicated good fortune—implying some power conjured against a lurking danger. Many participants wore squares of Mindanao cloth (*tubaos*) pulled over noses and mouths, a gesture originally intended both to protect against tear gas and conceal identity. Further intimations of danger could be found in the protest technology in evidence along the march. Many in the demonstration had festooned themselves with walkie-talkies and portable two-way radios, which linked them in a private and excluding dialogue, beyond the ear-shot—and beyond the economic reach—of working class marchers. Given these accents, one would not guess that the rally had been called to kick off a government campaign—in cooperation with, rather than against, state agencies.[6]

---

[4] One smaller ND rally occurred in front of the US embassy on July 4, 1984, and was dispersed by Philippine authorities. The Olalia funeral march, on the other hand, was a protracted week-long affair which culminated in a procession on November 20, 1986. Estimates of the number who participated in that march range from the *Manila Bulletin's* conservative 80,000 to *Malaya's* almost certainly exaggerated 500,000. From that point onward, however, ND rallies were resumed as a regular component of most Philippine mobilizations, beginning three days later when between 7,000 and 10,000 marched from Cubao to Camp Aguinaldo to protest the "resurgence of fascism" within the government. *Manila Chronicle*, November 24, 1986.

[5] The description in the *Manila Chronicle* following a Makati rally on October 16, 1986 names the political organizations participating in the march as Tambuli, Bandila, Atom-21, KASAPI [Kapulungan ng mga Sandigan ng Pilipinas], and the Liberal Party, all of which come from either liberal or social democratic movements. In addition to members of the Makati Chamber of Commerce, the Lion's Club, metro-Aids and "businessmen, clergy and secretaries . . . " joined the march. *Manila Chronicle*, October 17, 1986.

[6] This particular demonstration was largely sponsored and organized by the Quezon City Barangay Operation Center, an office of the local government. That office's new head, B. Montiel, had been recently released from prison, where as a KASAPI leader he had been held by the Marcos government. He staffed his office with experienced KASAPI organizers, who in

The proliferation of another sort of protest paraphernalia reinforces this discontinuity between movement form and purpose. By mid-1986, mini-vans routinely waded through demonstrations, air-conditioned reiterations of the open jeepneys that transport rally participants from the countryside and neighborhoods. Yet in contrast to the jeepneys, whose passengers alight to join the march, the vans became the primary mode of conduct along the march for a significant segment of the demonstration. For many, the protest march evolved thereby into a protest ride. Taken together, these two sorts of paraphernalia seem mutually contradictory; while some technology made rallies more comfortable and convenient, communications technology implied that participants must remain alert against (and *un*-comfortable in the presence of) some threat. Yet if the balance between danger and peace, radicalism and the status quo, seemed fine, a glance inside the vans, where matrons decked in yellow Cory T-shirts ("I stopped a Tank at EDSA") passed sandwiches to well-scrubbed children, would dispatch this illusion; the demonstrations' radical trope corresponded to neither the marchers' political agenda nor the danger they risked through participation in the protest action. [7]

Viewed as commemorations rather than acts of resistance, however, the assemblies become more intelligible. Communications equipment, for example, probably protected marchers less than they indicated EDSA veterans' status. At the time, historical commemoration—of Aquino's death, of the declaration of martial law, of Andres Bonifacio's life—proved more powerful than social or political grievances as a force to excite mobilization . As the various monuments to the EDSA struggle were erected—one thinks of the statue of Our Lady of EDSA and the Makati statue commemorating Benigno Aquino's assassination—"people power" (as the government insisted on calling it) increasingly meant the commemoration of the February uprising, often sponsored by and supportive of, the state.

The tensions which existed between the form and content of elite activism had an effect on relationships between the demonstrations' various class bases. As middle class activists conversed over two-way radios, megaphones spoke to a dustier and more ragged sort—the workers, farmers and slum dwellers who swelled these demonstrations. In part, these lower class participants validated the efforts of their higher class allies; they were important for their mass and their mass-ness. But their banners and chants also conveyed distinct and long-standing demands each notable in its appeal for tangible material improvement: land reform, new labor laws, and fair housing practices.

The apparent inconsistency between elite forms of protests and these grassroots demands reflects some uneasy alliances struck within and among the various political organizations of the popular movement. These alliances date back to the upsurge of spontaneous activism which crippled the Marcos state following Aquino's assassination in 1983. The broad protest which followed that murder swept many unorganized elites (newspaper editors, television personalities, and businesspeople) into the anti-dictatorship movement. These activists' substantial stature meant that, as a loosely coordinated political force, they soon dominated the

---

turn tapped their mass base areas for demonstration participants. From author's field notes, October 1987.

[7] EDSA [Epifanio de los Santos Avenue] refers to the location of protest gatherings which took place in February 1986; the shorthand abbreviation has come to refer to the "People Power" revolt of that year.

Aquino campaign, the post-election protest, and the immediate post-Marcos period.[8] Their ascendance, moreover, occasioned an activism which drove a wedge among the leaders of the long-standing political organizations—between those who sought to maximize the political opportunities which the hospitable but fluid state opened to them (even where these promised little immediate or direct benefit to mass constituencies) and those who stuck close to their constituencies, thereby risking marginalization from national political processes.

The very fluidity of this state heightened potential tensions within and between movement organizations. In contrast to the Marcos regime, whose firm and firmly repressive policies polarized society and inspired crisply drawn lines of opposition, the Aquino state was in every respect less defined. President Aquino—perhaps the only actor who clearly would be central in the emerging power structure—had by no means established her policy positions; this ambiguity made the standing of any movement demand (in the contest for influence in the emerging state) equally uncertain. The lines between the state and society were exceedingly obscure, and at the outset it was unclear whether activists or former Marcos leaders would dominate the emerging apparatus. Given this uncertain character, the state constituted both a target and arena of movement struggle. Each movement had to judge whether to forcefully assert mass demands, or to set such demands aside and ally with government against authoritarian aspirants. The choice itself exposed activists to competing risks. If they allied with government, they risked supporting an apparatus which might prove reactionary. On the other hand, if they imposed demands on the government, they risked weakening the state against (or driving it towards) conservative aspirants.

After the February 1986 uprising, the tactical alliance which had cemented the broad anti-Marcos movement became immediately more contentious. Organizations which formed basically in response to the growing political and economic crisis in the early eighties often perceived rapid and satisfactory change in the reconstitution of representative state structures. Indeed, the seventeen months following the popular uprising was a period of dramatic change: the Philippine state was restructured and acquired a new constitution, legislature, and several new national departments. Yet the social structure remained relatively unchanged by that transition, and organizations with a working class orientation continued to assert that economic disparity and poverty persisted under Aquino. Even where organizations developed some integrated perception of political change and social inertia (as most soon did) the relative importance (for praxis) of either participatory opportunities or social grievances was frequently in dispute. Often, although not always, these disputes divided along class lines.[9] That is, the conflict between an

---

[8] As Randolf David, an analyst and commentator who was involved in these movements, observed of the middle class's eventual assertion of hegemony over the anti-Marcos movement in the wake of Ninoy Aquino's eventual assassination: "In concrete terms, the emergence of the middle classes in the terrain of the anti-Marcos struggle meant that they would also dictate the symbols and class of the movement." Randolf S. David, "A Movement Dies, A Regime is Born (Notes on the Second Anniversary of the EDSA Uprising)" in *Kasarinlan* 3, 3 (1st Quarter, 1988): 3. This development in the movement carried over to the early Aquino years.

[9] I have elsewhere explored how disputes within a single organizational network's constituency corresponded both to the disputants' class and to their organizational affiliations. To summarize, grassroots working class organizations, mobilized into national political struggle, require that their participation produce material benefits within a relatively short

often middle class satisfaction with the national political transformation and a characteristically mass dismay at persistently ominous material conditions became a key dilemma for social movement organizations in the post-Marcos period.

The change accomplished by the 1986 transition (which inaugurated a procedurally liberal but politically undefined state), as well as the persistence of basic and long-standing grassroots demands, influenced and even transformed the inherent structures of all Philippine protest. Movement organizations responded to dilemmas posed by these structural changes in the way they chose among different tactics; these tactical choices, in turn, influenced subsequent politics. Three essential players were involved in making these choices—the movements' elite and middle class allies and constituents, its working class base of support, and its organizational cadres. At its height, the anti-dictatorship movement had forged alliances between the three which, as the movement ebbed, began to unravel. Much of subsequent movement politics represents cadres' efforts to stem this unraveling. The extent to which this dissent emerged in any one movement network, and its impact on movement politics, depends on the specific dynamics within given organizational networks.

Social democratic (SD) groups, both because of their strategic orientation and the relative dominance of economic elites in their leadership, were most divided by the attractions which participatory institutions worked on their middle class and elite members. SD leaders entered government office in significant numbers in Aquino's first two years, both through electoral campaigns and as appointees. These new avenues of political activity, however, were not regarded as deviations from the SD political line, which had long anticipated participation in a liberal government.[10] Still, not all members of the SD network looked favorably on these interaction with government, and some younger generation activists, deeply involved in grassroots activism, bolted from the group to form the democratic socialist organization, Pandayan (Pandayan para sa Sosyalistang Pilipinas. Forge of a Socialist Philippines).[11]

---

time. When national political struggle seems clearly unable to produce such benefits, disputes between working and middle class activists take place, and often acquire the sense of conflict between parochial and cosmopolitan political orientations. In this conception, parochialism is largely a product of material need expressed in a climate where national reform seems unlikely, while cosmopolitanism is the willingness to engage national participatory opportunities even where these produce little immediate advantage. I also note the rapid decline in middle class activism once Aquino's constitutional apparatus had been assembled. See Vincent Boudreau, "The Lider and the Cadre: Grassroots Organizations in the Philippine Socialist Movement" (PhD Dissertation, Cornell University, 1992).

[10] Karen Tanada, one SD leader, describes the movement's general orientation as one which views the acquisition of government office as a legitimate mode of movement struggle: "A socdem [SD] president two or three terms from now seems a feasible objective. Hence, socdems participate in elections and try to get positions in government in order to push the implementation of their minimum program, and also to support the movement in its mass organization work." in "An Overview of Social Democracy," Karen Tanada, *Conjuncture* 1, 3 (1987): 3.

[11] Pandayan would assess its troubled relationship with other social democratic forces in the following terms: "With the new-found democratic space also came new problems. One was the issue of whether to join or remain separate from the new government. Several SD-DS [social democrat-democratic socialist] personalities eventually joined government, leading to situations where they were at odds with their comrades in the streets. The dilemma continues

The legal national democratic (ND) movement never publicly regarded Aquino's brand of participatory democracy as particularly attractive. NDs assessed the Aquino government's class orientation and composition to be similar in most respects to that of Marcos.[12] Moreover, organizations like the Communist Party of the Philippines (CPP) and the New People's Army (NPA) had accumulated interests in and resources devoted to struggle. Given this counterweight to such opportunities, very few ND efforts sought access to or power within the government. Still, individual members—again many with middle class or elite origins—were drawn to these opportunities, and conflict between their perspective and official ND positions led many outside of the network's mainstream.[13] Their departure forestalled internal debates on strategy and tactics and allowed official ND policy to maintain a thoroughly oppositionist stance to the Aquino presidency, as well as to maintain its revolutionary state-power agenda. Furthermore, adherence to principles of democratic centralism, according to which the ND cadres could command mass participation at rallies, forestalled its own participatory crisis.[14]

Independent socialists in BISIG (Bukluran sa Ikauunlad ng Sosyalistang Isip at Gawa) as well as popular democrats (who from 1986 onward carved out an area of increasing autonomy and eventual independence from the ND movement) all expressed political visions based on leading a legal mass movement in the new political context. For these groups, as well as Pandayan, however, the potential tensions between different constituencies was perhaps the most pitched, for they had neither the authority of democratic centralism, nor so robust a belief in or capacity for government work so as to allow them to abandon protest. Such groups, therefore, most immediately experienced the divergence of class forces as a serious movement dilemma.[15]

---

to haunt the SD-DS movement to this day." Pandayan, *Batayan Kurso ng Kahanay: Unang Aklat* [Basic Members' Course, First Book], May 1994, p. 117.

[12] Loretta Ann P. Rosales, one of BAYAN's principle leaders during the period, expressed her organization's position in the following terms: " . . . the leadership that mobilized the people in their numbers to topple Mr. Marcos combined the Aquino camp of the elite and the traditional politicians, big business and conservative Church with Martial law implementors, now turned military rebels, Enrile and Ramos . . . Despite the rhetoric of constitutional democracy, the Aquino Regime shall enjoy the full protection of US imperialism for as long as it serves as imperialism's most effective mechanism for resisting change." Loretta Ann P. Rosales, "Understanding the `US-Aquino Regime,'" *Conjuncture* 1, 3 (1987): 3.

[13] Alex Padilla, who for a time was Customs director, had been an important BAYAN leader, and both Mita Pardo de Tavera [Secretary of Social Work and Development] and Nikki Coseteng [Congressional Representative to first the House, then the Senate] had been GABRIELA national officers during the Marcos period. Prominent ND allies included human rights lawyers Joker Arroyo and Augusto Sanchez, both of whom belonged to Aquino's very first cabinet.

[14] Immediately after the uprising, debates within the CPP questioned the party orthodoxy which, critics claimed, failed to respond to the "insurrectionary situation" building up to the uprising and failed to set the revolution's new tasks in light of emerging representative democracy. See, for instance, Carol Victoria, "A reply to the Resolution," August 1986, mimeograph.

[15]. For a more complete account of the concrete political expression of this dilemma, see Boudreau, *The Lider and the Cadre.*

THE CONJUNCTURAL DILEMMA

By 1987, the tension within movement organizations became much more pronounced. The relative consolidation of elite democracy moved the impetus for reform inside the framework of an institutional structure which was, both in itself and in its policy positions, inimical to popular influence. Although greatly indebted to the political movements for their initial power, government officials soon seemed intent on functioning in a more autonomous fashion, and decreased the extent to which they solicited popular participation in the policy process.[16] Nevertheless, at least in terms of procedure, things were generally running as a popularly approved constitution suggested they should. The overwhelming participation in parliamentary exercises demonstrated that the institutions of representative democracy captured the popular imagination; the constitutional plebiscite and 1987 national elections, for example, both drew over 80 percent of all registered voters. Yet the revolution in representative government had produced little of the social change which the movements' mass bases demanded; their grievances continued to provide the material basis for protest against government and (when middle class allies grew satisfied with representative institutions) dissent over movement praxis.

The events surrounding the 1987 Honasan coup attempt illustrate how, and to what effect, divisions opened between movement constituencies. A proposed national oil price hike at the time touched off significant public outcry; the hardships caused by increased fuel prices allowed movements to mobilize and especially encouraged working class activism. In consequence, the largest protests under Aquino occurred during August 1987. This unrest, coupled with a demonstrable public dissatisfaction with Philippine governance, created an opportunity for the coup conspirators: the Reform the Armed Forces Movement (RAM) stepped into the strike-born turmoil to make their play for state power. The militarist threat drew most political movements to support the very civilian leadership they had lately criticized and to abandon their oil price protests. Hence the sequence of events and reactions which moved from mass protest, to attempted coup, and from there to

---

[16] In July 1987, the Philippine legislature took office, marking the end of President Aquino's extraordinary legislative powers. Up to that point, Aquino could decree legislation, a power which greatly encouraged political movements to represent grievances to her: during this phase, a movement that could sway the president would thereby succeed in initiating reform. Hence extraordinary legislative powers promised extraordinary reforms. The week before congress took power, the popular movement made more and more urgent appeals; these demonstrations produced little substantial reform, however, and a measure such as the Comprehensive Agrarian Reform Program [CARP] was merely a declaration of the government's principled acceptance of agrarian reform. After July 1987, analysts writing for movement papers surveyed emerging representative institutions with increasing pessimism. The Institute for Popular Democracy, in its series on the 1987 elections, argued convincingly that the new solons were mainly from established and conservative political dynasties; see, for example, Antoinette, Raquiza, "Breaking up with Aquino," *Conjuncture* 1, 5&6 (1988): 1. According to Villenueva-Reyes: "The Cumulative erosion of the liberal-progressive flank in the cabinet has cleansed the Aquino administration of liberals and progressives." Pi Villenueva-Reyes, "Faded Rainbow Beginnings," *Conjuncture* 1, 4 (1988): 12. As another commentator reported on the congressional debate on agrarian reform, "When talk was out that the President would decree an agrarian reform policy before congress convened last July, conservative lawmakers in the House, in concert with the anti-reform lobby of organized landowners, demanded that Presidential initiative on the reform be halted, and the matter be left for Congress to settle . . . " in Joey Flora, "Congress Deliberates on Land Reform," *Conjuncture* 1, 1 (1987): 4.

defense of Aquino, raised serious tactical problems for movement cadres, since many people interpreted these events to mean that mass demands had inadvertently imperiled democratic gains. Cadres faced apparent (though by no means unresolvable) tensions between social advocacy and a defense of a largely democratic order. Moreover, as a closer examination of the events will reveal, both tactical programs had distinct class centers of gravity within the movements which rendered their synthesis still more problematic.

The strike against proposed oil price increases generated immense and immediate support, particularly in the urban centers. Transport workers defending their own diminishing profits enjoyed substantial public sympathy, for increased gas prices one month would surely mean increased fares the next. Resistance to oil price increases forestalled both prospects and cemented a unity between commuters and transport workers. Moreover, the strike made it virtually impossible for commuters to travel to work, and so every driver who refused to ply a route created dozens of de facto strikers, regardless of their actual sympathy. Still, the loosely organized middle class, so prominent in demonstrations just months earlier, was markedly absent from the groups which marched to support the strike; elements from this strata, in fact, staged their own explicitly separate demonstration on August 21 to commemorate Aquino's assassination. Despite this absence, the strike infused Philippine protest with a militancy that had been absent since Aquino's special legislative powers had lapsed.[17]

The clear and immediate material goals also rendered the strike an important collective activity. As representative government settled in, appeals for reform became less promising than they had been under the revolutionary government; mass constituents had less cause to expect any return on their collective efforts, and political organizers re-evaluated the wisdom of expensive demonstrations. The oil price strike, in its moment, resolved this dilemma. It set clear and attainable objectives and required an organizationally inexpensive strike (in which workers withheld labor power) instead of a demonstration (in which marchers must be brought to a specific site). Moreover, the strikers set out to maintain an existing policy rather than move the government to enact a reform, and so inertia lay with, rather than against, the movement campaign. The oil price hike seemed an appealing movement tactic, and organization cadres from BAYAN (Bagong Alyansang Makabayan. New Nationalist Alliance), BISIG, Pandayan, and Volunteers for Popular Democracy were therefore very active in its build-up and mobilization.[18]

---

[17] The *Philippine Daily Inquirer* on August 17 printed the transportation unions' claim that the strike had succeeded in paralyzing over 90 percent of transportation in Metro-Manila. Strike levels declined from that day until August 20. On August 20, "Transport workers in Metro-Manila were joined this time by bus drivers in what organizers described as a massive multi-sectoral protest action . . . " *Philippine Daily Inquirer [PDI]* August 21, 1987. On the following day, August 21, over 10,000 protesters (as distinct from the strikers) marched to the presidential palace. *PDI*, August 22, 1987. The strike activity peaked, however, by August 26, on which day, "Close to two million moderate and militant workers, drivers, public employees and students staged a protest highlighted by disbursements by water cannons and police, at which at least police arrested over forty protesters." According to the report, it was the single largest mass action since February of 1986. *PDI*, August 27, 1987.

[18] In its initial days, the strike action was mainly an affair entered into by labor and transport unions. By August 21, however, the broader working class constituencies, and political cadres, had joined the demonstrations as well. Ten thousand marched in on Aquino's death

The Honasan coup attempt cut the national strike short. Its intense initial assault overran several military bases and broadcast media stations, and shot apprehension through the movement. Organizers canceled the strike, both because any chaos would probably work to the advantage of the coup conspiracy, and because they had their own vulnerabilities.[19] Cadres across the political spectrum devoted their energies to securing their organizational apparatus against the advent of martial law or military government. They identified sanctuaries, assigned code names, and drafted contingency plans. Many simply slipped into a cautious semi-hiding to await the struggle's outcome. They did not, however, demonstrate to support civilian rule during the period when it was most at risk.[20]

The first anti-coup mobilization, the motorcade described in this paper's opening pages, lent clear and unambiguous support to Aquino's government. The demonstration, in fact, virtually excluded those who had recently challenged state policy and who threatened to muddy the clear message of support for Aquino with some criticism. At no point did the demonstration note or allude to the recent grievances which workers, slum dwellers, and movement cadres had brought before the government. Instead, in both its message and methodology, the motorcade suggested the growing gulf between the unorganized elite or middle-class yellow activists and the working class base on which most movement organizations rested. The demonstrators' celebration of existing civilian government and their programmatic break with the working class movement also marked a definitive end to the generalized popular intervention in national government that persisted after EDSA. In lauding the government victory, the motorized demonstration indicated that many were willing to accept that the Aquino state both should and could act more or less independently of any social mobilization. Indeed, this orientation owed much to the government itself , which during the coup urged citizens to stay at home and away from the battle.

More organized anti-coup activity began over two weeks into September with the Kilusang para sa Kalayaan at Demokrasya (Movement for Peace and Democracy, or KKD). The KKD sought explicitly to involve more established movement organizations (primarily social democratic, popular democratic, socialist and liberal

---

anniversary, and by the August 26 action, over 60,000 non-labor activists, many of whom were students and urban poor members, joined the protest action. *PDI*, August 27, 1987.

[19] Kilusang Mayo Uno leader, Crispin Beltran, commented on the matter. On September 1, Beltran granted an interview from his hide-out of four days: "Crispin Beltran declared that an arrest order is waiting for him, and that he would not come out of hiding until detained fellow leader Mario Roda is released from detention. Beltran told the *Inquirer* four days after he went into hiding that he would not give the government any chance to cripple the militant trade union movement by having him morally and illegally arrested." *PDI*, September 1, 1987. Striking organizations like the KMU, however, were not the only groups who spent August's last days preparing to go into hiding.

[20] The fact that no popular demonstrations took place in favor of the government, however, was not merely a result of the reticence of the political movements. Only hours after the coup was launched, stark black and white posters appeared throughout Manila, bearing the logo of the Philippine Information Agency. These signs urged citizens to remain in their houses, not to listen to gossip, and to tune to their radio stations for information. In effect, the government had chosen not to rely on popular support, and instead to meet the RAM's challenge with its own official state forces. Many have viewed this as a crucial turning point in Aquino's relationship with the popular political movements. See, for example, the BISIG statement deploring the government's decision not to involve popular forces, reported in *Philippine Daily Inquirer*, August 6, 1987.

organizations) and to establish a longer-term organizational presence. In many ways, however, its resembled the earlier spontaneous motorcade protest. Like the earlier motorcade, the KKD demonstrations relied heavily on several prominent personalities with only loose ties to any movement organization.[21] The KKD's class base, moreover, was more similar to the motorcade's than to the transportation strike's: the mini-vans and walkie-talkies were in evidence once more.[22] Its marches and rallies occurred after government troops had defeated RAM rebels (which was perhaps natural, from a logistical point of view). At last, the KKD launched several small rallies (eight hundred demonstrators, out of a projected 10,000, turned up for its inaugural mobilization) and disbanded about five weeks later after attracting indifferent support and generating little public attention: an offhand performance which thoroughly belied its pervasive rhetoric of vigilance and urgency.

National democratic groups did not participate in the KKD actions. ND statements at the time argued that the coup attempt represented a struggle between factions of an elite and authoritarian government, and that the people had no stake in its outcome.[23] Nevertheless, just after the KKD formed, the NDs launched their own coalitions, spurred on by the assassination of BAYAN Secretary-General Lean Alejandro. The National Movement for Civil Liberties (NMCL) refrained from lending any support to the existing civilian government, and concentrated instead on presenting resistance to government abridgments of civil and human rights.[24] Besides ND organizations, the NMCL contained independent socialists and popular democrats. It sponsored several small rallies and demonstrations which contained

---

[21] Another interesting parallel between the KKD and the August 28 motorcade was the KKD's September 21 rally in which yellow ribbon-bedecked cars were to drive around Makati to signal their support for Aquino. *PDI*, September 12, 1987.

[22] The organizations associated with the KKD were all relatively moderate, and included the Coalition for the Advancement of the People's Mandate [CAMP], the Federation of Democratic Socialist Movements [FDSM] the Philippine Democratic Socialist Party [PDSP], and Solidarity for People's Power [SPP]. Also featured in the organization were prominent figures such as newspaper magnate Don Chino Roces, and singers Leah Navarro and Jim Paredes. It's rally plans provide an indication of the KKD's dominant class base of support: the procession was to begin in the exclusive Greenhills suburb and march from there to the gates of Camp Aguinaldo. In a September 21 announcement of a subsequent KKD rally, the *PDI* reported that its membership had expanded to include, "The influential Catholic Bishops' Businessmen' Conference, The National Movement for Free Elections [NAMFREL] and ten other business organizations." *PDI*, September 21, 1987.

[23] On the very day that the Philippine press was announcing the formation of the KKD, ND organizations were signaling their disinclination to support similar efforts: "Leftists have rejected President Aquino's call for the people's support in stark contrast to members of moderate political groups who have vowed to side with the present regime in the time of crisis. `It is futile to think that Corazon Aquino is defending democracy,' A. Jimenez, secretary-general of the leftist Partido ng Bayan told the *Inquirer* yesterday. He said the president capitulated to the side of the military when she acceded to the soldiers' demand that the cabinet be purged of left-leaning members . . . .[and he continued] `It would be ironic to support a government that has already turned its back on the people's just demand for meaningful reform.'" *PDI*, September 12, 1987.

[24] According to Villenueva: "While most NMCL members believe that Honasan and company pose a grave fascist threat, they tend to focus more on the emerging authoritarian trend of the Aquino regime. Still, the NMCL hopes to draw into its ranks pro-Cory figures supportive of civil liberties." Eric Villenueva, "The Popular Forces: A Survey of Anti-Fascist Formations," *Conjuncture* 1, 2 (1987).

multi-class representatives, but lapsed into subsequent inactivity after several weeks.[25]

This sequence of events demonstrates a separation between the movement's class constituencies. Upper and middle class mobilization during Marcos's last three years had subsided, and activists from this strata generally returned to individual economic activity and lent little political or material support to collective actions. Even Honasan's threat to representative democracy met only fleeting opposition from such activists, and few indeed continued to demonstrate for agrarian reform, urban poor welfare, and labor rights. While these working class demands remained relatively undiminished and still could attract the mass support in evidence at the national strike, working class collectives as a whole were in a general retreat from the broad mobilization of months before. Specifically, strictly national political campaigns, despite the threat of military rule, seldom attracted the large mass support they had just months before. Strikers aroused prior to the Honasan coup mounted no demonstration in its aftermath. No KKD rally contained any substantial working class contingent, even from groups that had served as the SD mass base; the NMCL did mobilize working class associations, but did so mainly because of strict ND discipline. The most successful working class rallies made more concrete and material demands, of which the oil price strike is a defining example.

The events of mid-1987, and particularly the culminating failure of the anti-coup coalitions, placed cadres in a quandary. On the one hand, movement organizations seemed further and further from achieving substantial policy reform and could no longer reasonably expect that any imminent collective victory might concretely improve mass members' lives. Moreover, without the spontaneity which had propelled the mass movement until then, mobilization increasingly had to be orchestrated by movement cadres and underwritten by movement resources. Demonstration participants came more exclusively from political organizations' memberships, and the pool of non-organized sympathizers evaporated. The entire burden of demonstration-related expenses—transportation, food, publicity—fell on organization shoulders.[26] Hence, as such reform-directed mobilizations became less effective, they grew more expensive: a classic dilemma of diminishing utility.

A similar cost-benefit dilemma ran through problems of organization maintenance. Organizational solidarities, in particular cross-class solidarities upon

---

[25] In February 1988, the NMCL was re-launched as a broad human rights and political democracy coalition. Its second lease on life must be viewed as an essentially separate initiative from the original anti-coup tasks the coalition had adopted in September 1987.

[26] One leader of an urban poor organization from BISIG describes the sorts of processes and resources which political movements needed to command in order to mobilize supporters: "If there is a mobilization at 2:00, you tell me at 11:00. And then I would go to all of the areas. That's an instant mobilization. . . . I talk to the leaders. I would go to Bok (a nickname, like "buddy" which activists—more or less exclusively—use with one another) and say, "Bok, we need one hundred from you." I would go to the other place and say, "We need one hundred from you." In Bunggad, I would tell them to prepare fifty people. I would go to Project 7 for fifty, and to U.P. for fifty. I would give out the transportation expenses at that time. That's the way: when you go to the area, you have to take the money with you. You give half of the money to the leaders in the area, and when they come to the mobilization, with the correct number of people, then you give them the money to return home. If they arrive in numbers too small, then they must use the money that is left over as a part of their return transportation, and so there is nothing to collect back from the group. From recorded interview with B.M., July 21, 1988.

which Philippine ideological movements had constructed support, require maintenance. Impoverished activists have both the greatest material basis for resisting the status quo and the least material resources with which to mount such resistance. For working class or impoverished participants, activism which produces no collective or individual material improvement is both irrational and unsustainable. As the prospect of collective victories diminished, collective action aimed exclusively at large and inclusive goals—socialism, democracy, or the like— became less attractive investments. Social movement cadres needed to address more directly mass member concerns or risk losing this constituency.[27]

The dilemma that confronted movement cadres in 1987, therefore, had two faces. The first reflected an aspect of Philippine society: it showed that the opportunities for the sweeping reconfiguration of Philippine relations that seemed possible during 1986, while the structures of Philippine political and economic life remained somewhat suspended, had evaporated with the reinstitution of government. The dilemma's second face revealed a troublesome aspect of the SMO leadership's relationship with its mass base. Movement supporters could no longer afford the luxury of extraordinary movement participation which could promise no material improvement. Unless cadres took steps to decrease resource expenditure and increase the benefits that individuals gained from participation, they would likely have less success soliciting mass support or sustaining movement capacity, for national political activities would now require more effort.

THE LEFT'S RESPONSE

Across the left opposition, movement actors devised a range of solutions to their dilemma. While the underground left resumed armed struggle for state power, legal movements sought solutions in two organizational innovations. First, issue-based coalitions that represented narrow demands for specific reforms became the vehicles which most commonly sponsored demonstrations and protest. Before 1987 movement organizations had assembled their demands in the comparatively large categories of "democracy" and "socialism"; after 1987, they more frequently worked through sectoral-specific coalitions which advocated, for example, urban and agrarian land reform or labor rights. Sectoral coalitions attempted to solve the protest

---

[27] The process by which mass members argued for a program of struggle that more directly addressed grassroots concerns, of course, is intimately connected to specific relationships between cadres and mass members. Nor, obviously enough, should one anticipate that all working class members lost interest in political issues or demanded concrete advocacy. Nevertheless, I have elsewhere demonstrated how the systematic assertion of grassroots demands, conceived increasingly as existing in a zero-sum relationship with more political struggles, drove a wedge between BISIG and three of its affiliated mass organizations. Boudreau, *The Lider and the Cadre*. Similar developments occurred elsewhere. In an interview with the author, for example, an ND organizer in a Central Luzon farming community commented on how difficult it had become to mobilize organization members for demonstrations in the capitol: "A lot of it, of course has to do with the Mendiola Massacre [February 1987]. Many of the farmers who attended that rally came from this very area, and so they're not eager to go back. But even before then, something was changing in their orientation. Several leaders suggested that we try to set up a dialogue with provincial officials. Others began to advocate buying a community thresher. It's getting to the point where national protest—particularly for something as distant as justice or democracy—just isn't enough to sustain their interests anymore. So we need to decide how to integrate the political and the socio-economic." Author's interview, tape G-1, October 12, 1988.

movement's dilemma by extracting discrete demands from these larger packages, to more directly address a policy debate and more exactly represent mass member complaints. Second, movements began acting upon their members' need for material relief by delivering livelihood resources directly to mass constituencies through NGO-administered programs.

The Congress for a People's Agrarian Reform (CPAR) began during the second quarter of 1987 and was initially lauded as the very broadest coalition effort in contemporary Philippine movement history.[28] This praise implicitly compares CPAR with the previous high-water mark for unity-in-action: the anti-Marcos BAYAN initiative of 1985. In several significant respects, however, the comparison is not entirely appropriate. Sectoral coalitions sought specialized constituencies, segments of the underclass rather than its totality. They highlighted concrete demands previously subsumed within more comprehensive programs for Philippine society and attempted to build these into a coherent policy position. As sectoral coalitions more exactly represented mass grievances, they required fewer compromises from their constituents. Moreover, because their demands often centered around technical issues (e.g.. land retention limits or labor legislation) their organizers became specialists—NGO workers with technical areas of expertise—rather than the political generalists who serve on the leading committees of ideological movement organizations. Even where such specialists held different long-term visions for the Philippine state, they could frequently agree on a package of sectoral reforms. Hence precisely because sectoral coalitions were more manageable than political projects, they represented a partial solution to the movement's dilemma.

Whatever other benefits these sectoral coalitions offered the popular movement—and there is evidence that, at least under Aquino, they offered the distinct advantage of flexibility[29]—they also posed collective action in a manner that seemed most likely to yield concrete reforms, and in terms which most closely approximated mass complaints. At a time when demands for democracy, socialism, or nationalism elicited less and less attention in the public debate, these coalitions attempted to revive mass interest in collective action by advancing their respective sectors' economic struggles.

A second, and in many ways parallel attempt to solidify mass participation aimed even more directly at material grievances; from the middle of 1987, non-governmental organizations attached to Philippine social movements began sprouting like mushrooms on a humid summer night. Private volunteer organizations had actually existed for years in the Philippines as elsewhere, often

---

[28] Eduardo Tadem, who was among the coalition's prominent architects, periodically described CPAR to me as it unfolded during those months. According to him, it was a historic undertaking because it included a spectrum that ranged from a Marcos-created farmer organization (as it initially did) to the ND KMP, and that range made CPAR by far the broadest coalition. From field notes, May 16, 1987.

[29] Such coalitions (i.e. CPAR, LACC [Labor Alliance Consultative Committee], NACFAR [National Advocacy Committee for Fisheries and Aquatic Resources]) proved both broader and more flexible than outright political unions precisely because they explicitly postponed discussion of deeply rooted ideological issues that divided one movement network from another. Formally, and for the purpose of coalition activity, sectoral coalitions put a premium on specific reform campaigns, seeing these as critical points in the overall struggle for social transformation. Certainly participant groups maintained this longer term and instrumental conception of reform; nevertheless, ideological perspectives now set the parameters for coalition discussion and ceased to act as subjects of that discussion.

closely tied to church institutions and oriented towards charity work—the distribution of relief, resources, and religion. During martial law, some NGOs advocated a broader protection of human rights and provided free legal assistance; many shielded activists from direct state oppression by providing a legal institutional context for resistance activity. By 1986, and increasingly thereafter, however, a new wave of such groups devoted extraordinary attention to socioeconomic projects often funded by international donors and administered by community organizations.[30]

Under Aquino, NGOs offered movement cadres a new and perhaps more institutionally secure venue for their activity. Political movements had flourished as the exclusive counterpoint to the Marcos dictatorship, but enjoyed less widespread support as Aquino's representative rule depolarized society. NGOs, however, thrived in the new climate. They did not require broad popular support, relying instead on institutional grants obtained through specific and concrete project proposals. Such concrete programs, moreover, multiplied precisely because the transformation in state rule occasioned changes among international donor organizations; agencies which consented to fund political activities against the unpopular Marcos regime felt less compelled to do so after 1986.[31] Furthermore, as the domestic elite and middle class demobilized, they withdrew support for protest. NGOs, whose community-based programs accorded more with international development and domestic civic-mindedness, thus enjoyed a distinct advantage over outrightly political organizations in mobilizing resources.

NGOs also transformed the cost-benefit calculus of both cadres' and mass members' participation, and so were instrumental in sustaining movement organizations. As endowed offices, NGOs could employ their staffs, which allowed activists a source of livelihood—a consideration which grew more important as society routinized and provided less and less material support for activists. NGOs also provided mass participants with exogenous resources administered by movement cadres rather than achieved through collective success. Since participants obtained these resources from allies rather than adversaries, their material advancement—and so incentive to participate—ceased exclusively to depend on collective victories and rested more with their participation in the collective project. Resources administered by movement NGOs underwrote participation regardless of the political climate or collective successes. Hence, many political collectives reconfigured themselves into non-governmental organizations; cadres who struggled against Marcos recast themselves as NGO workers under Aquino, but associated, nonetheless, with essentially the same mass base.

These two organizational developments—the rise of sectoral coalitions and of NGOs—reinforced one another and together marked the main contours of evolving

---

[30] Particularly in the political afterglow of 1986, international agencies were eager to provide development assistance to the Philippines.

[31] This seems to have been the case of the Canadian and Dutch governments, which limited bilateral aid to the Marcos regime, choosing to work instead with their respective countries' NGOs doing work in the Philippines. When Aquino assumed power, things changed. The Canadian International Development Agency, for example, opened a bilateral program in 1986, committing as much as C$100 million over five years. Council for People's Development, "NGO Policy Advocacies of Official Development Assistance, Case Study of the Philippine-Canadian Human Resource Development Program and the Foundation for Philippine Environment," 1993.

movement politics. NGOs became central to sectoral coalitions as they more effectively controlled the technical expertise around which sectoral coalitions cemented their unities. Over time, as we shall see, NGOs within movement organizations asserted increasing autonomy and often even elaborated visions of social transformation that differed from those of any political organizations'. It would be a mistake, however, to read these later developments backwards to explain the initial NGO proliferation.[32] Whatever other roles NGOs have since acquired in Philippine society, they multiplied during the late 1980s within, and as part of, a demobilizing broad popular movement. As such, they represent experimental solutions to dilemmas which all movement organizations faced: how might they lead a mass base with immediate subsistence and security concerns in an atmosphere where movement access to, and influence within the polity was diminishing? Both the sectoral coalition and the NGO promised in some measure to resolve the dilemma by either tuning activism more exactly to mass needs and the larger political climate or by severing the connection between participatory incentives and collective benefits.

Though tactical experiments, these organizational innovations were in no sense politically neutral. Because sectoral coalitions strove for policy reforms, they anticipated some procedural democracy. As they worked toward the construction of community associations and self-help initiatives, NGOs perforce validated the (at least partly) civil character of society under Aquino. Both innovations, then, bore a significant political load, a situation which had two consequences. First, they worked to transform activism under Aquino. Second, the manner in which different movement organizations approached these new political expressions depended to a large extent on the character of their existing political arrangement and orientation. I will first examine the more general influences which the two innovations exercised, and then discuss their more particular expression within specific movement networks.

In important ways NGOs transformed activism. They frequently set out to implement some project—a socioeconomic or educational activity—for application to specific constituencies rather than on behalf of an entire class. NGO-based advocacy pursued the empowerment of communities to undertake their own development as an important collective end. This concentration on concrete accomplishments in specific communities soon acquired a coherence within movement discourse as a vision of social change alternative to the struggle for national power. Efforts to improve social and economic conditions incrementally captured the imagination of

---

[32] As NGOs helped resolved SMOs'[social movement organizations] mass-participation dilemma, they also provided a solution to a problem eating away at cadres themselves. During the 1985–86 upsurge, routine life in the Philippines had come to a virtual halt; in that extraordinary atmosphere, protest movements expanded by taking in thousands upon thousands of Filipinos who had few conflicting demands on their time. As the routines of society and the economy re-established themselves, even full time cadres needed to find some means of livelihood. Whereas guerrilla fighters sustain themselves through appropriations and donations, legal cadres in activist organizations required some living allowance. In the normal run of events, the political movement can perhaps afford to fund several full time organizers from its treasury, but few others. NGOs, however, incorporate staffing requirements into their grant proposals and can easily provide full time work. Many full time activists sustained their activism by taking up salaried positions in NGOs. The arrangement seemed to allow movements to retain full time workers and activists to secure a source of livelihood.

many, particularly as a ready answer to apparently failed statist transformative efforts elsewhere in the world.[33]

NGOs which worked in sectoral coalitions usually represented larger political movements; nevertheless, they also brought unique perspectives to coalition work and were particularly inclined to assume a more flexible stance towards government. As they acquired important positions within activist coalitions, NGOs therefore required that political activity not be exclusively a matter of protest and demonstration, and established that their main actors would bring consideration beyond broad mobilization of dissent to the fore.[34] Under NGO influence, coalitions incorporated a more explicit policy agenda into their advocacy, informed by the issues and experiences of communities. Besides indicating NGOs' greater facility with more technical approaches to advocacy, these shifts also suggest major transformations in the currency of power pursued by movement collectives.

While protest organizations cast themselves in adversarial relationships with state authorities, NGOs find points of cooperation. Community organizers building long-term economic structures like cooperatives need assurance that these structures would not encounter official harassment; moved by this need, many NGOs cultivate congenial rather than adversarial relationships with local authorities. Moreover, government line agencies have some discretion over and resources for policy implementation. As NGOs sought incrementally to resolve social problems, such official resources represented concrete and undeniable opportunities.[35] NGOs began increasingly to ask how they might solve problems, rather than how they might mobilize resistance to state authority. As they did so, internal organizational programs acquired an importance to mass associations independent of, and not reducible, to their ability to mobilize for protest.[36]

---

[33] Ronald Llamas summed up the NGO community's distinct advantage over political movements in these terms: "The NGO movement is especially strong not only because it has concrete projects and constituencies, but because it has permanent and employed cadres. It has concrete programs of activities, both immediate and medium-term, which the strategic political-ideological formations lack." Ronald Llamas, "Renewing the Struggle," in *Kasarinlan* 8, 2 (4th Quarter 1992): 48.

[34] Nowhere is the process by which NGO perspectives began to establish themselves in the broad movement more striking than in the debates surrounding sustainable development and environmentalism. While begun in the spirit of social criticism, increasingly throughout the late 1980s and early 1990s, groups such as the Green Forum and Convergence (themselves coalitions of NGOs and political organizations) and NGOs like the Philippine Rural Reconstruction Movement began to conceive of these positions as principles for their own activity. See, for example, "NGO Perspectives" (Quezon City: Council for People's Development, 1989).

[35] For example, while political organizations protested the government's sham agrarian reform program, as they did throughout the late 1980s, their affiliated NGOs increasingly availed themselves of resources and opportunities offered by that program—many induced their memberships to join government Barangay Agrarian Reform Councils [BARCs] or to obtain land under the program. See "CPAR Annual Coalition Report," unpublished document, Quezon City, 1988.

[36]. In fact, this became a common approach to solving long-standing socioeconomic problems. For instance, the Tripartite Program for Agrarian Reform and Rural Development [TriPARRD] was initiated by the Partnership for the Development of Human Resources in the Rural Areas [PHILDHRRA]. The project, which begun in 1989 included people's organizations [POs, as mass collectives increasingly came to be called], NGOs, and government organizations [GOs]; the POs were principally responsible for program implementation, NGOs assisted in organizing and maintaining POs as well as in coordinating the trisectoral activities, and GOs

As modes of activism changed under the influence of NGOs and sectoral coalitions, points of friction emerged between these newer institutions and more ideological movement organizations. The relationship between NGOs and funding agencies developed against what game theorists call the long shadow of the future; to systematically depart from technical and performance goals set forth in project proposals would prejudice an NGO's future access to funds, and so its viability. Funders could insist that NGOs comply with these standards,[37] and they often needed to do so to justify their overseas programs at home.[38] NGOs' institutional interests therefore became increasingly tied to performance and implementation standards, and while they enjoyed access to resources, NGOs could not endow political mobilizations. Material resources which previously had moved freely between movement institutions, less frequently underwrote political protest even as the once abundant social support for protest diminished. These constraints undercut the dominance of political protest in movement networks, especially relative to ascendant NGOs. Political protest ceased to represent the only expression of movement activity and in many cases was superseded by non-partisan community projects.[39]

Moreover, as NGOs developed extensive ties to mass populations, they became less inclined—given their pursuit of community-based programs—to expend human or material resources on massed national and political demonstrations or to quickly mobilize large and heterogeneous mass assemblies. NGOs usually limited their constituencies to sizes for which they could administer multi-faceted non-partisan community development programs. Such projects helped insure and enhance the bonds between NGO workers and their people's organizations. Unlike political cadres, NGO organizers preferred to develop more comprehensive community programs for smaller, but more coherent associations. As NGOs acquired prominence, they therefore transformed the character of mass associations within the movement.

---

saw to the programs legislative needs and support services. Maricel Almojuela, "Tripartism in Agrarian Reform" in *Development NGO Journal* 1, 1 (Third Quarter, 1992: 44.

[37] A case study about NGO interactions with bilateral donors noted: "As the NGOs are learning, negotiations basically must address the issues at hand, specifically at the project management level if they are to produce concrete results. Hence, whatever influence Philippine NGOs may exert during subsequent negotiations is circumscribed by the initial statement of the problem and opportunity, a statement which remains almost exclusively the prerogative of the ODA bureaucracy." CPD [Council for People's Development], "NGO Advocacies on Official Development Assistance," pp. 298–99.

[38] In 1988, moreover, then Minister of National Defence Fidel Ramos issued a series of press statements in which he accused overseas funding agencies of providing financial resources to insurgent and subversive organizations. As part of this effort, Ramos lobbied overseas governments to exert efforts to determine that their nationals not contribute to organizations which the Philippine state regarded as subversive. In response to this pressure, many funding organizations began to require that projects they funded have clear and concrete socio-economic components, and that some physical structure be built with project resources. Grants that had earlier been available for organizing or foundation building became extremely difficult to come by after that period. See, for example, *PDI*, May 26, 1988.

[39] This was particularly true during electoral campaigns. Whereas political organizations such as the Partido ng Bayan, BISIG, and the Movement for Popular Democracy campaigned for specific candidates, NGOs conducted non-partisan voters education and people's agenda building exercises.

If NGOs and sectoral coalitions transformed political activism, they did not do so at a uniform pace—or in uniform directions—for all movement organizations. These organizational innovations entered into existing movement relations and dynamics, and they tended to produce distinct political activity in different movement networks. ND organizations approached sectoral coalitions mainly as an opportunity to broaden their alliances and avoid isolation on the movement's left flank. ND organizations did not enter into these coalitions to maintain mass support, which was already provided for by democratic centralist policies. In consequence, the ND movement more easily subsumed individual and economic aspirations to larger political goals, and political cadres continued primarily to manage ND participation in sectoral coalitions. In fact, many ND organizations supported both sectoral and political demonstrations. The labor unions involved in the 1987 oil price strike, for instance, also turned out for NMCL rallies several weeks later, as did the Kilusang Magbubukid ng Pilipinas (KMP) which had marched in CPAR demonstrations weeks earlier.[40]

In contrast, virtually all movement networks to the right of the NDs ceded main elements of their representation in sectoral coalitions to NGO personnel, and key organizational leaders began to work out of NGOs. For instance, two of the popular democrats' three most prominent leaders, Horacio Morales and Isagani Serrano, operated out of the Philippine Rural Reconstruction Movement, and that office itself attained virtual pre-eminence in the PD movement. Likewise, BISIG's Karina David and Pandayan's Dina Abad, while retaining central influence in their political movements, also assumed leadership of NGOs. These developments indicate important shifts within movements, as both resources and political initiative moved from political councils towards NGOs, even as many who had recently identified themselves as primarily political cadres also shifted offices. Essentially this meant that for most movement organizations, the politics of resistance and progressive activism became more closely bound to the advocacy of specific policy demands through the medium of sectoral coalitions under the increasingly prominent leadership of non-governmental organizations.

The divergence between ND and non-ND organizational patterns of activity represent contrasting attempts to cope with demobilization. While NGOs and sectoral advocacy emerged in all movement organizations of the left, they achieved something like dominance only in non-ND groups. The very security of ND cadres' ties to their mass organizations insulated the movement apparatus from general trends away from protest and demonstration. In fact, the continued ability to mobilize large mass demonstrations with scant unorganized support arguably allowed NDs to envision for themselves a future which took little note of expanding civil and participatory opportunities, and wherein the redress of mass grievances continued to seem primarily dependent on state transformation. Predisposed to reject representative avenues proffered by what they viewed as a bourgeois state, comparatively few ND collectives seriously pursued reforms under Aquino, and instead concentrated their energies on the political confrontation with the State over national power. Groups with comparatively less ability to compel mass participation

---

[40] Internal documents of one ND movement reports on the respective attendance of its mass organizations at these different rallies. While for the most part sectoral rallies elicited support merely from potential beneficiaries, the NDs generally mobilized multi-sectoral support for political mobilizations such as NMCL rallies and electoral efforts. From "Summing Up Report Of Coalition Work, 1986-1990," unpublished document.

needed instead to coax it to the fore, and so to maintain organizational capacity. This effort drove them toward socioeconomic advocacy, produced both through less contentious civil demonstrations and self-help measures—both of which facilitated NGO proliferation, and more sharply transformed the character of activism. Hence while NDs relied on firm organizational discipline to maintain levels of overt activism, other groups attempted to wring participatory incentives from less contentious interactions with a liberalizing state.

The consequences for the demobilization of the Philippine legal movement seem twofold. On the one hand, the proliferation of NGOs produced an intricate honeycomb of institutions standing between grassroots communities and larger political structures. The far more centrally organized resistance to Marcos produced collective action which aggregated grievances into national programs and produced cross-class cooperation. NGOs continued to coordinate their activities in national policy positions, but increasing portions of their advocacy acquired a more specific and focused aspect. NGOs emphasized specific community problems and so took a narrower perspective on base-building and a more focused approach to the representation of grievances. Representation of bounded communities' grievances and the prosecution of community-based programs emerged as successors to complex multi-class programs. Moreover, as the Philippine state opened more participatory points of access, movement organizations and sectoral coalitions once oriented almost exclusively towards protest evolved more into some combination of interest groups and service centers. NGOs' orientation towards policy drew them into government deliberations and consultations.

This evolution completely altered the institutional structure which had previously functioned to mobilize mass demonstrations aimed at addressing a range of grievances. Before 1986, disparate grievances were assimilated into the general anti-Marcos chorus, with each discrete complaint representing an undifferentiated slice of national injustice; grievances were cast as interchangeable, which made them at once individually inexact and collectively equal. After 1987, advocacy became in most respects more precise, with narrowly defined issues, constituents, and audiences. This more exact representation of mass complaints, however, produced comparatively little incentive for cross-class solidarity and left many communities unrepresented. The new structures disaggregated resistance into discrete packages, and very likely will continue to do so. It is perhaps significant in this connection that water and electricity shortages during the early 1990s produced virtually no mass protest, despite the fundamental and material effect it produced over all social classes, including the bourgeoisie. Ironically, then, what began as two and a half years of the broadest Philippine mobilization since the turn of the century seems to have ended in structures which make "contagion"—Charles Tilly's description of protest which spreads like wild-fire throughout a nation—less likely in the future.[41]

A second result of this pattern of demobilization has become evident in recent years. Among the cross-bloc unities that have developed, a pattern has established itself according to which the members of different political movement cadres—the secretary-generals principally—have begun to work together with increasing frequency on political coalitions such as the NMCL and the 1992 AKBAYAN (Kaakbay ng Sambayanan) electoral coalition. Similarly, unities forged between

---

[41] Charles Tilly, *From Mobilization to Revolution* (Reading, MA: Addison-Wesley Publishing Co., 1978).

NGOs in such projects as the CODE-NGO (Caucus for Development—NGO) and the PCHRD (Philippines-Canada Human Resource Development Program) have grown deep and resilient, to the point where on several occasions they have superseded loyalties that exist between NGO workers and their political movements.[42] The pattern of demobilization which began in differential class responses to changing political conditions seems, therefore, to have taken on an organizational aspect as well, manifest at least to some extent in points of difference between NGOs and political organizations.[43]

CONCLUSION

I have endeavored to demonstrate that the proliferation of NGOs and consequent sectoral-specific approach to protest were responses to demobilization, and so it seems appropriate to conclude by redirecting attention from these tactical maneuvers back to demobilization itself. As I have described it, demobilization occurred as changes in the Philippine political structure upset the movement's constituent alliances. The procedurally open state influenced activists from the bourgeoisie to shift their political participation away from street protests and towards parliamentary avenues. Movement cadres also fell under the spell of new state institutions and needed at least to consider the opportunities proffered by participatory avenues in the new government. Yet despite these changes, movements' mass bases continued to labor under the weight of persistent socioeconomic and political grievances. The juxtaposition of liberal and representative political structures and socioeconomic hardship, then, represents the new terrain of movement activity which began to be shaped in 1986.

The most immediate reflection of these changes occurred in the division that opened between mass-based political organizations and the more spontaneous collectives of the urban bourgeoisie. The broad protest movement that unseated Marcos soon divided into two large groups, one intent on commemorating the EDSA struggle and the other committed to the prosecution of social restructuring based on a working class agenda. Even within this latter group, however, divisions emerged concerning how best to guide the organized left through the new political landscape.

New structural conditions forced a dilemma upon movement organizations which made existing patterns of protest untenable in the face of rapidly depleting resources. Before 1983, the movement grew slowly, and its leading organizations faced fairly limited resource requirements; the great post-1983 upsurge expanded the size of movement collectives, but also increased their social and material support.

---

[42] NGO leaders, from such agencies as CPD and the Philippine Business for Social Progress [PBSP] related incidents in which NGOs needed to assert their autonomy from political movements by criticizing moves which either undermined the spirit of development work or of their broad cooperation. The most dramatic such case occurred when NPA assassins killed a non-ND labor leader on December 10, 1990 (Human Rights Day!) on the Campus of Ateneo de Manila. On that occasion, the ND-CPD issued public criticisms of that act. Reported in "NGO Coalition Strategies" (Quezon City: Council for People's Development, 1990).

[43] In the face of the apparent divergence between NGOs and political organizations, Ronald Llamas called for a synthesis of the two formations' goals and functions: "The ideological-political forces must learn from the NGOs in terms of immediate, medium-term micro-programs. On the other hand, the NGOs must adopt strategic trajectories, long term structural anti-systemic targets. If such is not adopted, either their initiatives will be coopted, or their micro-alternatives will come out as failures." Ronald Llamas, "Renewing the Struggle," p. 8.

After 1986, however, middle class support (essential both as a source of resources and of influential popular pressure) waned as representative state institutions took root. This left movement organizations with fewer resources to use in directing their newly expanded mass collectives. Similar considerations influenced mass participation. Even during the height of the protest wave, a vision of material improvement, propelled by pervasive hardship, energized mass participation in protest movements. Members joined protest organizations as a cresting movement seemed to approach some definitive victory with tangible benefits. By 1987, however, three years of activism had produced scant material return, and many began looking beyond mere protest for other avenues to secure some relief. Some grassroots collectives fell into apparent inactivity and, as everyday conditions re-emerged, many adopted everyday forms of resistance. Significant sections of the broad mass base, however, sought material relief from within the movement structure, from a pool of movement resources (broadly conceived) rather than from adversaries.

I have argued that if all movement networks fell under similar structural influences, they responded in different manners. Where stronger organizational discipline existed, as in ND networks, cadres could fall back upon this organizational resource to bolster participation. In less disciplined collectives, cadres had more to meet mass material demands or expect that this mass constituency would shift allegiance away from them and turn elsewhere—to electoral candidates promising patronage, to village associations, to government programs—for such relief. For such movements—and increasingly even for ND organizations—sectoral coalitions and NGO-based development work represented the clearest solution to this dilemma. Both strategies were designed to address directly mass concerns and to grant movement collectives access to new pools of resources.

The extent to which the strategies have actually succeeded, of course, remain subject to debate. Some sympathetic observers have had to acknowledge that NGOs have often made little impact on mass communities,[44] while others make more sweeping claims of NGO successes.[45] I have demonstrated elsewhere that the extent or even validity of efforts to change directly mass members' socioeconomic prospects through the redistribution of collective resources is itself a contested issue within movement alliances. Even where organizations have set out deliberately to

---

[44] For instance, in an attempt to explain "donor fatigue" in a Canadian International Development Agency-sponsored forum held in Tagaytay, The Philippines, in June 1988, one officer from a Northern NGO stated that, "[D]isillusionment is building because despite their increased visibility and substantial resources, NGOs are not succeeding in effecting fundamental change. The traditional small-scale and scattered approach characteristic of NGOs is not adding up to significant and sustainable change." Tim Brodhead, "The Role of Foreign Development Agencies in Response to the Philippine Development Situation," paper presented to the steering committee of the Philippine-Canadian NGO Consultation, June 14, 1988.

[45] Morales Jr., the president of the Philippine Rural Reconstruction Movement [PRRM] summed up the NGO and community-based people's organizations' gains in the following terms: "Local communities, for instance, have improved their capacities, to mobilize and claim resources. In many cases, they have demonstrated substantial results in poverty alleviation through popular enterprises that increase productivity, income and job opportunities. In some areas, local capacity has reached a level of scale demonstration in integrated area development with measurable impact on the local economy as well as the microsystems. From the locality, nongovernmental and people's organizations have now moved up to the higher plane of public policy formation." Horacio Morales Jr., "The Role of Civil Society in Development," *Rural Reconstruction Forum*, October–November 1993, pp. 12–13.

provide resources for relief and rehabilitation, the mass communities may feel neglected and turn away from the movement.[46]

Nevertheless, the organizational legacy of NGOs and sectoral advocacy groups stands as one clear and clearly important result of the demobilization process. The institutionalization of NGOs has established structures that will likely influence Philippine protest for the foreseeable future. NGOs break the most collective expressions of mass grievance into more specific grievances which are then addressed through constituency-specific advocacy programs which can work directly to alleviate such grievances. As NGOs do more for specific sections of the Philippine underclass (i.e. their participant-beneficiaries) they also diminish the chances for broad and multi-class mobilization. Therefore, in place of the massed demonstrations with a broad national agenda of the sort which so often occurred during the mid-1980s, those who observe Philippine protest may look instead for smaller-scale and more specific patterns of interest representation. If these developments seem to promise a more civil pattern of interest representation, they perhaps also risk leaving the interests of unorganized sections of the working class unrepresented. Doubtlessly, however, the ground which these newer agencies and more ideological political movement organizations share will become one of the terrains where the future of Philippine protest is decided.[47]

---

[46] Boudreau, *Lider and the Cadre.*

[47] I wish gratefully to acknowledge the assistance of Ben Kerkvliet and two anonymous readers for their insightful comments on this piece. Antoinette Raquiza's heroic assistance probably helped save me from myself and added to the mountainous intellectual and personal debt I owe her. And, for some well-timed logistical help, my thanks to Woody.

BEYOND BOYCOTT:
THE PHILIPPINE LEFT AND
ELECTORAL POLITICS AFTER
1986

*Eva-Lotta E. Hedman**

INTRODUCTION

Beginning with the 1987 congressional and senatorial elections, the post-EDSA resurrection of formally democratic institutions and processes paved the way for what commentators have referred to as the "return of the oligarchs"[1] to political predominance in the Philippines. Subsequent elections appear to have further clinched the "continuing domination of political clans"[2] and thus strengthened the revival of the pre-Marcos "ancien regime."[3] Meanwhile, however, the Philippine Left—broadly defined—has begun to trespass upon the elite-controlled domain of electoral politics. In comparison with previous efforts to participate in elections by similarly oriented groups and organizations before the declaration of martial law in 1972,[4] moreover, these recent electoral interventions by the Philippine Left have tended to encompass a wider geographic scope and to draw on more diversified sectoral support.

* The author gratefully acknowledges her debts to several people who generously extended themselves and interrupted their busy schedules to share their insights into and experiences of progressive electoral intervention in recent Philippine elections. While the errors and opinions expressed below belong to the author, she would thus like to thank the following people for their best efforts: Fransisco Cinco, Lisa Dacanay, Eric Gutierrez, Liddy Nakpil-Alejandro, Toinette Raquiza, and Clark Soriano. In addition, she would like to thank two anonymous readers as well as Jojo Abinales, Doming Caouette, John Sidel, and Kathleen Weekley for helpful comments on previous drafts of this essay.

[1] Institute for Popular Democracy, *Political Clans & Electoral Politics: A Preliminary Research* (Quezon City: Institute of Popular Democracy, 1987), p. 95. EDSA [Epifanio de los Santos Avenue] is commonly used as a shorthand term to refer to the "People Power" revolt that took place in February 1986; protesters gathered on Epifanio de los Santos Avenue in Manila.

[2] Edicio de la Torre, "Structural Obstacles to Democratization in the Philippines," *Conjuncture* (July 1988).

[3] Benedict Anderson, "Cacique Democracy in the Philippines: Origins and Dreams," *New Left Review* 169 (May–June 1988): 28.

[4] See, for example, Masataka Kimura, "Philippine Peasant and Labor Organizations in Electoral Politics: Players of Transitional Politics," *Pilipinas: A Journal of Philippine Politics* 14 (Spring 1990): 29–78.

This essay focuses attention on problems of Left participation in Philippine electoral politics under the transitional regime of Corazon C. Aquino (1986–1992). While affected by the overall decline of and dissension within the Communist Party of the Philippines (CPP), the New People's Army (NPA), and the National Democratic (ND) movement at large during Aquino's presidential tenure,[5] the broad Philippine Left has not experienced a commensurate downward trend in the field of electoral politics in the same time period. While neither the organizational unity and strength of the dominant Left during the 1987 elections nor the more variegated approaches of the highly fragmented Left-of-Center forces in the 1992 elections have succeeded in dramatically altering the composition of elected representatives to date, they have nevertheless contributed to broaden significantly the spectrum of electoral politics in the post-EDSA Philippines. Thus, when viewed within the context of the dominant Left's widespread demobilization and deep division, examined elsewhere in this volume, the sustained efforts at electoral intervention by individuals, organizations, and coalitions identified with Left-of-Center politics present a compelling puzzle for investigation.

This essay examines the conditions—both external and internal—that combined to shape the Philippine Left's intervention in the 1987 congressional elections and the 1992 simultaneous local and national elections. It argues that the varying extent of anti-communist mobilization and degree of electoral entrenchment influenced both these efforts, as did the Philippine Left's own ideological orientation vis-à-vis, and actual experience of, elections. Based on this analytical framework, the essay also sketches some discernible trends for future Left electoral participation.

SITUATING THE QUESTION OF PHILIPPINE LEFT ELECTORAL INTERVENTION

Reflective of its American colonial legacy, Philippine electoralism in the pre-Marcos era discouraged the emergence both of third parties[6] and of issue-based or ideological party politics. Historically, there was no precedent of a Left party organized nationwide for purposes of fielding and/or supporting candidates before the declaration of martial law in the Philippines.[7] Moreover, with few significant exceptions, the Philippine Left largely refrained from organized electoral

---

[5] For more on this see the other essays in this volume, as well as, for example, Joel Rocamora, *Breaking Through: The Struggle within the Communist Party of the Philippines* (Manila: Anvil Publishing Inc., 1994).

[6] The most significant third parties to emerge in the pre-martial law period were the Democratic Alliance [DA] and the Philippine Progressive Party [PPP]. Whereas the former included both Huk guerrillas and members of the old communist party [Partido Komunista ng Pilipinas], the latter constituted a break-away faction from the Nacionalista Party during the presidency of Carlos P. Garcia by former affiliates of the Magsaysay for President Movement [MPM]. See Thomas Marion Pinckney, Jr., "Third Parties and the Philippine Party System" (PhD dissertation, University of Tennessee, 1971). For a brief summary, see also David Wurfel, *Filipino Politics: Development and Decay* (Ithaca: Cornell University Press, 1988), pp. 100–103.

[7] While enjoying some support in the capital region and elsewhere in the country, too, the Democratic Alliance scored its greatest success in Central Luzon in the 1946 elections. See Benedict Kerkvliet, *The Huk Rebellion: A Study of Peasant Revolt in the Philippines* (Berkeley: University of California Press, 1977), pp. 140–150. For a detailed discussion of the Democratic Alliance in the pre-election period, see also Ronald King Edgerton, "The Politics of Reconstruction in the Philippines: 1945–1948" (PhD dissertation, University of Michigan, 1975), pp. 276–292.

intervention before the 1987 national elections. Heavy-handed government intervention against the candidacies and support of the organized Left in the elections to the 1946 Congress[8] and, more importantly, to the 1978 National Assembly,[9] only served to validate the boycott position within the Philippine Left in the years between the official lifting of martial law in 1981 and the fall of Marcos in 1986. Thus, the boycott line essentially prevailed during the 1986 snap presidential election.[10]

However, in the immediate aftermath of EDSA, the Communist Party of the Philippines officially declared the decision to boycott the 1986 snap presidential elections a "tactical mistake."[11] The 1987 national elections then saw the emergence of the Partido ng Bayan (PnB) with its senatorial slate of former-CPP/ex-detainee candidates and its platform of "new politics." The ensuing electoral contests of 1988 and 1992, moreover, have witnessed an expansion of the electoral political spectrum to include both Left and Left-of-Center alliances and coalitions, some of which have linked up with more traditional political parties.

While noteworthy in and of itself, the Philippine Left's recent efforts at playing electoral politics have so far fallen short of both the rosy predictions of hopeful "Progressives"[12] and the doomsday prophesies of fearful "*trapos.*" Aside from a small (and far from monolithic) minority in Congress, electoral intervention at the national level has barely made a dent in the elite and clan-dominated Congress, for example.[13] With the exception of the Senate's rejection of the US-Bases Treaty in 1991, the broad Philippine Left has been unable to exert decisive influence on legislative issues of critical importance to its constituency, such as human rights, land-reform, and foreign debt.[14]

---

[8] First, during the 1946 electoral campaign, supporters and candidates of the Democratic Alliance [DA] suffered harassment by armed men. Thereafter, the six elected DA congressmen in Central Luzon were prevented from taking their seats because of alleged electoral fraud. See Kerkvliet, *The Huk Rebellion.*

[9] See, for example, Emmanuel de Dios, "The Erosion of the Dictatorship," in Emmanuel de Dios, Petronilo Bn. Daroy and Lorna Kalaw-Tirol, eds., *Dictatorship and Revolution: Roots of People's Power* (Metro Manila: Conspectus, 1988), pp. 70–71; and Gregg R. Jones, *Red Revolution: Inside the Philippine Guerrilla Movement* (Boulder, CO: Westview Press, 1989).

[10] For a brief discussion of the internal deliberations behind the Executive Committee's 1986 boycott decision, see Gregg R. Jones, *Red Revolution*, pp. 156–158.

[11] *Ang Bayan*, May 1986, reprinted as "Sum Up, Learn from Boycott Error," *Ang Katipunan* (San Francisco) (July 1986): 7. For further early Party assessments of the boycott error, see also the June 1986 issue of *Ang Bayan.*

[12] Before the 1987 national elections, for example, the newly created Institute for Popular Democracy [IPD] estimated that Partido ng Bayan would capture some 20 percent of the total votes for both Congress and Senate. See Institute for Popular Democracy, "Fearless Forecast," *Political Clans & Electoral Politics: A Preliminary Research* (Quezon City: Institute of Popular Democracy, 1987), p. 84.

[13] For a well-documented study of the post-1986 entrenchment of elite families, see Eric Gutierrez, Torrente, and Narca, eds., *All in the Family: A Study of Elites and Power Relations in the Philippines* (Quezon City: Institute for Popular Democracy, 1992). For an informative overview of the family and business ties of the present Congress, see also Eric Gutierrez, *The Ties that Bind: A Guide to Family, Business and Other Interests in the Ninth House of Representatives* (Manila: Philippine Center for Investigative Journalism, 1994).

[14] Clearly, the rejection of the US-Bases Treaty owed a great deal to Philippine senators' opposition to the unfavorable terms proposed by a recession-hit US government faced with mounting domestic pressures for post-Cold War peace dividends. At the same time, as a study

Rather than focusing on these obvious limitations, this essay instead proceeds with an examination of four factors that shaped in decisive ways the Philippine Left's efforts at playing electoral politics in the post-Marcos period. While for purposes of analytical clarity a distinction is made here between external versus internal conditions, such categorization clearly simplifies a more complicated and interactive political process. That is, developments in both government counter-insurgency measures and overall political stability have clearly had far-reaching consequences for the evolving debates over strategy and tactics within the Philippine Left. Similarly, the declining fortunes of the armed revolutionary movement have seen corresponding shifts both in government anti-communist policy and practice and in regime political polarization.

In any event, the following external and internal factors can be identified as decisive influences upon the nature and direction of the Philippine Left's intervention in the local and national elections since 1986. On the one hand, the degree of anti-communist mobilization and the entrenchment of Philippine electoralism comprise two factors external to the Philippine Left that have clearly contributed to shaping its involvement in electoral politics. On the other hand, the Philippine Left's ideological orientation toward and actual experience from elections constitute two important internal factors that have decisively conditioned its electoral performance.

ANTI-COMMUNIST MOBILIZATION

Despite the organized Left's political marginalization among the so-called "middle forces" in the aftermath of the 1986 boycott, the NPA's military strength remained essentially intact and caused influential elements both within the AFP (Armed Forces of the Philippines)[15] and the Reagan administration[16] to call for stepped up counterinsurgency measures within months of the Aquino administration's assumption of power. In the first year after EDSA, however, the

---

of Filipino opposition to the US military bases argues, "it cannot be denied that the Left performed the crucial role of providing the consistent, organized mass of opposition." Miriam Coronel-Ferrer, "Anti-Bases Coalition," in "Coalition Experiences" (unpublished mss., 1993), p. 22.

[15] For example, the AFP [Armed Forces of the Philippines] strongly endorsed relying on so-called "vigilantes," or paramilitary anti-communist civilian groups, as one means of intensifying the counterinsurgency. Thus, even at a time when "the Philippine armed forces were deeply divided, they were largely united in their support for vigilantes." Lawyers Committee for Human Rights, *Vigilantes in the Philippines: A Threat to Democratic Rule* (New York: The Lawyers Committee for Human Rights, 1988), p. xv.

[16] For a general discussion of US support of counterinsurgency in the Philippines, see Walden Bello, *Creating the Third Force: US-Sponsored Low-Intensity Conflict in the Philippines* (San Francisco: Institute for Food and Development Policy, 1987) and Gareth Porter, *The Politics of Counterinsurgency in the Philippines: Military and Political Options* (University of Hawaii: Philippine Studies Occasional Paper, no. 9, 1987). See also, Armitage, Statement to the Senate Foreign Relations Committee, June 3, 1986, p. 10, cited in Bello, *US-Sponsored Low-Intensity Conflict*, pp. 72–3; "US Wants Aquino to Toughen Stand on Insurgents," *New York Times*, September 1, 1986; Armitage, Statement before House Subcommittee on Asian and Pacific Affairs, March 17, 1987. See also Committee on Foreign Affairs, *US Assistance to the Philippines*, statement of John C. Monjo, deputy assistant secretary of state, before the Subcommittee on East Asia and Pacific Affairs at the House hearings, May 15, 1986, insisting that Aquino must "go strong on counterinsurgency".

civilian government avoided publicly committing itself to further militarizing[17] the conflict and instead lent support to political initiatives for national reconciliation[18]— the sixty-day national ceasefire in December 1986 and the February 1987 constitutional mandate to eliminate anti-communist vigilante groups.

However, after the NDF (National Democratic Front) left the peace talks in protest against the massacre of thirteen peasant demonstrators by Manila security forces in January 1987, the civilian government began to embrace publicly the military's preferred solution to the so-called "insurgency" problem. The activation of the National Capital Region District Command for purposes of establishing "an effective territorial defense"[19] in Metro Manila in January 1987 and the following month's declaration of the "Total War" policy against the insurgents reflected this shift. In her commencement speech at the Philippine Military Academy (PMA) in March 1987, for example, President Aquino declared that

[t]he answer to the terrorism of the left and the right is not social and economic reform but *police and military action*.[20]

In addition to "police and military action," moreover, the Philippine government now also publicly signaled its approval of military-backed anti-communist civilian groups known as "vigilantes," beginning with President Aquino's visit to one such group in Davao del Sur in late March.[21] In fact, the Department of Local Government "required all OIC [Officer-in-Charge] Governors in Mindanao to create similar community-based counter-guerrilla organizations by May 31, 1987, lest the OIC Governors lose their position."[22] Encouraged by this shift in the administration's position on right-wing civilian militias, such groups proliferated in subsequent months, and by the end of 1987, their number had grown to over two hundred.[23]

---

[17] However, Aquino's New Armed Forces of the Philippines [NAFP] were not issued any "defensive posture" orders during this period. Rather, Porter argues, "the NAFP's counterinsurgency plan, code-named 'Oplan Mamamayan,' which emerged full-blown from the office of the Chief of Staff only a few weeks after the ouster of Marcos, owes nothing to the influence of the democratic regime of Corazon Aquino . . . Originally drawn up in 1985 . . . [its] security portion . . . [is] basically the same as the one in its predecessor 'Oplan Katatagan.'" Porter, *The Politics of Counterinsurgency*, p. 86.

[18] The military's counterinsurgency strategy specified "a three-pronged approach which included not only security and development but national reconciliation as well." Hilario G. Davide et al., *The Final Report* (Manila: The Fact-Finding Commission, 1990), p. 59.

[19] AFP General Headquarters, Letter of Instruction 02787, January 20, 1987, cited in Lorenzo B. Ziga, "Military Checkpoints and the Rule of Law: An Unsettled Peace for Whom?" *Philippine Law Journal* 64, 3rd–4th quarter (September–December 1989): 242.

[20] President Aquino's commencement speech at the PMA, March 23, 1987, cited in Bello, *US-Sponsored Low-Intensity Conflict*, p. 74, emphasis added.

[21] Lawyers Committee for Human Rights [LCHR], *Vigilantes in the Philippines*, p. v.

[22] Free Legal Assistance Group, "Open Letter to Her Excellency Corazon C. Aquino," reprinted in *Malaya*, April 11, 1987, p. 16. The term OIC, or Officer in Charge, refers to the Aquino-appointed replacements for old Marcos loyalists in the interim period between the former dictator's ouster and the holding of local elections in January 1988.

[23] See, for example, the following *Malaya* articles: "Vigilantes to boost Cebu anti-Red drive," April 1, 1987, p. 1; "Counter death squads formed in S. Negros," April 4, 1987, p. 7; "Resist formation of vigilante units, Samarenos urged," April 9, 1987, p. 13; "Caution urged in arming vigilantes," April 10, 1987, pp. 1, 6; "PC, landowners form new vigilante group in Negros," April 22, 1987, p. 12. See also the "Open Letter to Her Excellency Corazon C. Aquino" from the

The May 1987 elections were thus held within the context of a mounting counterinsurgency drive by the Aquino administration and against the backdrop of a proliferation of so-called "vigilante groups," or anti-communist civilian militias. Employed by both police and military forces, vigilantes regularly performed "police and military activities such as armed patrols, manning of checkpoints, and search and seizure operations" throughout the Philippines.[24] In the course of 1987, and while enjoying wide support from the national top brass and operating with local military assistance,

> some of [these vigilante groups] tortured, maimed, mutilated, beheaded, shot and hacked to death people who they claimed support or sympathize with the NPA. Their victims included young children, infants, and the elderly.[25]

In this context of mounting anti-communist mobilization, the new legal left party in 1987—Partido ng Bayan (PnB)—and its Alliance for New Politics (ANP) were subjected to rampant red-baiting in the mainstream media and widespread harassment by armed groups. Thus, "[a]lmost all traditional parties and many key personalities of the right went public in voicing their apprehension and fear of the PnB."[26] Moreover, military and paramilitary armed groups reportedly harassed and even killed numerous PnB and ANP supporters—officials, candidates, campaign organizers and volunteers—during the 1987 election campaign.[27] Similarly, the PnB also saw its headquarters raided, supporters arrested and rallies disrupted by government officials.[28] In addition, the initial denial of accreditation as a legal party

---

Free Legal Assistance Group [FLAG] expressing the "deepest concern over the rise of armed paramilitary groups, counter-guerrilla groups, [and] vigilantes," reprinted in *Malaya*, April 4, 1987, p. 16, shortly after the news of a NAKASAKA-affiliate religious cult, Tadtad, chopping "to death a wounded rebel . . . drank his blood 'to ward off his ghost,' pierced his cheeks with rattan and carried his head to display in the . . . town square." "Vigilante group beheads, drinks blood of rebel," *Hong Kong AFP*, April 1, 1987, reprinted in Lawyers Committee for Human Rights, *Vigilantes in the Philippines*, p. 144.

[24] Senate Committee on Justice and Human Rights, *Report on Vigilante Groups* (Quezon City: Philippine Congress, April 1988), cited in Ziga, "Military Checkpoints and the Rule of Law," p. 242. This report unequivocally calls for the dismantling of vigilante groups in the Philippines.

[25] Lawyers Committee for Human Rights, *Vigilantes in the Philippines*, p. xi.

[26] Eric Gutierrez, "Electoral Coalitions for the 1992 Elections," "Coalition Experiences" (unpublished mss, 1993), p. 96. According to then-chair of PnB, Fidel Agcaoilil, the anti-PnB and ANP [Alliance for New Politics] propaganda in the 1987 election campaign even included a "comic booklet [in which] the ANP people were portrayed as satanists," cited in Benjamin Pimentel, Jr., "What's Left of New Politics?" *Midweek*, September 23, 1987, p. 7.

[27] See, for example, the following *Malaya* articles: "PnB man killed in Aklan, another nabbed in Navotas," April 1, 1987; "More ANP bets cry harassment," April 9, 1987, pp. 1, 6; "Two campaign workers of ANP believed killed," April 10, 1987, pp. 1, 6; "Stop harassment of ANP, government urged," April 11, 1987, pp. 1, 7; "4PnB campaigners are missing," April 14, 1987, pp. 1,6; "ANP worker attacked by armed group," April 25, 1987; and "Increase in military harassment cases noted," May 1, 1987. A paid advertisement by PAHRA [Institute for Political and Electoral Reform], POTENT, KMU, KMP, LFS, KPML, and KAP claims that 24 "officials, campaigners and supporters of the Alliance for New Politics have been killed while 54 others have been arrested, abducted and mauled . . . ," "Another Rape of Democracy?," *Malaya*, May 11, 1987, p. 7.

[28] See, for example, the *Malaya* articles cited above.

to the PnB[29] and the eventual removal of many candidates' ANP affiliation from official COMELEC (Commission on Elections) lists of registered candidates, for example, have been cited as further evidence of possible anti-Left intervention by COMELEC officials at both the national and local levels in the 1987 elections.[30]

The following statement by the PnB Secretary-General on the 1988 local elections summarizes the argument advanced here that, against the backdrop of Aquino's Total War policy, Left-leaning electoral efforts were bound to run up against not merely the usual election-related violence for which Philippine polls have gained such notoriety but also against more selective repression as a result of widespread anti-communist mobilization:

> Efforts by the Left and other progressive forces to contest the local elections not only would involve them in the fierce and bloody fighting among traditional political rivals for their power bases, but also pit them in direct and more intense confrontation . . . with the Aquino regime. . . .[31]

By comparison, the May 1992 elections were held without the widespread anti-communist hysteria and repression that marked the 1987 electoral exercise. By 1992, most vigilante groups had been demobilized or disbanded altogether and the majority of paramilitary forces known as CAFGUs (Civilian Armed Forces Geographical Units) operated as private armies at the behest of individual local politicians rather than in the service of a national government crusade against communism, thus making above-ground Left affiliates less privileged targets of repression. That is, Left candidates faced much the same pressures due to election-related violence and harassment—which remained salient features of the electoral process in many parts of the Philippines—as did other contestants in 1992. In short, the relative decline of government-backed anti-communist mobilization allowed for greater visibility and activism on the part of above-ground progressive forces, thus favoring electoral intervention by individuals and organizations identified with the Philippine Left.[32]

ENTRENCHMENT OF ELECTORALISM

Despite the authoritarian legacies of Marcos's martial law years and the "revolutionary" origins of the Aquino regime, the swift political comeback of old

---

[29] See, for example, Jun F. Sibal, "Newcomer in the Arena," *Midweek*, March 18, 1987, pp. 3–7.

[30] For example, there were reports of "Comelec lists in polling booths [that] failed to identify PnB, Bayan and Volunteers for Popular Democracy candidates as ANP coalition candidates." *Malaya*, May 12, 1987, p. 3.

[31] Alan Jazmines, "Areas of Contention: Aquino's Total War and the Local Elections," *National Midweek*, January 20, 1988, p. 33.

[32] However, the PnB's internal election report cited "heavy military operations throughout the electoral period" as the main reason why the party refrained from reactivating its Partido Kordilyera and PnB-Metro Baguio chapters in Regions One and Two. See Partido ng Bayan, *Grassroots Electoral Politics: An Evaluation of the Electoral Performance of PnB and Allied Organizations in the 1987 and 1992 Elections* (Quezon City: Partido ng Bayan, April 1993), p. 39. See also, for example, "Lull before the long war," *Manila Chronicle*, December 28, 1991–January 2, 1992, p. 10. Significantly, William Claver, a congressional representative identified with progressive politics, failed to gain reelection in his district in Kalinga-Apayao.

elites and the resounding popular endorsement of the new constitution seemed to pave the way for the successful entrenchment of electoralism in the post-EDSA Philippines. As in the pre-martial law period, formally democratic institutions and procedures once again presented obvious opportunities for a national agro-industrial oligarchy[33] and local political bosses[34] to rejuvenate and legitimize stable elite rule through regular and popular elections. The massive turnout and endorsement—in sharp contrast to the dominant Left's official boycott and "no" positions—in the 1986 snap presidential elections and the 1987 constitutional plebiscite, respectively, also appeared to confirm the safe return of electoral politics in the post-Marcos Philippines.[35]

However, extra-electoral forms of political mobilization nurtured by conditions under martial law continued to pose a challenge for the consolidation of Philippine electoralism even as the 1987 senatorial and congressional election campaigns gained momentum. In fact, these elections were held within a context characterized by widespread political uncertainty as to the sturdiness of the "rule of law," especially in the face of persistent military adventurism and revolutionary mobilization. Thus, the ravages of civil war and the continued presence of both a vastly expanded armed forces and Asia's largest contemporary communist movement contributed to a highly polarized political environment during the time of the 1987 elections.[36]

The most serious challenges to the entrenchment of electoralism in the early post-Marcos years stemmed from extra-electoral mobilization from both the Right and the Left. During its first eighteen months in power, for example, the Aquino administration faced down six separate coup attempts by so-called "rebel" soldiers or Marcos "loyalist" troops.[37] Meanwhile, the New People's Army remained essentially intact and retained significant control over some 20 percent of all

---

[33] See, for example, Temario Campos Rivera, "Class, The State and Foreign Capital: The Politics of Philippine Industrialization, 1950–1986" (PhD dissertation, University of Wisconsin-Madison, 1991).

[34] See, for example, John T. Sidel, "Coercion, Capital and the Post-Colonial State: Bossism in the Postwar Philippines" (PhD dissertation, Cornell University, 1995).

[35] While Marcos, too, held "elections" and "plebiscites" under martial law, these served essentially as auxiliary public relations measures (designed as much for target audiences in US foreign policy circles and international lending institutions as for local consumption) under his reign of "constitutional authoritarianism." See, for example, Raul P. de Guzman, "Citizen Participation and Decision-Making under the Martial Law Administration: A Search for a Viable Political System," *Philippine Journal of Public Administration* 21, 1 (January 1977).

[36] For a brief account that vividly captures the "vigil" of the early Aquino regime, see, for example, Marites Danguilan-Vitug, "An endless vigil: Philippine democracy under siege," in *Kudeta: The Challenge to Philippine Democracy* (Manila: Philippine Center for Investigative Journalism, 1990), pp. 153–160. Another recent PCIJ publication provides an introductory anthology of sorts to various manifestations of what one contributor refers to as the apocalypse-now mentality characteristic of these "siege" years. For more on this, see PCIJ, *Coups, Cults & Cannibals* (Manila: PCIJ, 1993).

[37] The government-appointed investigation released a lengthy report which lists these attempts: "The first coup attempt against the Aquino administration was staged by civilians and military elements loyal to the deposed President Marcos by taking over the Manila Hotel in July 1986. Subsequent attempts were the November 1986 'God Save The Queen' plot, the January 1987 GMA-7 attempt, the April 1987 Black Saturday incident, the July 1987 takeover plot at the Manila International Airport [and] the August 1987 [attempt]." Davide, *The Final Report*, p. 21, fn. 1. See also Fransisco Nemenzo, "A Season of Coups: Reflections on the Military in Politics," *Kasarinlan* 2, 4, (1987): 9–14.

barangays in the Philippines.[38] In addition, while essentially pursuing parliamentary politics by other means, striking workers[39] and demonstrating peasants[40] (especially those identified with the organized Left) nevertheless presented a challenge for the Philippines' resurrected elite democracy by publicly exposing its narrowly conservative political parameters. Despite widespread popular support for the widow-housewife president, the constitutional foundations of the Aquino regime came under increasing public attack in 1987. For example, the Aquino administration's efforts to promote a new draft constitution ran up against strong protests from "representative[s] of the radical Left, nationalist, cause-oriented groups, and the extreme Right, particularly the military."[41] Significantly, the Communist Party of the Philippines called for a "No" vote in the plebiscite on the ratification of the new Constitution, which was also reportedly voted down in several military camps in the country.[42]

In the weeks before the February 1987 constitutional plebiscite, moreover, Manila witnessed the Channel 7 military coup attempt, the Mendiola Massacre of peasant protesters, and a series of popular demonstrations, all of which underlined the political precariousness of the regime at the time. Although the constitution won roughly 75 percent popular approval, the political mobilization of what have been

---

[38] At the time, the AFP reportedly estimated "NPA strength to 24,000–25,000 regulars, half of whom are thought to be armed. The insurgents are thought to be operating in at least sixty-eight out of the nation's seventy-two provinces, and to exert significant influence over 20 percent of the nation's 40,000 villages." Lawyers Committee for Human Rights, *Vigilantes in the Philippines*, p. 3.

[39] According to one estimate, "strikes increased in 1986 to 581, 248 (43 percent) of which were reportedly led by KMU-affiliated unions," Bureau of International Affairs, Department of Labor, *Foreign Labor Trends: Philippines 1986* (Washington DC.: Department of Labor, 1987), p. 10. KMU, which is short for the Kilusang Mayo Uno, is the most radical national federation of Philippine workers. The 1986 strikes, moreover, reportedly involved 169,379 workers, a dramatic increase compared to the calculated 20,902 workers who participated in the sixty-two strikes recorded for the year 1980. "Most of the 1986 strikes were called by the KMU." Fransisco Nemenzo, "The Philippine Labour Movement and the Continuing Struggle for Democracy," paper presented at the Conference on Labour Movements in Transition to Democracy, Kellogg Institute for International Studies, University of Notre Dame, April 1988, p. 41.

[40] The founding in 1986 of the Kilusang Magbubukid ng Pilipinas [KMP] as a peasant counterpart to the KMU—both of which are affiliates of the above-ground umbrella organization for the national democratic left, Bagong Alyansang Makabayan [BAYAN]—signaled a new development as "the KMP launched nationwide 'organized land occupations' on 26 September 1986. Other peasant organizations also decided to occupy idle and abandoned land in an attempt to force the government to make good its promises for reform," James Putzel, *A Captive Land: The Politics of Agrarian Reform in the Philippines* (Quezon City: Ateneo de Manila University, 1992), p. 219.

[41] Luzviminda G. Tancangco and Roger L. Mendoza, "Elections and the Crisis of Legitimacy in the Philippines: A Comparative View of the Marcos and Aquino Regimes," *Philippine Journal of Public Administration* 32, 3–4 (July–October 1988): 291.

[42] "After the plebiscite, . . . considerable concern was expressed over the conviction and persuasion of the military which supported the Constitution by a mere 60 percent to 40 percent margin. The 40 percent was viewed as a significant number. The 'no' vote was in fact larger in certain military camps." Tancangco and Mendoza, "Elections and the Crisis of Legitimacy in the Philippines, p. 292.

referred to elsewhere as elements of the "disloyal opposition"[43] continued to undermine the consolidation of Philippine electoralism throughout the 1987 congressional campaign and inauguration.

On the one hand, renegade military troops continued to plot and to launch coup attempts during this period, as evidenced by the following three incidents recorded between April and August 1987: the April 18 Black Saturday occupation of Fort Bonifacio; the July 2 failed Manila International Airport takeover; and the August 28 coordinated attacks on the Malacanang presidential palace, the Camp Aguinaldo AFP headquarters, the Villamor Air Force base and the Quezon City government TV station.[44] On the other hand, as the ceasefire between government and underground troops broke down in January 1987, the Politburo of the CPP resolved to "regularize" and intensify the armed struggle in a "strategic counter-offensive"[45] and the Party's public voice, *Ang Bayan*, began to call for opposition to "the US-Aquino scheme to stabilize the reactionary ruling order."[46] In addition, NPA "tactical offensives were escalated throughout the archipelago."[47] According to *Ang Bayan*, for example,

> the NPA took for its main targets the CHDF [the Civilian Home Defense Forces, the government militia], paramilitary right-wing groups, warlord armies, death squads, and armed fanatical sects, as well as units of reactionary armed forces associated with the deposed dictator.[48]

This early escalation of NPA tactical offensives, moreover, was reportedly "followed by a coordinated anti-LIC (low intensity conflict) campaign in July–September 1987 [with] more than 600 small and big guerrilla operations . . . launched by the NPA throughout the country."[49]

In the aftermath of the May elections, non-violent collective mobilization from both the Right and the Left also added to the challenge against Philippine electoralism. Leaders of the rightist Grand Alliance for Democracy (GAD), for example, including former Defense Minister Juan Ponce Enrile, held a mass protest

---

[43] While loaded, the term "disloyal opposition" nevertheless captures the idea of more or less organized resistance to and/or assault upon not merely a particular politician, party, or administration, but an entire regime or, put differently, the "rules of the game." See, Juan Linz, *The Breakdown of Authoritarian Regimes: Crisis, Breakdown, and Reequilibration* (Baltimore: Johns Hopkins University Press, 1978).

[44] Over 2,000 troops reportedly took part in the August 28 coup attempt (and many more allegedly hedged their bets until the end), making it the most serious military threat during Aquino's first eighteen months in power. Beyond Metro Manila, "[r]enegade troops also took over the military commands in at least six provinces and mobilized their supporters among the cadets of the Philippine Military Academy." Sheila S. Coronel, "A Coup Before Dawn," *Manila Chronicle*, December 31, 1987, reprinted in Sheila S. Coronel, *Coups, Cults & Cannibals: Chronicles of a Troubled Decade* (Manila: Anvil Publishing House, 1993), p. 71. For more on these coup attempts, see also the government-appointed Davide Commission's report: Davide et al., *Final Report*. See also the PCIJ-collection, *Kudeta*, and Criselda Yabes, *The Boys from the Barracks: The Philippine Military after EDSA* (Manila: Anvil Publishing, 1991).

[45] Paco Arguelles, "Pagbabalik-aral: A-priorism Reaffirmed," *Debate* 7 (August 1993): 69.

[46] "Oppose the US-Aquino Scheme to Stabilize the Reactionary Ruling Order," *Ang Bayan*, January 1987, pp. 1–3.

[47] Arguelles, "Pagbabalik-aral."

[48] "People's War Advances, Confronts Total War," *Ang Bayan*, March 1987, pp. 2–3.

[49] Arguelles, "Pagbabalik-aral."

outside the AFP and PC (Philippine Constabulary) camps on EDSA soon after the May 11 elections and distributed leaflets urging soldiers to take action against alleged electoral fraud perpetrated by the Aquino administration. Two months later, moreover, a radical "parliament of the streets" confronted the official inauguration of the newly elected elite- and clan-dominated Congress with its own mass ceremony:

> At noon, various people's organizations started to congregate. . . including militants from BAYAN [Bagong Alyansang Makabayan], KMU [Kilusang Mayo Uno], KMP [Kilusang Magbubukid ng Pilipinas], KAIBA. . . . The rallyists peaked at more than 3,000 but they were prevented from approaching Congress by anti-riot police who encircled them. . . . The demonstrators version of Congress—a Congress of the streets—was highlighted by their own State of the Nation address which was delivered by BAYAN secretary-general Lean Alejandro. . . . [50]

Escalating political violence in Metro Manila itself also attested to the instability and vulnerability of the Aquino regime in the months surrounding the May 1987 elections. Contributing to the heightened levels of armed confrontation in Metro Manila—the center of economic and political power in the Philippines—the AFP activated the National Capital Region District Command "to conduct security operations, . . . establish an effective territorial defense, [and] maintain peace and order."[51] Responding in part to increased counterinsurgency operations by government forces, the NPA's urban "sparrow units" stepped up their own tactical offensives in the National Capital Region.[52] As a result, according to one source, in 1987,

> the most devastating effects of NPA violence—traditionally largely confined to the provinces—came to Manila. As many as one hundred people were executed by NPA urban 'sparrow units'—assassination squads; almost all of the victims were police or military personnel.[53]

Overall, the mounting extra-electoral mobilization and deepening political polarization that surrounded the May 1987 elections contributed to delimit the nature and scope of the Philippine Left's participation in these polls. The escalation of both government and underground military (and paramilitary) campaigns in the aftermath of the failed peace negotiations, and the concomitant centrifugal trajectory of the rebel Right and the revolutionary Left away from "critical collaboration" within Centrist parameters, militated against electoral intervention by the Philippine Left. In fact, given the continued obstacles to the entrenchment of electoralism discussed above, the 1987 elections constituted only one among several arenas of contestation for the Philippine Left. As the CPP's renewed emphasis on military efforts hampered planning and coordination concerning all other areas of work, it has been suggested, "[t]hese organizational problems fed into a long series of

---

[50] Melanie Manlogon, "The Day Congress Came Back," *Midweek*, August 19, 1987, p.46.

[51] AFP General Headquarters, Letter of Instruction 02787, January 20, 1987, cited in Ziga, "Military Checkpoints and the Rule of Law," p. 242.

[52] Porter, *The Politics of Counterinsurgency*, p. 8.

[53] Lawyers Committee for Human Rights, *Vigilantes in the Philippines*, pp. 9–10.

propaganda disasters [including] the defeat of Partido ng Bayan candidates in the 1987 congressional elections."[54] With the consolidation of Philippine electoralism still uncertain, the Left's 1987 electoral strategists and activists thus never resolved "whether the [Pnb/ANP] campaign should primarily be aimed at winning seats, at using the elections to 'educate the masses' or both."[55]

In 1992, by contrast, elections were firmly established as *the* route to power and influence in the Philippines. Threats of coups no longer posed a credible challenge to the regime, especially in light of the demilitarization of the Philippine Constabulary and the creation of a Philippine National Police (PNP) removed from control and supervision of the AFP and the Department of National Defense (DND).[56] As a further deterrent to military adventurism,

> the government after December 1989 [also] built up its defenses, including forming an anti-coup force and an extensive counterintelligence unit especially to thwart rebel attempts.[57]

Moreover, due to government counterinsurgency efforts as well as internal conflicts, the severely decimated underground Left, and its much-depleted "united front" affiliates, no longer posed an acute challenge for the consolidation of Philippine resurrected electoralism. According to its own estimates, for example, between 1987 and 1990,

> Party membership decreased by 15 percent, the total number of barrios under its coverage by 16 percent, the total number of members of the people's army by 28 percent, and the total membership in the rural mass organizations by 60 percent [and] big number of cadres at the provincial, front and district levels were lost due to arrests, death, or demoralization.[58]

However, this period also allowed for the simultaneous growth and proliferation of smaller above-ground Left-of-Center groups and organizations for which progressive electoral struggle constituted a sine qua non: "Opening 'yan na dapat ine-exploit."[59] While clearly less enthused by the prospect, the largest legal left mass organization also recognized the imperative of electoral participation in 1992: "We

---

[54] Rocamora, *Breaking Through*, p. 93.

[55] *Conjuncture*, February–March 1988: 17.

[56] See, for example, Rod B. Gutang, *Pulisya: The Inside Story of Law Enforcement in the Philippines* (Quezon City: Daraga Press, 1991). Congressman and former PC Brigadier General Gutang drafted the bill to demilitarize the police force which went into effect as R.A. 6975 on January 1, 1991.

[57] Roberto D. Tiglao, "Rebellion from the Barracks: The Military as Political Force," in *Kudeta: The Challenge to Philippine Democracy* (Manila: Philippine Center for Investigative Journalism, 1990), p. 21.

[58] Arguelles, "Pagbabalik-aral," p. 78.

[59] Interview with Ronald Llamas of Bukluran sa Ikauunlad ng Sosyalistang Isip at Gawa [BISIG] by Ces Ochoa, "New politics: Is it worth another try?" *Midweek*, May 16, 1990, p. 23. This statement is echoed by many other individuals and groups identified with the above-ground progressive Left.

will have to participate."[60] The entrenchment of electoralism thus contributed to create a new set of incentives for participation in elections by the Philippine Left. Against this backdrop, the following section will briefly outline the Philippine Left's evolving ideological orientation on the question of electoral struggle.

IDEOLOGICAL ORIENTATION

In terms of the ideological orientation and cohesion of the Philippine Left, the 1987 and 1992 elections offer a study in contrasts. Ideology has obviously been an important "internal" factor conditioning the Philippine Left's electoral involvement in the post-EDSA period. Whereas some developments leading up to the 1987 national elections suggested the increasing significance of legal and electoral forms of struggle, the dominant organized Left continued to emphasize both the primacy of armed struggle and the 'vanguard' role of the Party leadership in relation to its above-ground affiliates, with direct consequences for the "new politics" election campaigns. By 1992, however, the deepening ideological differences within the Party itself, as well as the emergence of a plethora of so-called "cause-oriented" groups with links to Left-of-Center organizations, allowed for a more variegated electoral intervention.[61]

Historically, the Maoist orientation of the CPP has been a decisive factor shaping its involvement—or lack thereof—in electoral politics.[62] The following excerpt from founding chairman Sison's "revolutionary bible" illustrates this strong influence of Mao Zedong Thought on the CPP:

> The main force of the Philippine revolution is the peasantry. It is the largest mass force in a semi-colonial and semi-feudal country. Without its powerful support, the people's democratic revolution can never succeed. . . . There is no solution to the peasant problem but to wage armed struggle, conduct agrarian revolution and build revolutionary base areas.[63]

Thus, from its inception as a breakaway Maoist faction from the old Partido Komunista ng Pilipinas (PKP), the CPP's "rejection of the cities in favor of the countryside led it, on a theoretical plane, to equate urban struggle with parliamentary or legal struggle, and hence with revisionism."[64]

In addition, it has been argued, the "revisionist" PKP's old cadres served as influential "teachers by negative example"[65] for the new generation of middle-class intellectual recruits who formed the core of the CPP. This is reflected in another key

---

[60] Interview with Bayan chair Nelia Sancho by Rodney Tasker, "Grassroot support: Left to help some candidates in local polls," *Far Eastern Economic Review*, March 12, 1992, p. 20.

[61] For more detailed and nuanced accounts of the nature and direction of the Philippine Left in this period, see Arguelles, "Pagbabalik-Aral."

[62] See, for example, Armando Malay, Jr., "The Legal vs. the Illegal in CPP-ML Strategy and Tactics," *Asian Studies* 20 (1982): 122–142.

[63] Amado Guerrero, *Philippine Society And Revolution* (Hong Kong: Ta Kung Pao, 1971), p. 280.

[64] Armando Malay, Jr., "The Influence of Mao Zedong Thought on the Communist Party of the Philippines Marxist Leninist," in Theresa C. Carino, ed., *China and Southeast Asia: Contemporary Politics and Economics* (Manila: La Salle University Press, 1984), p. 48.

[65] Ibid., p. 42.

document titled "Rectify Errors and Rebuild the Party,"[66] which is as much a critique of "PKP leaderships for their alleged ignorance or non-application of Mao Zedong Thought [and] of the previous PKP leaderships, from Crisanto Evangelista down to Jesus Lava, as it is an enunciation of the CPP-ML's (Communist Party of the Philippines—Marxist-Leninist) theses for revolution."[67]

Leninist principles of "democratic centralism," scholars have suggested, discouraged debate over—or deviation from—the Maoist party line.[68] In fact, despite the much celebrated policy of "centralized leadership, decentralized operations," successful local adaptations by regional and sectoral cadres, it has been argued, "rarely worked their way 'upwards' as ideas that prompted a re-thinking of the central tenets of Party thought."[69] The binding nature of sanctions by higher Party organs upon subordinate cadres—reflected in practices of suppression and self-policing—thus insulated Maoist doctrine from internal "revisionist" challenges.

Finally, the relative isolation from international communist movements, it has been noted, further shielded the CPP from any serious critical challenges to its position that "political power grows out of the barrel of a gun." Thus, as a Maoist splinter party, "Philippine communists have had relatively little access to on-going debates within other, broader Marxist circles in the world."[70] In fact, several critics have linked the relative isolation of the CPP to its "purist" orientation in favor of a protracted people's war in the countryside (and at the expense of legal or parliamentary urban struggles).[71]

While internally debated and opposed,[72] the Party leadership's ideological orientation in 1987 essentially reflected a back-to-basics approach—"building on the movement's strength in rural armed struggle and union organizing, then waiting for the [urban] 'middle forces' to return"[73]—which downplayed the significance of electoral struggle. At the same time, however, the Party reportedly authorized the foundation of the Partido ng Bayan (PnB) as a new progressive legal party, which was subsequently "organized by prominent former party leaders, including founding Chairman Sison and the first NPA Chief Bernabe Buscayno."[74]

---

[66] This document was adopted at the CPP "Congress of Reestablishment" in December of 1968. See, for example, Fransisco Nemenzo, "Rectification Process in the Philippine Communist Movement," in Lim Joo Jock and S. Vani, eds., *Armed Communist Movements in Southeast Asia* (Hampshire, England: Gower, 1984), pp. 75–79.

[67] Malay, "The Influence of Mao Zedong Thought," pp. 47–48.

[68] Gareth Porter, "Strategic Debates and Dilemmas in the Philippine Communist Movement," *Pilipinas* 13 (Fall 1989): 19–40.

[69] Kathleen Weekley, "A Tale of Two Boycott Debates: Some Notes on the Roots of the Crisis of the Communist Party of the Philippines," in this volume. The CPP's official publication, moreover, has argued that on "occasions, at various levels, when we were not able to correctly enforce democratic centralism . . . our unity was unstable and our advance obstructed." "Party Members Urged to Review Basics of Democratic Centralism," *Ang Bayan* (English ed.)17, 4 (June 1986): 8.

[70] Weekley, "A Tale of Two Boycott Debates," p. 3.

[71] See, for example, Rene Ciria Cruz, "Why the Philippine Left Must Take the Parliamentary Road," *Debate* 2 (March 1992): 9, and Marty Villalobos (pseudonym), former high-ranking Party member, "For a Politico-Military Framework," unpublished paper, February 23, 1987.

[72] See, for example, Marty Villalobos, "For a Politico-Military Framework."

[73] Rocamora, *Breaking Through*, p. 84.

[74] Porter, *The Politics of Counterinsurgency*, p. 44. Jose Maria Sison chaired PnB's Preparatory Committee, while several other former CPP cadres and ex-detainees became prominent PnB

Thus identified with—though not identical to—the underground Left, the PnB's electoral agenda was allegedly still considered "secondary" to armed struggle.[75] For example, a key PnB figure and ANP senatorial candidate claimed that the "primary campaign goal was to educate the electorate and to broaden the policy debate."[76] Another prominent PnB personality also admitted "very strong reservations about participating in the 1987 elections."[77] Many PnB insiders, moreover, "noted that their strategists and activists were less than united on the objectives of their participation."[78]

Organizationally, PnB also had a difficult time instituting and enforcing the national council's decisions, particularly among the base organizations that openly supported the party. Many of the party directives, for instance, were not awarded enough attention by local chapters and constituent organizations, which were understandably engaged in other campaigns and commitments. This could be seen as a reflection of how elections are accorded strategic significance in the rank and file of ND organizations.[79]

Compared to the PnB's "propaganda campaign" in 1987, its new motto, "field to win," seemed to point in a new direction for the Left in the 1988 local elections. However, reflective in part of the heavy toll suffered by its supporters in 1987—both in terms of electoral defeat and personal injury—the PnB also declared that in the 1988 elections "only chapters that are able to ensure the safety of their candidates are campaigning actively, resulting in few reported PnB casualties this year compared to last year. . . ."[80] The party thus reportedly fielded fewer than a hundred PnB candidates for the positions of municipal mayor and councilor, while expressing support for some 3,000 candidates of different party-affiliations and reputed opposition to the government's counter-insurgency policies. In addition to official guidelines limiting the PnB's electoral participation to areas where supporters could receive adequate protection, media reports that "Communist guerrillas have confirmed for the first time that they are receiving money from candidates . . . for safe-conduct passes in guerrilla-controlled areas"[81] also underlined the continued significance of armed struggle for the Philippine Left during the 1988 elections.

---

personalities, including, for example, Secretary-General Romeo Candazo and senatorial candidates Bernabe "Dante" Buscayno, Horacio "Boy" Morales, and Nelia Sancho.

[75] See, for example, Jose Maria Sison, "Political Report," presented to PnB's founding convention on August 30, 1986, cited in Porter, *The Politics of Counterinsurgency*, p. 53, fn. 47.

[76] Francisco Lara, Jr. and Horacio R. Morales, Jr., "The Peasant Movement and the Challenge of Rural Democratisation in the Philippines," *Journal of Development Studies* 26, 4 (July 1990): 149. Morales was one of ANP's seven senatorial candidates in the 1987 election.

[77] Interview with Etta Rosales by Ces Ochoa, "New politics: Is it worth another try?" *Midweek*, May 16, 1990, p. 8.

[78] *Conjuncture*, February–March 1988, p. 17.

[79] Eric Gutierrez, "Electoral Coalitions for the 1992 Elections," unpubl. mss., author's file, p. 96.

[80] Interview with Lui Gamit, PnB deputy secretary-general for operations, by Yasmin Arquiza, "PnB adopts new poll motto: field to win," *Malaya*, January 15, 1988, p. 6.

[81] "Rebs admit bets gave them money," *Malaya*, January 15, 1988, p. 1. Other contemporary reports claimed that "several municipal and provincial candidates in Quezon province yesterday said the NPA was collecting 'tong' from the candidates to raise funds . . . The

In short, the dominant Left's orientation towards elections in the aftermath of the "tactical mistakes" of the 1986 boycott and 1987 "no" campaigns continues to reflect the secondary importance accorded to legal progressive efforts in the electoral arena as opposed to the primacy of armed revolutionary struggle. The following statement in *Ang Bayan* captures the extent to which considerations of an essentially tactical nature guided the Party's move toward a "beyond boycott" position on the question of electoral participation in the 1987 and 1988 elections:

> The Party should never allow itself to be preoccupied with and divided over any debate on the question of boycott or participation in any voting exercise . . . [but] counter . . . by using revolutionary dual tactics and encouraging the legal progressive parties to expose the limits of the voting exercise and, at the same time, use it to gain advantages for the people.[82]

By 1992, by contrast, the internal debates within the Party and the growth of the extra-Party left reflected far-reaching reassessments and critiques of the Left's revolutionary program. The 1992 elections saw, for example, "the disjointed . . . ND forces, with PnB calling for 'active participation,' BAYAN-MMR [Bagong Alyansang Makabayan—Metro Manila-Rizal] calling for 'Rebolusyon, hindi eleksyon' and BAYAN-National asserting 'walang ilusyon sa eleksyon.'"[83] Thus, contrasting the revived PnB of 1992 with its predecessor in 1987, the new chair emphasized a shift toward "a more long-term view of our role in parliamentary work."[84] The following statement further underlines the PnB's changing electoral agenda for the 1992 elections:

> The 1987 PnB had Alliance for New Politics, at the national level, but this was actually made up of kindred spirits. Now we are trying to broaden the coalitions. We have talks with traditional parties. We have coalitions with progressive candidates at the local level. . . .[85]

The growth and proliferation of progressive forces more or less autonomous of the dominant underground Left have also contributed to a wide array of Left-of-Center initiatives aimed at intensifying and expanding electoral struggle since 1987. For example, while the 1987 electoral coalition of broad progressive forces (led by

---

candidates, who requested anonymity, said the rebels were asking P5,000 from councilors, P10,000–P30,000 from mayors and P100,000 from gubernatorial bets. Several candidates have already been forced to pay up because the rebels were prohibiting them from campaigning . . ." *Manila Chronicle*, January 5, 1988, p. 6. See also, for example, "A must for candidates: NPA pass," *Malaya*, January 13, 1988; and the front-page picture and caption of "a New People's Army safe conduct pass," *Manila Chronicle*, January 15, 1988.

[82] *Ang Bayan*, December 1988, p. 16.

[83] Partido ng Bayan, *Grassroots Electoral Politics: An Evaluation of the Electoral Performance of PnB and Allied Organizations in the 1987 and 1992 Elections*, (Quezon City: Partido ng Bayan, April 1993), p. 54.

[84] "PnB with a Difference," *Conjuncture* 5, 2 (February 1992): 5.

[85] Interview with PnB chair Loretta Ann "Etta" Rosales, in "PnB with a difference," *Conjuncture* 5, 2 (February 1992): 5.

popular democrats[86]), the Movement for New Politics, was superseded by the more orthodox Alliance for New Politics (led by national democrats[87]), the 1992 elections saw the participation of a broad spectrum of Left-of-Center groups and coalitions in both the local and national elections. Thus, despite the staying power of the "guns, goons and gold" of traditional party politics and the absence of a unified electoral coalition/strategy of the broad Left, many among the latter took the position that "the parliamentary arena must be maximized to bring progressive issues, if not leadership, closer to the people."[88] In the 1992 elections, for example, the Koalisyong Pambansa (National Coalition)—which included the Liberal Party (LP), the Pilipino Democratic Party Lakas ng Bansa (PDPLABAN), and the Kaakbay ng Sambayanan (AKBAYAN)[89]—constituted the most ambitious effort to bring established political parties together with cause-oriented and non-governmental organizations around a national platform of progressive politics.

ELECTORAL EXPERIENCE

Finally, in terms of electoral experience, the Philippine Left had little to no actual experience of involvement in electoral politics in 1987. In the words of the PnB's chairman: "Hindi pa talaga kami sanay."[90] Again, with few exceptions, election-boycott campaigns constituted the Left's most organized efforts at electoral intervention since Independence and mass suffrage. In addition to lacking much useful experience for purposes of fielding and/or supporting candidates, moreover, the Philippine Left's collective memory of one or two previous attempts at playing electoral politics further shaped its involvement in the 1987 elections.[91]

In 1992, by contrast, the Philippine Left could draw on its own record of electoral experiences which included both participation in the 1987 national and 1988 local elections, as well as the subsequent incumbency of a few municipal and congressional "Progressives." The so-called "Progressive Bloc" in Congress after 1987, for example, influenced not merely legislation but also government appointments, pork-barrel, and national debates which added to the Left's experience of Philippine electoralism.[92] Internal evaluations, moreover, argued that

---

[86] Popular democrats, or "popdems": Volunteers for Popular Democracy [VPD] and Bukluran sa Ikauunlad ng Sosyalistang Isip at Gawa [BISIG].

[87] See Rocamora, *Breaking Through*, pp. 139–169, on "natdems."

[88] Toinette Raquiza, "Is a democratic transition possible?" *Conjuncture* 5, 2 (February 1992): 11.

[89] AKBAYAN [Kaakbay ng Sambayanan] drew on three socialist-oriented groups for its leadership (BISIG, Pandayan, and MPD [Movement for Popular Democracy]) and on NGOs, labor, peasant, and urban poor groups.

[90] Interview with PnB chair Fidel Agcaoili by Benjamin Pimentel Jr., "What's left of New Politics?" *Midweek*, September 23, 1987, p. 41.

[91] While the old communist party—the Partido Komunista ng Pilipinas [PKP]—emphasized "legal and parliamentary struggle" in the early post-war period, there appears to be little residue of this experience in contemporary debates on progressive electoral intervention. For a brief discussion of the "rebelliousness" of the Manila-Rizal Committee in regards to the 1978 elections, however, see Armando Malay, Jr., "The Dialectics of Kaluwagan: Echoes of a 1978 Debate," Third World Studies Center, *Marxism in the Philippines* (Quezon City: University of the Philippines, 1988), pp. 1–21. See also, Benjamin Pimentel, *Rebolusyon! A Generation of Struggle in the Philippines* (New York: Monthly Review Press, 1991), pp. 218–231.

[92] For more on the "progressive bloc" in Congress, see, for example, "The Progressives," *Midweek*, June 14, 1989, pp. 3–6. This article identifies Representatives Bonifacio Gillego, Oscar

the "participation as propaganda" line characteristic of much of the Left's electoral efforts in 1987 backfired with the dismal performance of PnB and ANP candidates. In addition, the lessons of the 1987 electoral campaign underscored the significance of i) linking up local constituents to the national leadership through an organizational "machine"[93]; ii) translating sectoral support into territorially mobilized votes[94]; iii) and mobilizing resources to last the entire campaign—from candidate posters before to ballot-watch vigils after election day.[95] Finally, the Philippine Left's experience in the elections before 1992 underlined the importance of electoral reforms to progressive politics.

Mindful of the PnB/ANP's weak and uncoordinated electoral machinery in 1987, and its consequent failure to translate local support into national votes, the Philippine Left adopted two approaches aimed at overcoming or circumventing this problem in the 1992 elections. First of all, the Left-of-Center Koalisyong Pambansa and the PnB-BAYAN TAPAT network presented two separate efforts at linking local constituencies to national platforms by means of a political machine. The former linked local cause-oriented and non-governmental organizations, united under a socialist-oriented umbrella group, to the political machineries of two national parties.[96] The latter mobilized the mass base of BAYAN and other ND formations in support of a nationwide campaign—"Tañada Para sa Tao" (TAPAT)—to elect Bobby Tañada to the Senate.[97] Second, the broad Philippine Left placed much greater emphasis upon local than national level electoral efforts in 1992.

The PnB/ANP campaigns also highlighted another salient issue for the Philippine Left's electoral intervention in 1992—the problem of translating sectoral support into actual votes within given territorial boundaries (municipalities, congressional districts etc.). In view of the PnB/ANP's failure to mobilize a labor, peasant, or urban poor vote in 1987, for example, Philippine progressive electoral initiatives in 1992 included organized efforts at building electoral coalitions out of existing non-governmental and people's organizations. One example was the formation in Bataan province of the local electoral coalition (Kabalikatan) from an

---

Rodriguez, Florencio Abad, Gregorio Andolana, Nikki Coseteng and Edcel Lagman as the core of this bloc and goes on to list Oscar Santos, Milagros Laurel-Trinidad, Enrico Dayang-hirang, Eduardo Joson, William Claver, and Ciriaco Alfelor as other progressives.

[93] The following excerpt from an internal PnB report dated April 5–15, 1987, assessed the party's operation in the provinces of Agusan Norte, Agusan Sur, Surigao Norte, Misamis Oriental, Bukidonon, Misamis Occidental, and Zamboanga del Sur: "Organizationally, the PnB also had a difficult time instituting and reinforcing the national council's decisions, particularly among the base organizations that openly supported the party. Many of the party directives, for instance, were not awarded enough attention by local chapters and constituent organizations, which were understandably engaged in other campaigns and commitments. This could be seen as a reflection of how elections are accorded strategic significance in the rank and file of ND organizations." Cited in Gutierrez, "Electoral Coalitions," p. 96.

[94] See, for example, Benjamin Pimentel, Jr., "Interview: Fidel Agcaoili," *Midweek*, September 23, 1987, pp. 6,7,41.

[95] "Capulong admitted that the lack of campaign funds had been the major problem of the party . . . [For example,] the Pnb could only afford a minimal printing of one group campaign poster." Cited in *Midweek*, June 14, 1989, p. 13.

[96] See, for example, Cristina Jayme Montiel, "Organizational Dynamics in a Left-of-Center National Coalition: The Salonga-Pimentel Campaign," paper presented to the Fourth International Philippine Studies Conference at the Australian National University, July 1, 1992.

[97] See, for example, PnB, *Grassroots Electoral Politics*, p. 40.

already established developmental NGO (Balikatan) linked to the Movement of Popular Democracy.[98] Another example was the launching in Davao City of KAPATIRAN (Kilusan ng Alternatibong Pulitika para sa Inang Bayan) as an effort to channel broad-based national democratic forces into an electoral coalition "for campaigning for progressive candidates."[99]

The Philippine Left's electoral intervention prior to 1992 also underlined the importance of mobilizing salient resources for each stage of the election campaign. By combining their own volunteer recruitment and training efforts with the resources available to local candidates of established political parties, for example, progressive electoral coalitions proved more successful at fielding and keeping poll watchers throughout the vote count and canvassing procedures in certain parts of the country in 1992.[100] In addition, Philippine progressive forces showed greater appreciation for the political significance of registering voters, checking the official voters' lists, and providing sample ballots, for example, in the 1992 elections.

While publicly proclaiming its emphasis on voter education and political propaganda in 1987, the PnB/ANP campaign actually devoted scanty attention and resources to developing or disseminating a progressive agenda for electoral reform in this election. By contrast, the 1992 elections saw the broad Left-of-Center undertake a plethora of initiatives—ranging from immediate measures such as candidate/platform evaluation seminars to long-term demands for proportional representation—aimed at reforming the legal provisions, administrative procedures and political culture underpinning Philippine electoral democracy. For example, several more or less successful progressive efforts at promoting organized voters education and ballot watching accompanied the 1992 elections: the PnB and BAYAN supported Institute for Political and Electoral Reforms (IPER)[101] and KAPATIRAN,[102] Projects 1992 and 2001,[103] and COMPEL (Citizens for Meaningful

---

[98] In 1992, the MPD included, among other "popdem" NGOs, the Philippine Rural Reconstruction Movement [PRRM] and the Institute for Popular Democracy [IPD]. While not a direct participant in the 1992 elections, PRRM, which has its largest branch in Bataan province, lent several of its people to work on Kabalikatan's campaign. For a case study of PRRM in Bataan, see Philippine Rural Reconstruction Movement, *Bataan: A Case on Ecosystem Approach to Sustainable Development in the Philippines* (Quezon City: PRRM, 1991).

[99] PnB, *Grassroots Electoral Politics*, p. 53. Among the supporting organizations for the Kilusan ng Alternatibong Pulitika para sa Inang Bayan [KAPATIRAN] were: the Alliance for Concerned Teachers [ACT], Bagong Alyansang Makabayan [BAYAN], Kilsang Magbubukid ng Pilipinas [KMP], League of Filipino Students [LFS] and PRRM, according to a KAPATIRAN flyer on "What to ask the candidates".

[100] See, for example, Fransisco Cinco, *Experiences during the Local Elections in Bataan*, (Quezon City: Institute for Popular Democracy, 1993).

[101] See, for example, IPER's "Pagsasanay pang-instruktor para sa batayang edukasyong pambotante," author's file.

[102] See, for example, KAPATIRAN organizational material, author's file.

[103] The three socialist-oriented groups BISIG, Pandayan, and MPD formed the core of Project 1992. Project 2001 brought together the Caucus for Development NGOs [CODE-NGO], allegedly the largest NGO federation in the Philippines, and "virtually formalize[d] NGO involvement in electoral politics." Gutierrez, "Electoral Coalitions," p. 101. The MPD-supported Institute for Popular Democracy, together with the PRRM, also developed and organized voters education seminars. See, for example, PRRM and IPD's *Voters Education Training Module*, author's file. BISIG's Institute for Electoral Education also prepared "educational modules," for example.

and Peaceful Elections).[104] In addition, an International Observer Mission was invited to watch and report on the 1992 electoral exercise.[105] Another area of electoral reform which saw the intervention of progressive forces concerned the COMELEC's exemption of the paramilitary CAFGUs from the gun ban. After petitions from the PnB and public pressures from other progressive elements, the COMELEC eventually reversed its decision less than a week before election day.

These efforts constituted novel additions to the more traditional clean-election campaigns that have emerged at critical junctures in the past (NAMFREL in 1953, CNEA in 1969, and NAMFREL in 1986) with the backing of opposition supporters, business elites, and church organizations, and that appear to have become a permanent fixture in Philippine electoral contests after the highly publicized Bantay ng Bayan crusade in 1986 (NAMFREL in 1987 and 1988, PPCRV-MCQC in 1992).[106] As a result, the 1992 election campaign might very well have been the most issue-oriented to date with progressive forces contributing to focus public debate on questions of substantive electoral reform and programmatic party politics. However, reflective of the disunity among individuals, groups, and organizations identified with Left-of-Center politics, the proliferation of such efforts also reveal a lack of coordination that hampered progressive intervention in the 1992 elections.

THE 1987 NATIONAL ELECTIONS

In terms of the four factors discussed above, the elections for congressional representatives in 1987 and for municipal and gubernatorial positions in 1988 proceeded under circumstances highly unfavorable to successful participation by the then relatively strong and united Philippine Left. First of all, in the context of mounting anti-communist mobilization, supporters of the legal left party were targets of right-wing propaganda and military-backed repression. Second, against the backdrop of persistent challenges to the new constitutional regime from both the military Right and the armed Left, the 1987 and 1988 parliamentary exercises presented themselves less as critical mechanisms for wielding power than as

---

[104] From its origins as the "Covenant for Orderly, Meaningful and Peaceful Elections" and to its eventual "Citizens for Meaningful and Peaceful Elections," COMPEL drew on the support from the Ateneo Center for Social Policy and Public Affairs [ACSPPA], the much criticized NAMFREL and the government appointed COMELEC, among others. It focused on broader electoral reforms, as well as on voters education and poll-watch volunteer training. See, for example, "Electoral Reforms," *People's Agenda for Development and Democracy* (Quezon City: ACSPPA, 1992), pp. 59–61.

[105] See, for example, Tezza O. Parel, "Memo from election monitors," *Midweek*, June 10, 1992, pp. 6–8; "Foreign observers to monitor polls," *Philippine Daily Inquirer*, May 11, 1992, pp. 1, 13; "Int'l group to monitor elections," *Daily Globe*, May 11, 1992, p. 3. Officially invited by the Council for People's Development, the Ecumenical Bishops Forum, the Philippine Independent Church, and the local chapter of the Women's International League for Peace and Freedom, the IMO [International Mission of Observers] thirteen-person delegation of "church workers, academics, journalists, and officials from government and non-government organizations" contributed perhaps a more critical international perspective than that offered by the mostly American foreign observer teams that have descended on precincts all over the archipelago in previous elections. IMO, "Preliminary Report," author's file.

[106] NAMFREL in the early 1950s refers to the National Movement for Free Elections; in the 1980s, it refers to the National Citizens Movement for Free Elections. CNEA refers to Citizen National Electoral Assembly. PPCRV-MCQC refers to Parish Pastoral Council for Responsible Voting–Media Citizens Quick Count.

opportunities for political education and organizational consolidation of the mass base for the dominant Philippine Left. Third, in light of the Communist Party's strong influence upon the nature and direction of the PnB and ANP's electoral intervention, and the Party's ideological stance on the primacy of armed struggle, the Left, on the whole, made little organized effort to translate its mass base and resources into a serious political machine. Fourth, and finally, after a succession of election-boycott campaigns, the Left's extremely limited electoral experience served as poor preparation for participation in polls enveloped in the politics of "guns, goons, and gold."

Thus, relative to the Philippine Left's overall armed strength and mass support at the time, very few PnB/ANP candidates won election in 1987 and 1988. In 1987, for example, none of the "Magnificent Seven" candidates running under the ANP's banner succeeded in capturing a senate seat.[107] Moreover, despite reports of pre-election surveys that estimated at fifty the number of districts with ANP or ANP-supported candidates in the lead, or "in a good second place, with a chance to win," and with sixteen identified as "almost sure" winners, fewer than "twenty congressional winners [were] supported by the ANP."[108] Of thirty-six fielded, only two PnB congressional candidates—whose districts fell within NPA strongholds—won election in 1987. Finally, only eighteen out of 144 PnB candidates were elected to municipal governments in 1988.[109]

Suggestive of the significance of armed Left support for progressive electoral intervention in 1987, PnB candidates Garduce and Andolana captured Western Samar's sole and North Cotabato's first congressional districts, respectively. However, despite public pledges that "NPA guerrillas 'will adopt measures to protect voters and civilians' from being harassed and intimidated" in so-called "red zones" elsewhere in the country, no other electoral gains for the Left occurred in such areas.[110] In this regard, Andolana's victory in North Cotabato contrasts with PnB candidate Ireneo Escandor's failed bid to represent the second congressional district of Sorsogon (another province considered an NPA stronghold at the time) and, according to one study, highlights the role of pre-existing grassroots networks in mobilizing and protecting progressive votes in the 1987 elections.[111]

THE 1992 SYNCHRONIZED LOCAL AND NATIONAL ELECTIONS

In contrast with the early post-Marcos electoral exercises, the 1992 synchronized local and national elections saw different external and internal conditions influencing the electoral interventions by a more fragmented and diminished Philippine Left. First of all, with anti-communist mobilization on the wane, supporters of the broad legal Left rarely faced the systematic and discriminatory treatment accorded the PnB in 1987. Second, given the entrenchment of Philippine electoralism and the

---

[107] The top ANP senatorial candidate polled only about 1.7 million votes nationwide.

[108] IPD, *Political Clans*, pp. 84, 87.

[109] This figure does not include candidates who enjoyed the endorsement or support of PnB but who ran under other political parties.

[110] See, for example, "NDF pledges to protect voters in coming polls," *Malaya*, April 13, 1987, p. 4.

[111] See Jenny Franco, "Philippine Electoral Politics and the Peasant-Based Civic Movement in the 1980s," draft mss., 1993.

elimination of serious armed threats to the stability of the regime, elections now unquestionably constituted the key mechanism for exerting influence and power, a reality even the harshest critics of "bourgeois democracy" could not afford to ignore entirely without risking virtual political marginalization. Third, reflective of the growing ideological dissension within the Party as well as the emergence of alternative Left and Left-of-Center groups and coalitions, the 1992 elections saw a variety of more or less effective efforts at electoral participation, ranging from ideological education to pragmatic politicking. Fourth, and finally, with the lessons of 1987 and the example of the Progressive Bloc in Congress, the Philippine Left's expanded electoral experience provided relatively greater insights into both the costs and rewards involved in "working the system."

> The left, in effect, worked the clientelist system. National leaders, as well as leaders of provincial affiliates such as labor unions, made short-term alliances with candidates at national and local levels and so operated like vote brokers.[112]

Thus, compared to the dominant Left's overall decline and dissension at the time, the intervention of broader Left-of-Center forces in the 1992 elections indicated the continued significance of progressive politics in the electoral arena. A reactivated PnB, for example, fielded or supported candidates in seven major cities and twenty-three provinces in eleven out of the thirteen regions. While only two out of eleven senatorial and four out of twenty-nine congressional candidates endorsed by the PnB at the national level won election, individual PnB chapters who entered into local electoral alliances with other political parties reportedly supported twenty-eight winning bets to the House, eleven of whom "are considered ND/ND allies and the rest are open and can be approached on an issue-to-issue basis."[113] Counting not merely congressional candidacies, but also other PnB fielded and/or supported winning bets at the local level (reportedly including, among others, "forty-four councilors in five provinces and four cities," "seventeen vice-mayors in seven provinces and two cities," "forty-one mayors in ten provinces," "forty board members in fifteen provinces," as well as a few vice-governors and governors[114]), the PnB's own assessment of the 1992 elections identified 622 successful candidacies, or "3.6 percent of the total number of candidates who won,"[115] as having received the

---

[112] Rosanne Rutten, "Courting the Worker's Vote: Rhetoric and Response in a Philippine Hacienda Region" (Center for Studies of Social Change, New School for Social Research: Working Paper no. 176, 1993), p. 4. Rutten's analysis of the worker's vote in the 1992 elections focuses on the province of Negros Occidental.

[113] PnB, *Grassroots Electoral Politics*, p. 38. While the successful senatorial candidacies of Bobby Tañada and Nikki Coseteng enjoyed the PnB's endorsement, their incumbent status (as Senator and Congressional Representative of Quezon City's district 3, respectively) as well as other resources (the Tañada family name and Danding Cojuangco's Nationalist People's Coalition political machinery, respectively) significantly advanced these reelectionist bids. In terms of the four winning PnB-endorsed congressional bets, moreover, three of them— Bonifacio Gillego, Edcel Lagman, and Gregorio Andolana—ran as reelectionist candidates in their respective districts, while the fourth, Juan Ponce Enrile, was a former Senator.

[114] PnB, *Grassroots Electoral Politics*, p. 38.

[115] Ibid., p.43. In addition to leaving unexamined both the question of what, if anything, the PnB contributed to these 622 winning candidacies and the issue of the 260 odd seats out of those 622 for which no internal assessments had been completed, this report also falls short of

party's active support. While perhaps overly generous and certainly difficult to evaluate without further research into specific local election campaigns, this internal report nevertheless underscores the extent to which the Philippine Left's post-EDSA trajectory points toward expanding rather than contracting electoral intervention.

Indicative of the increasing significance of so-called "development NGOs" to Left-of-Center political forces and agendas in the Philippines, some notably successful efforts at progressive intervention in the 1992 elections focused on building electoral coalitions around pre-existing local community groups and associations with ties to regional or national development-oriented non-governmental organizations. For example, political candidates identified with NGO-linked groups reportedly performed "credibly" in Angeles City, Cebu City, Pasig, Quezon City (districts two and four) and Davao City, and won seats in "two municipalities in Bataan, San Luis, Aurora; Roxas, Oriental Mindoro; Irosin, Sorsogon; and North Cotabato."[116] While manifesting salient variations from case to case, these progressive electoral advances typically resulted from a combination of, on the one hand, sustained efforts to promote economic development (by NGOs) and political organizing (by so-called "people's organizations" [POs] or more mainstream "cause-oriented groups [COGs]) among local communities and, on the other hand, pre-election initiatives to form strategic alliances with individuals and groups identified with mainstream municipal/ provincial politics.

The local elections in Bataan province, for example, highlighted the significance and role of NGOs and POs for progressive electoral intervention.[117] Prior to the 1992 election campaign, for instance, the PO-NGO community in the Bataan municipality of Orani—which elected a mayor, a vice-mayor and four councilors identified with a local progressive electoral coalition—allegedly counted 12 percent of the total voting

---

identifying by name and party affiliation these alleged ND or issue-based allies. Such shortcomings make it difficult to evaluate claims that "[o]ut of the 364 winning candidates accounted for, 1/3 or 118 are ND/ND allies while 2/3 or 246 are issue-based allies." PnB, *Grassroots Electoral Politics*, p. 49.

[116] Julio P. Macuja, "The Mass Movement and the Elections," *Philippine Political Update*, April–July, 1992, p. 5. However, Macuja also notes that the two candidates with the strongest ties to development NGOs, former Acting Secretary of Agrarian Reform Florencio "Butch" Abad and Polytechnic University of the Philippines President Nemesio "Doc" Prudente, failed in their respective senatorial bids. Other progressive incumbents, moreover, lost in Davao Oriental, Pampanga, South Cotabato, and General Santos City. Interestingly, losing incumbent candidates Governor Mike Sueno of South Cotabato and Mayor Lita Nuñez of General Santos City allegedly "lost their highly dedicated mass base and the informal but influential support of the local Catholic Church" after switching party affiliation from the AKBAYAN-supported PDP-LABAN [Partido Demokratiko Pilipino-Lakas ng Bayan] to Danding Cojuangco's NPC [Nationalist People's Coalition]. See Montiel, "Organizational Dynamics in a Left-of-Center National Coalition," p. 6.

[117] For an insightful inside analysis of progressive electoral intervention in Bataan's first congressional district in the 1992 elections, see Fransisco Cinco, *Experiences during the Local Elections in Bataan* (Quezon City: Institute for Popular Democracy, 1993). See also, by the same author, the brief post-election summary "Kilusang Electoral sa Bataan: NGOs-POs Tumaya sa Halalang Panlokal," *Conjuncture* 5, 6–7 (June–July 1992): 7–8. For some background on Balikatan, see also PRRM, *Bataan: A Case*, especially pp. 46–47, 76–83.

population among its members.[118] Targeted as a priority area by both the PRRM, a major NGO committed to sustainable development, and the IPD, a Manila-based organization engaged in electoral research and training, Bataan province (particularly the first congressional district) thus saw the emergence of Kabalikatan, a local coalition which fielded its own progressive, and supported other allied, political candidates in the 1992 elections. As a result, three municipalities in the first congressional district of Bataan province elected a combined total of three mayors, two vice-mayors and nine councilors identified with Kabalikatan.[119]

The relative success of Jovito Salonga's presidential bid in the province of Camarines Sur (where he, in sharp contrast to placing fifth in the national tally, captured the lead) has also been linked to the intervention by progressive electoral coalitions of NGO-PO-COGs and established political parties in the 1992 elections.[120] That is, the so-called "NagaPopDems," a few Liberal Party stalwarts, and the PnB contributed to Salonga's campaign by, for example, organizing voters education seminars, brokering the province's Salonga-Pimentel Movement, supplying sample ballots, and training poll watchers. While electoral coalitions forged around local communities already organized into sectoral, political, and/or cause-oriented groups have contributed to some progressive gains in the 1992 elections, many such efforts also floundered. For example, former PnB chair Romeo Capulong failed in his bid for the first congressional district of Nueva Ecija, despite support from both local NGOs and the province-wide coalition BALANE, which in turn linked up to the national party of Danding Cojuangco.[121] In part, such failures resulted from the difficulties involved in transforming sectoral and issue-based organizations into electoral machines. As noted on the Nueva Ecija elections:

> NGOs and people's organizations campaigned in the early part of the electoral period towards information dissemination among voters including grassroots voters' education activities. Unfortunately, as election day neared, active individuals in the same NGOs and POs . . . ceased these activities to campaign for their own candidates in various posts."[122]

The outcome of the 1992 elections, while hardly a decisive victory for the broad Left, nevertheless signaled a deepening of its 1987 electoral involvement, especially

---

[118] J. Clark Soriano, *Selected Case Studies: NGO-PO-GO Interfaces in Local Governance* (Quezon City: Institute for Popular Democracy, 1993), p. 28. In absolute terms, according to Soriano, the NGO-PO community in Orani counted some 3,000 members in a voting population of approximately 24,000 people.

[119] Of the three elected mayors, Dr. Mario Zuniga was fielded as a Kabalikatan candidate in Orani while the two successful contenders for the highest municipal office in Abucay and Morong both received direct backing from the same progressive electoral coalition. Kabalikatan also supported the successful candidates for Orani and Morong's vice-mayorship positions and several elected councilors in Abucay (five) and Orani (four).

[120] Soliman M. Santos Jr., "The local face of the national campaign," *Conjuncture* 5, 6–7 (June–July 1992): 9.

[121] Laura L. Gonzaga, "Interview: Romeo Capulong," *Midweek*, May 13, 1992, pp. 3–5.

[122] Excerpt from a report on the 1992 elections in Cabanatuan City, and the towns of Zaragosa, Talavera and Quezon, Nueva Ecija, prepared by the International Observer Mission's Nueva Ecija team, headed by Ruth Cadwallader, p. 8. See also, for example, "Memo from election monitors," *Midweek*, June 10, 1992, pp. 6–8.

in light of its widespread decline and disarray. As noted above, one candidate strongly identified with the Left, Bobby Tañada, won reelection to the Senate; a number of Left-of-Center candidates won election as congressmen, governors, mayors, and councilors. Moreover, in contrast with the 1987 election, the Left showed greater flexibility and pragmatism in its electoral tactics and strategies, endorsing candidates running under established national political parties and entering into various alliances with local politicians and party formations, as well as building a national progressive coalition with LP-PDP-LABAN.

LOOKING AHEAD TO FUTURE ELECTIONS

Looking ahead to upcoming elections, the following developments can be discerned in terms of the four factors that have so far decisively shaped the Philippine Left's electoral participation in the post-EDSA period. First of all, the legalization of the Communist Party and the renewal of the AFP-NPA peace process under the new Ramos administration signal a more hospitable political environment for so-called "progressive" forces in elections to come.[123] Second, the successful neutralization of threats of coups and revolution as well as the peaceful transition of power from Aquino to her anointed general underscore the extent to which elections define future arenas of struggle for the Philippine Left. Third, the casualties of the Party's internal debates and the government's counterinsurgency efforts, in combination with the "NGO-ization" of the Philippine Left, have set the stage for more pragmatic and flexible electoral intervention by a wide array of forces ranging from the Left to the so-called "progressive mainstream." Fourth, and finally, in addition to first-hand experiences at the polls since 1986, recent developments within the Philippine Left and progressive mainstream—ranging from voters' education seminars, ballot-watch manuals, election studies, coalition-building efforts, and lobbying activities—underline a stronger appreciation for—as well as commitment to—the requisites of competitive electoral politics.

CONCLUSION

In conclusion, whereas the "reaffirmationist" faction of the Communist Party might succeed in closing down the internal debate and ousting its "heretics," and thus possibly consigning itself to indefinite political marginalization, the broader Philippine Left is now increasingly recognizing the primacy of legal and parliamentary struggle.[124] While noteworthy in and of itself, however, the Left's emergence on the electoral scene hardly resolves the political dilemma of cooptation

---

[123] Executive Order no. 125 issued on September 15, 1993, outlines the Ramos administration's vision of "comprehensive peace efforts."

[124] A recent paper discussing the "unfolding drama of the Philippine Left" argued that a "highly predictable outcome of the debate, such as it is, between radicals and moderates is this: nothing will be settled [and] both will remain entrenched in their 'non-negotiable' positions..." Armando Malay, Jr., "Old Reflexes, New Slogans: The Mid-Life Crisis of the Philippine Left," paper presented at the Second Philippine Studies Conference, University of London, April 1994. For a statement broadly representative of the "moderate" left's position on elections, see, for example, R. Ciria Cruz, "Why the Philippine Left Must Take the Parliamentary Road," *Kasarinlan* 7, 4 (1992): 51–61.

versus contestation. The following quote from a recent so-called "popular democratic" publication captures this dilemma:

> [T]he broad Left must position itself firmly within the national current—the better to expose the limits of elite democracy, if not to gain entry into mainstream political life.[125]

In other words, rather than posing a counterhegemonic challenge to Philippine elite democracy, the Left's participation in elections may end up simply conferring legitimacy upon the existing political order. Moreover, rather than redefining the parameters of Philippine electoralism, the Left itself may end up (re)defined by the limitations of procedural democracy.

In general, the logic of electoralism, it has been noted, is inherently demobilizing, based as it is on a periodic one-person, one-vote symbolic enactment of political citizenship. Procedural democracy thus privileges elections as the most legitimate form of political participation, while delegitimizing—or coopting—extra-electoral forms of popular collective action. In the Philippine case, moreover, the American colonial legacy of machine politics and the absence of proportional representation decisively structure both the means and ends of electoral participation by the Left.

In terms of the means, several reports of local election initiatives by the broad Left in 1992, for example, cited the key role of so-called "electoral technology"—or, in the words of one community organizer, the "dirty-tricks department"—for a successful campaign.[126] In terms of the ends, moreover, another organizer working on an election-campaign for progressive politics in Bataan noted that while before 1992 he thought

> that winning an election or 'seizing the state' was the most difficult effort of any organizing effort. . .[n]ow he argues that this is chicken feed compared to the task of governing. . . because they are commitment-bound to govern in a new way [which] involves new roles for government officials, PO leaders, and NGO development workers.[127]

Similarly, progressives who won election to municipal office or to Congress, for example, have since encountered difficulties in realizing their "progressive" constituencies' goals without running up against the interests of the local landowners who provided critical backing for their election bids.

On this note, and by way of concluding, the following quote culled from a post-1992 election document by the PnB-affiliated Institute for Political and Electoral Reform aptly captures, on the one hand, the Philippine Left's interest in acquiring relevant skills and accessing legal institutions, and, on the other hand, its wariness of submitting to the shortcomings and the dangers of Philippine electoralism.

---

[125] Editorial, "Uniting the broad left around electoral reforms," *Conjuncture* 4, 4 (April 1991): 1.

[126] See, for example, Fransisco Cinco, "NGOs-POs Tumaya sa Halalang Panlokal," *Conjuncture* 5, 6–7 (June–July 1992): 7–8.

[127] J. Clark Soriano, "Selected Case Studies: NGO-PO Interfaces in Local Governance," unpublished manuscript, Institute for Popular Democracy, June 1993, p. 32.

Lobby work is something we have to live with or work on. If we want to know the system, then let us plunge into this system of governance and make it as a field of action or an arena of struggle. But let us not also forget how to swim or else we will get drowned.[128]

---

[128] Antonio R. Villasor, Policy Officer, PAHRA, "Lobby Work: The Pahra Experience," *Consultations on Parliamentary and Electoral Work,* unpublished document, Institute for Political and Electoral Reform, 1993.

POPULAR SUPPORT FOR THE REVOLUTIONARY MOVEMENT CPP-NPA: EXPERIENCES IN A HACIENDA IN NEGROS OCCIDENTAL, 1978-1995

Rosanne Rutten

INTRODUCTION

Why did peasants and rural workers support the revolutionary movement CPP-NPA (Communist Party of the Philippines-New People's Army, henceforth called NPA)? The question is hardly trivial: without the support of more than a million people in Philippine villages and towns who supplied manpower, food, cash, and intelligence, the NPA would never have developed by the mid-1980s into a powerful challenger to the state. This sizable popular support for the NPA was one sign of a "revolutionary situation" in the Philippines, a situation that, as Tilly says, is characterized by the appearance of contenders with exclusive claims to state power, the "commitment to these claims by a significant segment of the citizenry," and the "incapacity or unwillingness of rulers" to suppress these contenders.[1] Here I deal with the second aspect, that of popular commitment, and seek to explain the rise (and decline) of support for the NPA among hacienda-worker families in Negros Occidental, one of the provinces where the NPA gained considerable influence and support.[2]

---

[1] Charles Tilly, *European Revolutions, 1492-1992* (Oxford and Cambridge: Blackwell, 1993), p. 10.

[2] Research was financed through a grant from the Royal Netherlands Academy of Arts and Sciences. While in the Philippines in January-November 1992, I was affiliated with the Institute of Philippine Culture, Ateneo de Manila University. An earlier version of this paper was written while I was a Visiting Researcher at the Center for Studies of Social Change (CSSC), New School for Social Research, New York, in 1993-94. I wish to thank Charles Tilly and the members of his Proseminar on Political Mobilization and Conflict at the CSSC for their comments and for the opportunity to develop my argument in an intellectually stimulating atmosphere. Thanks are also due to Patricio Abinales, Rod Aya, Ben Kerkvliet, Vina Lanzona, Kim Scipes, John Wiersma, and Frank de Zwart for critical comments and suggestions.

A common view has it that Philippine rural poor were pushed into the arms of the NPA because they were "desperate and outraged"[3] at increasing poverty, repression, and the lack of legal means to seek redress of grievances; and that their outrage was channeled by the NPA. Porter, for instance, cites "disaffection from the government arising from a number of sources: the inequalities of the existing landowning system, the process of landgrabbing by wealthy and politically influential figures, the insensitivity of the Marcos regime to the interests of poor farmers, the arbitrary and repressive local political and administrative structure, and the abuses of the military."[4] Such explanations list "invidious conditions of state and society" that supposedly cause people to join or support a revolutionary movement, but give little evidence that such aggregate conditions actually motivate or constrain them to do so. [5]

To find out what leads people to support the NPA, we need to focus on the level at which people interact, trace the microprocesses that produce this support, and start by analyzing the sequence of key interactions in which people actually decide to contribute to the NPA. Simply stated, most contributions to the NPA are solicited and provided in interactions between mobilizers and villagers. Taking these interactions as a starting point, we can then consider whether and how specific "invidious conditions" motivate people to provide these concrete contributions, what other considerations are at work, and how people's motives for support may change over time. At this level of personal interaction we can also explore how people's involvement in social networks of community, family, peers, and activists, and their connections to larger social environments, influence their mobilization and commitment.

Two considerations inform this perspective. First, we should avoid looking around for "big" causes (for instance, a wide gap between rich and poor, or a deep socioeconomic crisis) to explain a "big" change (massive support for a revolutionary movement) but consider, instead, the accumulation of microprocesses out of which a specific large change is built.[6]

Second, we need to acknowledge that revolutionary activists may have considerable influence on why, how, and when villagers support a revolutionary movement. Like most party-led and rural-based revolutionary movements this century, the NPA gains rural support through the mobilizing work of activists, who combine ideological work, organization, and coercion in an effort to reshape communities into support bases for the NPA. The initiatives come primarily from mobilizers; the actions of villagers are primarily reactions to those initiatives. In the course of mobilization, villagers may not only enhance their capabilities to act upon their grievances and perceive new opportunities for taking such actions. They may also redefine their grievances and change their aspirations as they acquire new

[3] David Rosenberg, "The Philippines," *Revolution and Political Change in the Third World*, Barry M. Schutz and Robert O. Slater, eds. (Boulder and London: Lynne Riener Publishers, 1990), p. 165.

[4] Gareth Porter, "The Politics of Counterinsurgency in the Philippines: Military and Political Options," *Philippine Studies Occasional Paper* no. 9 (Honolulu: Center for Philippine Studies, University of Hawaii, 1987), p. 25.

[5] Rod Aya, *Rethinking Revolutions and Collective Violence: Studies on Concept, Theory and Method* (Amsterdam: Het Spinhuis, 1990), p. 12.

[6] cf. Arthur Stinchcombe, *Theoretical Methods in Social History* (New York: Academic Press, 1978), pp. 61–62.

perspectives on society and their place in it, and as the balance of power shifts somewhat in their favor. Moreover, the very presence of armed mobilizers confronts villagers with new incentives and pressures to support the movement.[7]

This paper, then, seeks to explain rural support for the NPA by taking the actual process of face-to-face mobilization as the starting point of analysis. My focus on mobilizers and mobilized is not an attempt to dust off and reintroduce the "outside agitator" approach, but an effort to place the interactions between activists and villagers center stage.

In Hacienda Milagros (a pseudonym), a plantation in the vast sugarcane producing region of Negros Occidental, workers' involvement with the NPA had ranged from active participation to reluctant support. I had informal interviews with women and men of the hacienda when I lived there (with one of the hacienda families) for nine months in 1992 and one month in 1995. Most people of Milagros knew me well from previous fieldwork in 1977–78, and with several families I had maintained close personal ties. Taking my previous research as a starting point, I tried to reconstruct the mobilization histories of individual persons, families, and the community as a whole.[8] This account of experiences in Milagros does not pretend to be complete or typical of the rise and decline of community support for the NPA elsewhere, but rather suggests ways of analyzing it. Broadly similar processes of mobilization did take place, though under varying conditions and with diverse outcomes, in haciendas near Milagros, as well as in an upland village in southern Negros Occidental where I did additional fieldwork.[9]

The province of Negros Occidental—its hacienda lowlands and marginal uplands—was one of the main centers of NPA mass support in the 1980s. Located in the lowlands, Hda. Milagros was fully organized and controlled by the NPA by the mid-1980s, as were most of the surrounding haciendas. By 1992 the balance of power in the area had shifted in favor of the military, planters, and the government, and revolutionary support by the hacienda population had declined.

THE QUESTIONS "WHY" AND "HOW"

In his analysis of revolutionary movements in Latin America, Wickham-Crowley notes a shift in perspective from studies that emphasize "the *causal* role of . . .

---

[7] On changing capabilities and opportunities, see Tarrow, *Power in Movement: Social Movements, Collective Action and Politics* (New York: Cambridge University Press, 1994) and Charles Tilly, *From Mobilization to Revolution* (New York: Random House, 1978). On pressures exerted by armed mobilizers, see Norma J. Kriger, *Zimbabwe's Guerrilla War: Peasant Voices* (Cambridge: Cambridge University Press, 1992) on Zimbabwe.

[8] In Hda. Milagros, I had the opportunity to talk to both supporters and critics of the NPA since, by 1992, neither the NPA nor the government, through its military forces fully controlled the hacienda. Though I was viewed as sympathetic to the political left, partly because in the 1970s I was introduced in the hacienda by progressive Catholic nuns, I believe I was not closely identified with any one party during the research. Initially, I spent most time with old friends among the worker population who were former activists and who were, as such, relatively independent of the NPA apparatus. Gradually, I could reestablish old contacts and friendships on various sides.

[9] Although I focus on the hacienda, my understanding of support for the NPA also profited from interviews around the province with (former) NPAs, planters, military men, government officials, union leaders, and priests; analysis of provincial newspapers; and fieldwork in an upland village in 1992 and 1995.

discontent in fomenting movements," to studies "describing . . . the *processes* of mobilization. They seem to have replaced the 'why?' of an earlier generation of movement theorists . . . with a 'how to?'"[10] Focusing on the issue of popular support for revolutionary movements, I would argue that the why and how questions are interlinked. Because mobilization processes partly shape the circumstances under which people decide to support a movement, we need to know how they were mobilized to understand why they provide support.[11]

Two approaches to peasant support for revolutionary movements are relevant in this respect. The first has a strong "why" and a weak "how" component. Studies by Gould[12] and Kerkvliet,[13] for instance, attribute villagers' support primarily to villagers' grievances against landed elites and the state, and their self-generated struggle for subsistence security and land. In the cases they discuss, villagers make an "alliance" with a revolutionary movement and retain some autonomy vis-à-vis that movement. These studies provide important insight in indigenous perceptions, grievances, and aspirations (in particular the restoration of traditional subsistence rights), local leadership, and preexisting peasant solidarities.[14] They deal sparingly, however, with actual community mobilization, in particular whether village-based mobilizers exert control, change local perceptions, and institutionalize the movement within communities, all of which may affect villagers' decisions to provide support.

Authors who follow the second approach, in contrast, contend that answering the "how" of peasant mobilization explains the "why" of their support.[15] They argue that party-led revolutionary movements develop village-based organizations that provide incentives and sanctions to induce local support. Villagers weigh their individual contributions to the movement against the benefits provided, which may include access to land, protection, and positions of power and status in the movement's organization.[16] Referring to Olson's concept of "selective incentives,"[17]

---

[10] Timothy P. Wickham-Crowley, *Exploring Revolution: Essays on Latin American Insurgency and Revolutionary Theory* (London: M. E. Sharpe, 1991), p. 7.

[11] Cf. Alvin H. Scaff on former members of the Huk movement in Central Luzon: "Why they joined the Huks is inseparable from the process of how they joined, for motivation includes the entire complex of action in becoming a Huk and not simply the reasons which one may give for joining or the appealing aspects of the Huk propaganda. Becoming a Huk is a series of interlocking acts, one leading to another like links in a chain." Alvin H. Scaff, *The Philippine Answer to Communism* (Stanford: Stanford University Press, 1955).

[12] Jeffrey L. Gould, *To Lead as Equals: Rural Protest and Political Consciousness in Chinandega, Nicaragua, 1912–1979* (Chapel Hill and London: The University of North Carolina, 1990).

[13] Benedict Kerkvliet, *The Huk Rebellion: A Study of Peasant Revolt in the Philippines* (Berkeley: University of California Press, 1977).

[14] James C. Scott, "Peasant Revolution: A Dismal Science," review article, *Comparative Politics* 9 (1977): 231–48. Also James C. Scott, "Revolution in the Revolution: Peasants and Commissars," *Theory and Society* 7 (1979): 97–134.

[15] Joel S. Migdal, *Peasants, Politics, and Revolution: Pressures Toward Political and Social Change in the Third World* (Princeton: Princeton University Press, 1974). Also Samuel Popkin, "Political Entrepreneurs and Peasant Movements in Vietnam," *Rationality and Revolution*, Michael Taylor, ed. (Cambridge: Cambridge University Press, 1988). Also Jeffrey Race, *War Comes to Long An: Revolutionary Conflict in a Vietnamese Province* (Berkeley: University of California Press, 1972). Also Michael Taylor, "Rationality and Revolutionary Collective Action," *Rationality and Revolution*, Michael Taylor, ed. (Cambridge: Cambridge University Press, 1988).

[16] Race, *War Comes to Long An*, pp. 174–75.

[17] Mancur Olson, *The Logic of Collective Action* (Cambridge: Harvard University Press, 1965).

they note that activists supply rewards selectively to promote individual participation and combat free-riding, and make rewards contingent on villagers' ongoing support.[18] Inspired by organizational theory, they give valuable insight into the dynamics of community mobilization. They pay little attention, however, to villagers' notions of justice and rights, how these notions are articulated and changed, and how social networks in which villagers are embedded influence their decisions to extend support.

My own discussion of mobilization and popular support for the revolutionary movement NPA explores in particular the *interplay* between people's own perceptions, experiences, solidarities, and actions on the one hand, and, on the other, new ideas, opportunities and constraints, organizational forms and collective actions, introduced by mobilizers.[19]

That workers in the hacienda region of Negros Occidental were mobilized at all by the NPA depended on two conditions at least: party strategy and the opportunities of activists to operate in the hacienda region. These also affected how hacienda workers were mobilized. It is to these two aspects that I turn first.

RURAL MOBILIZATION AS PARTY STRATEGY

Activists based at Manila universities allied with a group of peasant guerrillas and established the Communist Party of the Philippines-New People's Army (CPP-NPA) as a Maoist revolutionary movement in 1968–69.[20] The movement consists of a political arm (CPP), a military arm (NPA), and a united front organization (NDF or National Democratic Front) which includes legal organizations such as labor unions and peasant associations. Here I will call the CPP-NPA, in most cases, simply "NPA" because the general population uses that term, many low-level cadres are not Communist party members, and the "NPA" does not present itself as communist to its sympathizers.

The student activists were influenced by Philippine nationalist ideology and were part of the worldwide wave of radical student movements of the 1960s. They adopted Mao Zedong's blueprint for a peasant-based revolution as the only means to change the elite-dominated and corrupt political system in the country and achieve national and social liberation.[21] Their focus on the countryside was based on ideological and practical considerations. Following Mao's analysis of pre-revolutionary China, they defined Philippine society as "semi-feudal and semi-

---

[18] Migdal, *Peasants, Politics, and Revolution*, p. 274; and Race, *War Comes to Long An*, p. 15.

[19] There are similarities with social-movement studies on micro-mobilization that provide a sequential analysis, take account of small-group settings, include a concern for changing perceptions and social identities, and pay attention to the wider social context in which mobilization takes place. For a good overview of the literature, see Doug McAdam, John D. McCarthy, and Mayer N. Zald, "Social Movements," *Handbook of Sociology*, Neil J. Smelser, ed. (Newbury Park, CA: Sage Publications, 1988).

[20] Both had been linked to the old Partido Komunista ng Pilipinas (PKP), whose leadership had abandoned the idea of guerrilla struggle after the PKP-controlled peasant guerrilla movement Hukbalahap (Huk) was practically defeated in the 1950s. Francisco Nemenzo, "Rectification Process in the Philippine Communist Movement," *Armed Communist Movements in Southeast Asia*, Lim Jao Jock, ed. (Hampshire: Gower Publishing Company, 1984).

[21] Gregg R. Jones, *Red Revolution: Inside the Philippine Guerrilla Movement* (Boulder: Westview Press, 1989) and Nemenzo, "Rectification Process in the Philippine Communist Movement."

colonial," with peasantry and workers a potential revolutionary force against landlords, capitalists, and imperialists.[22] Encircling the cities from the countryside seemed a feasible strategy since it is in the countryside "where the widest area of maneuver is available and where armed strength can be accumulated," as CPP head Jose Maria Sison noted.[23] Moreover, lacking external funds and external sanctuary, the NPA depended heavily on the peasantry for food, cash, and shelter. With the proclamation of martial law in 1972, sanctuary in distant rural areas became all the more pressing. The rural poor would form the main mass base of the movement and supply much of the manpower for the guerrilla army and the lower positions in the NPA's political and administrative apparatus. The strategy of a rural-based "protracted people's war" has, since then, been subject to numerous debates and policy changes. By the 1980s the NPA had expanded its mass mobilization efforts from the countryside to the fast-growing cities, partly through legal organizations.

Mobilizing a rural mass base remained, however, a top priority. Activists eventually followed a standardized plan of community mobilization that was refined over the years. When successful, their work progressed as follows. After a "social investigation," through a trusted contact, of the socioeconomic structure and main problems in a community, activists organized the first group of villagers by holding political seminars in villagers' homes. They invited interested persons to join so-called Organizing Groups of women, men, and youth of peasant and farm-worker background, and helped organize small-scale collective actions around local problems. Interested and capable members, tasked with recruiting fellow villagers, were brought together in an Organizing Committee, which was eventually formed into a Party Branch directly linked to the CPP's organizational hierarchy. In the process, villagers became local activists for the NPA as they accepted positions in the party branch and related village committees responsible for organization, education (ideological seminars), finance (collecting rice and money for the movement), health, and security. Persuasion in the early stages of mobilization was combined with coercion in later stages to force unwilling residents into compliance and neutralize community-based power holders unsympathetic to the NPA. With the basic unit of the shadow government in place, the cadres would move to another area. Activists eventually developed a state-like political organization, loosely centralized, that reached from the national level down to region, district, section, and village, with party committees staffed by local women and men.[24]

Within rural communities the NPA acquired control over vital resources: villagers' contributions in food, cash, and information for both the political and military cadres; as well as manpower for part-time positions in the village or full-time posts as mobile cadres or armed fighters. Other "contributions" consisted of participation in collective actions such as rallies and pickets in nearby cities,

---

[22] Amado Guerrero, *Philippine Society and Revolution*, 3rd ed. (Oakland, CA: International Association of Filipino Patriots, 1979).

[23] Jose Maria Sison, with Rainer Werning, *The Philippine Revolution: The Leader's View* (New York: Crane Russak, 1989), p. 165.

[24] See also William Chapman, *Inside the Philippine Revolution* (New York: W. W. Norton, 1987), pp. 125–27, and Victor N. Corpus, *Silent War* (Quezon City: VNC Enterprises, 1989), pp. 36–43, and Jones, *Red Revolution*, pp. 13–14, 185–99, on community mobilization by the NPA.

sometimes under the cover of legal organizations, which made public the extent of rural mass support for the broad left-wing cause.[25]

In each region of the Philippine archipelago, the NPA enjoys some autonomy, and is self-sufficient regarding personnel, funding, and arms. It recruits its personnel locally, gets funds mainly by taxing the poor and extorting the rich, and acquires most of its arms by ambushing members of the Philippine Army or raiding army camps.

In 1988, the NPA had some 24,000 guerrillas in sixty of the country's seventy-three provinces.[26] Estimates of civilian sympathizers and supporters range from more than 1.7 million people in 1986[27] to roughly half a million in 1988.[28] Another source mentions in 1989 that some 20 percent of the country's *barangay* (villages and urban neighborhoods) were "controlled" by the NPA.[29] By 1993, the number of guerrillas had dropped to an estimated 10,600, and the percentage of NPA controlled or influenced *barangay* had dwindled to 1,300, or 3 percent.[30] This decline was partly due to an intensive counterinsurgency campaign that combined military operations with an amnesty program and forced community-based 'surrenders' of civilian supporters.[31] The nationwide split within the CPP-NPA in 1992–93 on issues of strategy and leadership further weakened the movement. As CPP founder Jose Maria Sison dictated the strategy of rural-based protracted people's war, his opponents propagated more emphasis on legal struggle (using the expanded democratic space in the post-Marcos era) and/or more emphasis on urban insurrectionist activities, and deplored Sison's stifling of party debates.[32]

---

[25] It is crucial for any social movement to make public displays of its "numbers, determination, unity, and worthiness" in order to become, and remain, a political force acknowledged by powerholders and the wider public, if not by its own followers. CPP documents on mass mobilization specifically state, by period, what issues activists should focus on when mobilizing workers, peasants, students, and other sectors. They also specify short- and long-term demands by sector (higher wages, genuine land reform, for example), time-tables for specific rallies, pickets, and other forms of collective action, and slogans to be used (e.g. Negros Regional Party Committee 1987). Quote from Charles Tilly, "Social Movements as Historically Specific Clusters of Political Performances," *Berkeley Journal of Sociology* 38 (1993–94): 8.

[26] Jones, *Red Revolution*, p. 297.

[27] Alfred McCoy, "Low Intensity Conflict in the Philippines," *Low Intensity Conflict: Theory and Practice in Central America and South-East Asia*, Barry Carr and Elaine McKay, eds. (Melbourne: La Trobe University, Institute of Latin American Studies, and Monash University, Centre of Southeast Asian Studies, 1988), p. 61.

[28] Jones, *Red Revolution*, p. 297.

[29] Douglas S. Blaufarb and George K. Tanham, "Deadly Combat Without End—The Philippines Today," *Who Will Win?: A Key to the Puzzle of Revolutionary War* (New York: Crane Russak, 1989), chapter 7, p. 117.

[30] John McBeth, "Internal Contradictions: Support for Communists Wanes as Party Splits," *Far Eastern Economic Review* (August 26, 1993).

[31] Rosanne Rutten, "'Mass Surrenders' in Negros Occidental: Ideology, Force and Accommodation in a Counterinsurgency Program," Paper for the 4th International Philippine Studies Conference, July 1–3, 1992, Australian National University, Canberra.

[32] McBeth, "Internal Contradictions," and Joel Rocamora, *Breaking Through: The Struggle Within the Communist Party of the Philippines* (Pasig, Metro Manila: Anvil Publishing Inc., 1994).

MOBILIZING HACIENDA WORKERS IN NEGROS OCCIDENTAL: OPPORTUNITIES AND CONSTRAINTS

The province of Negros Occidental is one of the main sugar-producing regions in Southeast Asia. The product of its several thousand sugarcane haciendas and some fifteen sugar centrals is sold on export and domestic markets. The haciendas range in size from about twenty to over a thousand hectares (the majority falls in the 20–150 hectares range), and are mostly owned by planter families that live in the province's towns or Manila. Some 200,000 wage-dependent workers (women and men) do back-breaking labor in the canefields and survive precariously on low and irregular wages. Permanent workers living with their families on hacienda premises, and casual workers living on or near haciendas, plow, plant, weed, and cut the ripe cane, and are joined by migrant canecutters in the harvesting season. The lowland sugarcane-growing plain is bordered by hills and mountains to the east and south, where marginal haciendas exist alongside peasant subsistence farms.

The hardship of hacienda workers, which contrasts sharply with the wealth of so-called sugar barons, has long been an issue in progressive and social-minded circles in Manila, particularly since the 1960s–70s when newspaper articles, Church publications, and a movie made it the symbol of exploitation and injustice in the Philippine countryside.[33] To CPP chairman Jose Maria Sison (alias Amado Guerrero), the revolutionary potential of sugar workers in Negros was obvious. He stated in 1969 in a letter to *The Manila Times*:.

> When we consider the magnitude of the land owned by so few (few in relation to the masses of the people) and the long history of exploitative relations between the landlords on one hand and the peasants and farm workers on the other, Negros Occidental is, indeed, ripe for social revolution. It is only a matter of time that the exploited masses will gather force and rise up to resist the feudal and semi-feudal oppression that they suffer.[34]

Studies on pre-NPA Negros show divergent views on the potential for worker militancy in the hacienda region. Some rate the potential high because of severe poverty, stark class differences, exploitation and repression, which all produce a fertile ground for grievances; and because of the solidary, close-knit type of proletarian hacienda community, which provides capabilities for collective action.[35] Others rate it low, and view hacienda workers in pre-NPA times as "apathetic" and "disorganized,"[36] under tight planter control, vulnerable to planter repression,

---

[33] Arsenio C. Jesena, SJ, "The Sacadas of Sugarland," *Action Now* 1, 44 (1969): 4–11. Also Antonio Ledesma, Gerry Bulatao, Nini Abarquez, Felix Pasquin, Rufino Suplido, eds., *Liberation in Sugarland: Readings on Social Problems in the Sugar Industry* (Manila: Kilusan ng Bayang Pilipino, 1971).

[34] Amado Guerrero, "Letter to the Editor: CPP Leader Writes on Negros Landlords," *The Manila Times*, September 22, 1969.

[35] Frank Lynch, SJ, *A Bittersweet Taste of Sugar: A Preliminary Report of the Sugar Industry in Negros Occidental* (Quezon City: Ateneo de Manila University Press, 1970), p. 31. Also Norman Schul, "A Philippine Sugar Cane Plantation: Land Tenure and Sugar Cane Production," *Economic Geography* 43 (1967): 168-69.

[36] John A. Larkin, *Sugar and the Origins of Modern Philippine Society* (Berkeley: University of California Press, 1993), p. 235.

lacking a tradition of organized protest, and, in each hacienda, divided among themselves by their personalized ties of dependency with their planter.[37]

The constraints imposed by the hacienda system—compounded by planter control of provincial politics, the judiciary, and the police—were indeed severe. With little protection from unions or the state, workers with insistent claims could be refused work, ousted from the hacienda, put in jail by local police, or physically threatened. Many overseers carried a handgun (up to the declaration of martial law) to keep the upper hand over workers who outnumbered each individual overseer, and whose cleavers could turn into weapons. The options open to workers were either to lodge a complaint with the overseer and hope for planter benevolence, or, individually, to move out to a better-paying hacienda or to the upland frontier. Union activists found haciendas extremely difficult to penetrate. Besides several short-lived attempts to organize hacienda workers, unions tended to concentrate until the 1960s on sugar-mill workers and upland peasants.[38]

However, by the mid-1980s the lowland hacienda region had become one of the centers of NPA activity in the country. By 1986, the NPA had mobilized island-wide in 586 haciendas and 352 villages, organized some 100,000 hacienda workers and peasants into mass organizations, and established 251 party branches. It had twenty-seven guerrilla squads and several teams and squads of snipers fielded across the island. And it assisted in staging numerous protests, strikes, and rallies.[39] Left-wing Labor Day rallies drew thousands of hacienda workers to the provincial capital.

Did the sugar crises of 1976–79 and 1984–85 (triggered by slumps in the world market price of sugar) force workers out of submissiveness? In those periods, planters cut back rigorously on work, wages, and the subsistence credit that tides workers over the lean season in cane cultivation, and large planters began to mechanize more cultivation tasks. Porter notes, "in Negros Occidental . . . most popular support for the NPA has been the result of years of denial of sugar workers' rights by plantation owners, massive unemployment in the industry, and the collapse of social services for workers."[40] McCoy states that "battling against market forces that are robbing them of their social role and respect, the Negros workers have

---

[37] John Adkins, "Land Control and Political Behavior in the Philippines: A Comparative Assessment of the Impact of Land Usage Patterns on Socio-political Relationships and Behavior in Occidental and Oriental Negros," (PhD dissertation, University of Michigan, 1975).

[38] In the 1930s–50s, the militant labor union Federacion Obrera de Filipinas concentrated primarily on workers in sugar centrals. The Negros chapter of the Federation of Free Farmers made short-lived attempts to organize hacienda workers and migrant laborers in the late 1950s-early 1960s in several milling districts but, as these were thwarted by planter repression, shifted by the early 1970s to organizing small upland farmers victimized by landgrabbing. See AMRSP, *The Sugar Workers of Negros* (Metro Manila: Association of Major Religious Superiors in the Philippines, 1976), pp. 103–04; Alfred W. McCoy, *Priests on Trial* (Victoria: Penguin Books Australia, 1984), pp. 115–18, 134-36; and Alfred W. McCoy, "The Restoration of Planter Power in La Carlota City," *From Marcos to Aquino: Local Perspectives on Political Transition in the Philippines*, Benedict J. Kerkvliet and Resil B. Mojares, eds. (Honolulu: University of Hawaii Press, 1991), pp. 112–13.

[39] Miguel Coronel, *Pro-Democracy People's War* (Quezon City: Vanmarc Ventures, 1991), pp. 658, 660, 665–66.

[40] Porter, "The Politics of Counterinsurgency," p. 20. See also Chapman, *Inside the Philippine Revolution*, p. 128.

turned to [progressive] Catholic priests and Communist guerrillas in a desperate quest for survival."[41]

But subsistence problems as such have poor explanatory value. We cannot assume a direct relation between increasing economic hardships and militancy, since these may weaken tactical capacities and may not be translated into kinds of grievances necessary for confrontational action. By attributing the expansion of hacienda-worker support for the NPA mainly to hardships caused by the sugar crisis of the mid-1980s, moreover, one may easily ignore other factors that were at work at the time. In my research area, for instance, NPA policy to seek a tactical alliance with planters and overseers in its campaign against the Marcos regime facilitated NPA mobilization in haciendas as it lowered opposition among hacienda management. Since mobilization processes intervene between adversities and support for the NPA, we need to turn to the interactions between hacienda workers and mobilizers.

Where NPA activists are unable to operate, mass support for the NPA remains negligible. Two preconditions for mobilization, then, need to be discussed first: activists' access to hacienda workers, in this case through social networks that reached into haciendas; and activists' room to maneuver in the hacienda region, which depended on the so-called political opportunity structure, in particular the extent of repression and other counter-actions by planters and the state.[42]

The small group of NPA activists sent from Manila to Negros in 1969—to open up the first NPA expansion area outside of Luzon—lacked any organizational link with hacienda workers. These activists, led by two Central Committee members and including several Huk-guerrilla veterans, "were either jailed or shot or forced to flee the province after only a few days work among the laborers," and apparently "laborers themselves informed authorities of the activities and location of the organizers."[43] Unable to speak the local language and lacking a political base, they were vulnerable to capture when the guerrillas killed and wounded several policemen.

The second group of NPA activists, which arrived from Manila in 1971, took care to develop a network of cadres and supporters first. They were student activists who linked up with small groups of activist students in the provincial capital Bacolod City. Though they initially noted "the absence of even a single representative from the labor sector" among their early contacts,[44] the category of NPA cadres eventually expanded from students at city campuses to peasants recruited in the southern

---

[41] McCoy, *Priests on Trial*, p. 73.

[42] The concept of "political opportunity structure" refers to the "receptivity or vulnerability of the political system to organized protest by a given challenging group" which provides "incentives for people to undertake collective action by affecting their expectations for success or failure." Quote from McAdam, et al., "Social Movements," p. 699. See also Tarrow, *Power in Movement*, p. 85. Skocpol, for instance, emphasizes this aspect when she argues that peasant support for institutionalized revolutionary movements depends on whether revolutionary cadres can "operate effectively in the countryside" and "address peasant needs successfully" and relates these conditions to the strength of state power. See Theda Skocpol, "What Makes Peasants Revolutionary?," *Power and Protest in the Countryside: Studies of Rural Unrest in Asia, Europe, and Latin America* (Durham, NC: Duke University Press, 1982), pp. 169–72.

[43] John Adkins, "Land Control and Political Behavior," p. 225. See also Primo Esleyer, "Social Justice and the Thompson Sub-Machine Guns," *Sugarland: A Magazine for the Sugar Industry* (Bacolod City) 6, 8 (1969): 39; and Jones, *Red Revolution*, pp. 91–92.

[44] Leonardo S. Nicdao, "History of the Establishment of the CPP/NPA in Negros Occidental," typescript, n.d., p. 1.

uplands that formed the NPA's first rural base, and finally to a large number of workers recruited from and based in the province's haciendas.

This outcome was by no means assured at the onset. Initially, the Manila activists operated through the militant youth organization Kabataang Makabayan (KM, Patriotic Youth), whose reach was limited to city colleges and high schools. In contrast, its rival in the province, the moderate urban Christian-socialist youth movement Khi Rho, was linked to the Federation of Free Farmers (FFF) which staged actions in behalf of peasants and hacienda workers and had close connections with progressive Roman Catholic clergy who undertook social-action programs for the poor.[45] KM labeled Khi Rho "clerico-fascist," kept far from its social network, and so remained isolated from the poor whose interests they sought to represent.[46] Only when KM connected with Khi Rho and its rural activist contacts, after the declaration of martial law when KM and several moderate activists went underground, could the NPA expand into the Negros countryside.[47]

The early activists, then, eventually reached hacienda workers by linking up with social networks of Church and unions that reached into many haciendas and villages in the province.[48] Moreover, they connected to Liberation Theology which matched to a large degree the ideological frame of the NPA. The CPP-NPA nationwide had developed an interest in Roman Catholic clergy opposed to the martial-law regime and committed to Vatican II's call for social justice. In Negros Occidental, progressive priests and nuns supported two militant unions, the Federation of Free Farmers (FFF, primarily active among upland peasants victimized by landgrabbing) and the labor union National Federation of Sugar Workers (NFSW, active among hacienda workers). Since the 1970s, they also helped organize hacienda workers and upland villagers into emancipatory Basic Christian Communities (BCCs). Confronted with repression and ineffectiveness of legal claims, as well as with NPA recruitment efforts, several priests and nuns joined the NPA and went underground, reaching influential positions in the party hierarchy; many more became sympathetic to the NPA.[49] As a member of the clergy in Negros states in

[45] Fr. Hector Mauri, SJ, one of the early leaders of the FFF [Federation of Free Farmers] in Negros, introduced Khi Rho members to the social activism of the FFF: "I found them a little bit vague in their idealism with no concrete program, so I invited some of them to work with me for something positive and clear that may uplift the sugar workers in their own province, instead of talking about national and international problems." "Sworn Statement of Fr. Hector Mauri before Supv Agt Dionicio A Lapus of CITF, C2 Division, HPC, Camp Crame, Queon City this 12th Day of December 1972 in the Office of CITF." Mimeographed copy of typescript, p. 2.

[46] In pre-martial law days, the conflict in Manila between radical (KM) and moderate student movements carried over to the provinces. Cf. Benjamin Pimentel, Jr., *Edjop: The Unusual Journey of Edgar Jopson* (Quezon City: Ken Inc., 1989).

[47] Interview with Nemesio Demafelis, former chairman of the Negros Island Regional Party Committee, Bacolod City, March 17, 1995; and with a former Khi Rho member, Bacolod City, March 15, 1995.

[48] Nicdao, "History of the Establishment of the CPP/NPA," p. 5.

[49] Cf. "The Makings of Revolutionaries," *Viewpoints* (Badolod City) 2, 5 (1987): 4–7, 14. Also Vicente Pelobello, "Talambuhay ni Ka Seloy" [Life Story of Comrade Seloy], a typed copy of the autobiography of Fr. Vicente Pelobello, among documents captured by the Philippine Constabulary at a CPP training camp in Gawahon, Victorias, Negros Occidental, July 1, 1987. Date of manuscript, 1984. The NPA's early ally was Fr. Luis Jalandoni, son of a planter family who, as the chaplain of the Federation of Free Farmers and director of the Social Action Center of the Diocese, experienced the powerlessness of the poor in court as well as in peaceful

retrospect, "the active leadership of these priests, or at least their blessing, was a vital factor in strengthening the revolution in Negros, an island which is 90 percent Catholic and where the Church, in spite of everything, is still the most credible institution around."[50] NPA activists eventually began to recruit among local organizers of Basic Christian Communities and the labor union. In the hacienda lowlands, many of these organizers were sons and daughters of hacienda workers or overseers. Such local organizers, from poor backgrounds, knowledgeable of hacienda life, and rooted in hacienda society, eventually became the main NPA activists in the haciendas.

The activists' room for maneuvering was constrained by harassment and violent repression on the part of authorities and planters. The declaration of martial law did partly undermine the coercive power of planters and local authorities as a gun-ban affected overseers, planters' guards, and *barangay* captains, and as the municipal police was placed under the control of the Philippine Constabulary (PC). But the PC intensified its crackdown on suspected "subversives" and by the mid-1970s a militia force (the Civilian Home Defense Force, CHDF) was at the disposal of local authorities and influential Marcos-loyalist planters. An increasing number of abuses were committed by members of the PC, CHDF, and later the Philippine army as well (Long Range Patrol, Scout Rangers, and several army battalions deployed in the province).[51] Among the victims of military abuse were local organizers of the union NFSW and of Basic Christian Communities (BCCs), who were tagged as subversives, harassed, and a number brutally killed.

What did allow NPA activists some maneuvering space in the lowlands was the legal cover, often unwittingly, of the BCCs and union (despite harassment of its organizers). Moreover, up to the mid-1980s, much of the hacienda lowlands were spared militarization. The Philippine army focused on the isolated uplands in the south and along the eastern mountain range, where the guerrilla army was initially confined. In the hacienda lowlands, NPA activists developed a political mass base while avoiding armed confrontations. Planters, living in towns and cities, often realized the extent of NPA influence in their haciendas only when the NPA had already established considerable control there. To avoid NPA retaliations (burning of their canefields, for instance) many planters eventually opted for accommodation.[52] Many were hesitant to make a forceful alliance with the military during the Marcos regime, not in the least because of their anti-Marcos sentiment (fueled by Marcos's curtailment of their influence and the appropriation of sugar profits through a state

---

collective actions. He joined the NPA in the early 1970s. Charismatic and widely respected, he helped persuade a number of other priests and nuns. Jalandoni later became a member of the CPP Central Committee and director of the NDF international office in the Netherlands.

[50] Niall O'Brien, *Island of Tears, Island of Hope: Living the Gospel in a Revolutionary Situation* (New York: Orbis Books, 1993), p. 52.

[51] For instance, in 1977 at least twenty-six civilians were killed and thirty tortured by military forces in Negros Occidental. See *Itum: Bitter Times in the Land of Sugar*, n.p. (Task Force Detainees of the Philippines, 1979), p. 5. In 1985, at least sixty-two civilians were killed, including twenty workers, peasants, and students who participated in a "people's strike" rally in the northern town of Escalante. See "A Diary of Terror in Sugarlandia," *Singgit* (Bacolod City) 4, 3, (1985): 15. Published by Task Force Detainees of the Philippines-Negros.

[52] Nanette G. Dungo, "Changing Social Relations in the Negros Sugar Hacienda: The Eroding Relation of Patronage Between the Hacendero and Worker in the Context of Developments in the Wider Political Economic Milieu," (PhD dissertation, University of the Philippines, Quezon City, 1993), p. 244.

sugar-trade monopoly). As the NPA established hacienda-based monitoring systems against military personnel and began to kill or threaten suspected informers, local authorities had increasing difficulties monitoring and curbing NPA mobilization. Meanwhile, as McCoy notes for the country as a whole, "local [military] commands yielded the countryside to insurgents" as military leaders were absorbed by internal factional strife, military personnel were ill-paid and ill-motivated, and support by local power holders was wanting.[53]

In the research municipality in the north-central part of the province, armed activists enjoyed an expanding room for maneuver by the mid-1980s. NPAs raided hacienda warehouses and killed several hacienda overseers and policemen. Many lowland haciendas were organized by the NPA or had NPA influence. Police were hesitant to set foot in the area. Planters had stopped visiting their haciendas, and when the NPA held up several jeeps carrying payroll money, many planters transferred the weekly payment of wages from their haciendas to the nearby town.

A marked turnaround occurred during Corazon Aquino's presidency when, in 1987, Aquino sanctioned a concerted counterinsurgency campaign, and provincial elites, having recaptured control over their provinces with bicameral and provincial elections in 1987–88, and alarmed by the increasing influence and audacity of the NPA, allied with regional military commanders to support this campaign.[54] In Negros Occidental, the provincial commander of the Philippine Constabulary, Col. Miguel Coronel, coordinated a counter-movement to the NPA in the north-central part of the province that included planters, journalists, politicians, and several former provincial NPA leaders who had surrendered and become vocal anti-NPA activists.[55] Planters helped establish the paramilitary Philippine Constabulary Forward Command (PCFC), and by 1988 paid a compulsory contribution to the so-called Sugar Development Foundation that funded the PCFCs. The PCFCs eventually numbered about 1,600 men occupying 52 patrol bases throughout the north-central part of the province.[56]

Counterinsurgency targeting the political base of the NPA intensified in the lowlands. In 1987–89, in particular, it involved selective terror by PC, police, paramilitary PCFCs, and vigilante groups, combined with virulent anti-NPA propaganda and the labeling of Church personnel and left-wing organizations (including the union NFSW) as NPA members and communist front organizations.[57] Several presidents of hacienda-based NFSW chapters were among the victims of military and vigilante killings (e.g. Amnesty 1988, 1991). Military and paramilitary units were spread out over the lowlands in small detachments, each patrolling the surrounding areas in an effort to cut off the NPA from its mass base.

By 1989, the focus had shifted towards a mass surrender program managed by the Philippine army, aimed at NPA-influenced communities and individual NPA activists. Except for large military operations against NPA bases in the uplands, military violence decreased as the surrender strategy involved force and persuasion

[53] McCoy, "Low Intensity Conflict in the Philippines," p. 60.

[54] McCoy, "The Restoration of Planter Power in La Carlota City," pp. 141–42.

[55] Coronel, *Pro-Democracy People's War*.

[56] Ibid., p. 728.

[57] Coronel, *Pro-Democracy People's War*. Also McCoy, "The Restoration of Planter Power in La Carlota City." Also TFPD [Task Force Detainees of the Philippines], *Vigilantism in Negros* (Bacolod City: Task Force Detainees of the Philippines-Negros, 1988).

(coupled to an amnesty program) rather than violent coercion. From 1987 to September 1994, according to provincial police sources, 11,966 "rebels" surrendered to the authorities.[58] Haciendas may now count former NPAs who became government informers or paramilitary men (members of the Civilian Armed Force Geographical Units, CAFGU). In recent years, then, the activists' room for maneuver in the hacienda lowlands has narrowed considerably.

HACIENDA MILAGROS: CONFLICT AND ACCOMMODATION

Hacienda Milagros is an average-sized sugarcane hacienda (130 hectares) located in the north-central part of the province's lowlands, with some sixty wage-earning families living and working on its land. The planter lives with his family in the provincial capital, a half-hour jeep ride away. A resident overseer and two or three foremen make up the local management; they are, together with several drivers of trucks and tractors, the only salaried employees (*empleados*) in the hacienda. The resident workers or *dumaan* (women, men, teenagers, and some children) are paid daily or piece-rate wages. Their low and irregular income has long spelled poverty for the hacienda families, marked by malnourishment, illnesses like tuberculosis, and low levels of education. Conditions have somewhat improved in the last twenty years, partly brought about by workers' successful collective actions: infant mortality declined, more children are able to attend high school, and several worker and *empleado* families presently own battery-powered television sets. But most families still cannot cover basic costs of medicine and education, the cramped houses lack latrines and electricity, and making ends meet remains a constant worry.

Workers were already involved in protracted conflicts with the planter long before activists began to operate in the hacienda. These conflicts concerned their right to year-round family subsistence in return for the availability of their labor. This traditional social contract, acknowledged by planters and workers throughout the hacienda region, included the right of resident workers to (minimal) subsistence credit during the lean season, free housing (small dwellings made of bamboo and palmleaf), and emergency credit for medical costs. Though many planters tried to economize on these expenses, the tacit contract as such provided workers a standard to which they could appeal. When workers of Hda. Milagros experienced regular drops in planter patronage, they confronted the overseer, individually or in small groups, with persistent pleas and complaints. They had a good potential to act collectively: they depended on the same planter, were linked by ties of kinship, friendship, and neighborhood, worked together in the canefields, and spent leisure time together at the many small hacienda stores.

But workers depended on their individual good standing with planter and overseer in order to secure work, credit, and any possible improvement in their families' life chances, which limited workers' capabilities for collective claim-making and fostered disunity. The planter, who also distributed small gifts at Christmas and arranged regular Catholic masses in the hacienda, expected from his workers unconditional loyalty. Seeking to avoid "trouble," workers limited their protests to complaints addressed to the overseer. The *empleados*, on their part, tended to favor the status quo to maintain the meager privileges they enjoyed. So did the many

---

[58] They were classified as 495 party members, 5,402 mass activists, and 6,069 sympathizers and supporters. *The Visayan Daily Star* (Bacolod City), November 8, 1994.

worker-relatives of the overseer, whom the overseer sometimes favored when allocating work and house repair materials. Workers' concern with family subsistence and smooth relationships with planter and overseer was underpinned by a worldview that was thoroughly personalistic: there were "good" and "bad" planters, not a bad planter class as such, and one could leave a bad planter and try to link up with a more generous one.

How activists addressed these interests, and how workers responded, will be further discussed below. The account is more or less chronological, and activities of Church and left-wing union are included. Workers themselves view their organization by Church, union, and NPA as interrelated: the messages were broadly similar, social networks on the local level overlapped, and key activists from Milagros moved from Church and union to the NPA. Workers of Milagros first organized into a Basic Christian Community in the mid-1970s, then joined a moderate labor union to claim legal benefits (13th month pay) which the planter finally provided after he had locked out several active union members. They subsequently joined the left-wing union NFSW which helped improve labor conditions, and were eventually mobilized to support the NPA. By the mid-1980s the NPA considered the hacienda a "consolidated area."

CREDIBILITY OF LOCAL ACTIVISTS

Respected community leaders and local organizers played an important role in the early stages of NPA mobilization. After all, political mobilizers need to be credible and capable in the eyes of their potential following.[59] One such leader in Milagros was former overseer Rafael. Soft-spoken, well-respected, a "very persuasive talker," and with a large network of kin and ritual kin, he helped to convince many workers and *empleados* to support the movement.

He was a vital link in a chain of mobilizers in the hacienda which started in the mid-1970s, before NPA mobilization in the area, with a respected left-wing parish priest and his sacristans who held seminars in the hacienda and established a Basic Christian Community (BCC). Their work was carried on by progressive nuns, who recruited two young single men from Milagros and an overseer's daughter from a neighboring hacienda as BCC activists in the area. These three activists began to double as organizers for the Church-supported left-wing labor union, and eventually joined the NPA in the late 1970s against the explicit will of the nuns. They had mobilized a core group of supporters in Hda. Milagros when former overseer Rafael became willing to join.

What moved these hacienda youths into NPA activism was a process of conversion among the young Church activists in the municipality who regularly gathered at the *convento* (presbytery) in town. As they experienced their powerlessness as organizers in the face of repression of workers, learned of repression and military abuses elsewhere in the province through Church seminars and rallies, had lengthy talks with NPA recruiters (friends of friends) who presented revolutionary struggle as a viable alternative, and read revolutionary literature that

---

[59] Cf. Popkin, "Political Entrepreneurs and Peasant Movements in Vietnam."

made this alternative seem credible and scientifically based,[60] they became jointly convinced that revolution was the only way out. From Liberation Theology it was but a small step toward revolutionary ideology, and the step was facilitated by student-activist friends and small-group pressures. Eager and committed activists, they argued that the nuns merely focused on "conscientization" and, unlike the NPA, lacked a clear program of action. The madres strongly objected to their radicalization, and heated discussions in the *convento* preceded their break-up.

Personal grievances, humanist proclivities, and contact with mobilizers prompted former overseer Rafael into activism. Son of a foreman and planter's protégé, he was houseboy of the planter when young and eventually appointed overseer when still in his twenties. A religious person, and kin and friend of many workers, he felt burdened by his inability to help workers in lean months. Demoted to the position of foreman during the sugar crisis of 1976–79 (allegedly to make room for a better-educated outsider who could help rationalize the production process), he was all the more attracted by the Church's teachings on social justice. No longer hampered by loyalty to the planter, he contacted the three local Church activists and began to promote Church and union organizing in Milagros. When the planter had him jailed for two weeks on charges of padding the payroll (Rafael claimed the "padding" was accidental), he quit his job as a foreman and became a full-time activist, first for the union, later in the service of the NPA, where he eventually reached the position of secretary of a district committee.

These four local mobilizers recruited other activists from among their kin and friends in the hacienda, and eased the introduction of visiting NPA cadres, including members of Propaganda Organizing Teams, instructors of advanced ideological seminars, and eventually teams of mobile guerrilla fighters. Tasked to mobilize by persuasion, they were respectful and soft-spoken, visited workers in the evenings for long talks, and, above all, made workers courteous personal requests: to attend ideological seminars or rallies in the city, or do some task for the movement. Such face-to-face requests were often hard to refuse.

As a rule, local activists avoid any mention of the Communist Party in their contact with potential supporters. They present themselves as members of the *hublag* ("the movement") and of "the NPA, the genuine army of the poor" (*ang matuod-tuod gid nga army sg pumuluyo*) that helps to defend the interests of the poor against "despotic" landlords and an oppressive government. The reason is simple: "the masses are against communism," as one former activist said, "the old people fear they will be killed under communism and made into *betsin* (food seasoning)." Others feared they would have to share the few belongings they had. Confronted with the result of decades of anti-communist propaganda, the mobilizers' strategy is to initially deny any connection to communism, and only gradually inform selected people of CPP "guidance" and eventually invite these into the party.

IDEOLOGICAL WORK: REFRAMING

The willingness of most people of Milagros to support the NPA did not arise naturally from their experiences as hacienda workers. The conceptions they had of

---

[60] In particular the study by CPP founder and former university lecturer Jose Ma. Sison, alias Amado Guerrero, *Philippine Society and Revolution*, first published in 1970. Reprinted (Oakland, CA: International Association of Filipino Patriots, 1979).

their own position in society, including their vulnerability vis-à-vis the powerful, favored (grudging) accommodation with the planter and state authorities or, in case of conflict, leaving and settling elsewhere.

Activists had to overcome workers' reluctance toward confrontational collective action. They tried to convince workers that it was in their own interest to act collectively, "to move," as they put it. They sought to change people's perceptions in order to inspire action: they (re)defined workers' condition as unjust, identified the people or structures that were to blame, argued that workers, when organized, could do something about it, and outlined a course of action. In presenting such "collective action frames," [61] they connected to the existing standard of justice among hacienda workers—the right to subsistence—but expanded workers' notions of rights to include the right to a true and lasting improvement in their life chances.

Workers of Milagros, by themselves, certainly had grievances enough against the planter. But, as a worker recounted, "we lacked a 'voice' to protest (*reklamo*)." Their notion of subsistence rights was closely tied to personal dependency on the planter and their claim-making was limited to presenting complaints to the overseer and waiting for a benevolent reply. What they lacked was a forceful language to make claims, an ideology that legitimized confrontational claim-making, and an organizational format that enabled them actually to make these claims.

All activists, including the early Church and union organizers, tried to provide this protest "voice." They all used seminars to do so. Their analysis was Marxist and nationalist: not "bad" planters or personal failures caused workers' poverty, but an exploitative system represented by planters, supported by the government, and backed up by imperialist powers. "Oppression" was the key word; it suggested the cause, the people to blame, and the solution to workers' misery. Seminars of Church and union[62] familiarized the workers with the image of Philippine society as a pyramid (drawn in chalk on battered blackboards) with "ninety percent" of the population forming the broad base of poor and destitute people, and a small percentage made up of landlords, capitalists, and government leaders forming the top, who were in turn under the yoke of imperialists. It would only require a united effort of the poor, the activists said, to turn the pyramid upside down and produce a truly liberated society without oppressive structures. The activists redefined the shared identity of workers from "we, the poor (*mga imol*)" into "we, the oppressed (*pumuluyong pigos*)," and sketched how hacienda workers, scattered in hundreds of separate haciendas, were part of a nationwide category of oppressed people. They called for class-based unity and action.

---

[61] On collective action frames, see David A. Snow and Robert D. Benford, "Master Frames and Cycles of Protest," *Frontiers of Social Movement Theory,* Aldon Morris and Carol Muller, eds. (New Haven, CT: Yale University Press, 1992) and William A. Gamson, *Talking Politics* (New York: Cambridge University Press, 1992). Gamson discusses three components of collective action frames: injustice, agency, and identity, which refer, respectively, to the "moral indignation expressed," the "consciousness that it is possible to alter conditions or policies through collective action," and the "process of defining [a] 'we,' typically in opposition to some 'they' who have different interests and value." Gamson, *Talking Politics,* p. 7.

[62] The so-called "Self-Discovery Seminar" organized by the progressive clergy in the Catholic high school or *convento* in town, and the "General Trade Union" seminar held by union organizers in the hacienda.

So when the NPA began to recruit in the hacienda, the workers were already, in a sense, "culturally prepared," to borrow Ileto's formulation.[63] NPA activists needed to take the analysis by Church and union one step further to convince workers of the necessity of armed struggle. In places where union actions were not successful, they argued there was another, more effective way to fight landlords. In Milagros, where union actions had success, they argued union gains would be tenuous unless a "people's army" would defend these gains and eventually overhaul the whole oppressive system to provide genuine long-term improvements. Through seminars, workers were persuaded to shift their focus from the so-called *partikular* (worker-planter relations within their own hacienda) to the *universal* (the encompassing system of exploitation represented by "feudalism, bureaucrat capitalism, and imperialism"), to ensure their continuing support for the struggle even if their own conditions would improve.[64]

The oppression frame used by Church, union, and NPA was new to workers of Milagros in that it provided a systemic rather than a personalistic worldview and called for collective confrontational action. It was, however, linked to familiar notions. The clergy in town, for instance, once portrayed the liberation of hacienda workers from planter oppression by staging an adapted version of "Exodus." NPA activists connected to folk notions of the good life—notions that emphasized subsistence security, family well-being, and basic human dignity—by envisioning liberated society as a place in which "all will be equal, no poor, no rich" (*palareho tanan tanan, wala pigado, wala manggaranon*), "no slaves, no masters" (*wala sg ulipon, wala sg amo*), and defining genuine freedom and independence as freedom from landlord control and free access to land.

The activists' call to action, then, was not just to defend traditional rights to subsistence, but to claim new rights that could finally deliver workers from poverty. Clergy and union focused on workers' legislated rights—which workers had only been partially aware of. Legitimate by definition, these provided a powerful rallying point. NPA activists, on the other hand, stressed much broader self-defined rights to land and to political influence, and sought to convince workers of the legitimacy of these claims in at least the following ways:

Simply stated, they argued that workers had a right to a better life and should not accept current conditions. "You are victims of injustice. You earn too little to cover your needs. Do you want the same miserable life for your children?" former overseer Rafael said in his activist role. Legislated wages and benefits were not enough, and true improvement of workers' livelihood was impossible under current conditions, the activists argued. Using the labor theory of value they carefully computed cane yields and profits per hectare to convince workers they had a right to planter profits.

They delegitimized planters (as the descendants of Spanish landgrabbers) and government leaders and so denied them the right to land ownership and state power. They referred to the constitutional right of citizens to government services and asked workers what the government did to solve their problems of poverty, illness, and lack of education. Very little, indeed. After the seminars of Church and

---

[63] Renaldo Clemeña Ileto, *Pasyon and Revolution: Popular Movements in the Philippines, 1840–1910* (Quezon City: Ateneo de Manila University Press, 1979), p. 24.

[64] For similar observations in another region, see Chapman, *Inside the Philippine Revolution*, pp. 134–35.

union had firmly introduced the notion of legislated rights, the NPA seminars emphasized that these rights were trampled upon, and workers began to feel shortchanged of rights they had only recently been informed about.[65]

The claim to land—which appealed most to workers of Milagros as it embodied, they said, the end to planter oppression and the possibility of true improvement—may illustrate this point. The notion that workers had a right to hacienda land did not come from the workers themselves. As descendants of migrant laborers from Panay island who had settled in Milagros after serving in other haciendas as well, workers of Milagros used to accept the planter's right to private property as self-evident. After the Japanese Occupation, for instance, resident workers returned to the planter, without a grudge, the hacienda land they had planted to subsistence crops when cane cultivation had ceased. "Of course we returned the land, we had just borrowed it," they recounted, and they had welcomed the opportunity to earn a wage again. In the course of mobilization, they started to link the planter's regular disregard of their subsistence rights to systematic planter oppression and began to perceive land reform as the only way to end it. The growing influence of the NPA in the 1980s in the province and country at large suggested that this goal could be realized.[66] Not all workers went along with this. An elderly woman, for instance, objected that the planter had rightfully inherited the land from his father, but an activist worker criticized her for being "satisfied" with her present condition.

The NPA seminars formed the backbone of mobilization in the hacienda. Held regularly in one of the hacienda houses for women, men, and teenagers, they brought hacienda residents together in small-group settings conducive to conversion. The seminars were intensive social affairs that lasted from one day to more than three days, and they were live-in events, which fostered a strong sense of camaraderie. The so-called "instructors" were familiar figures: the former overseer, and eventually other women and men of Milagros who were schooled in the new ideology. The seminars introduced people step by step deeper into the movement, and marked the trajectory of entrance and upward mobility in the NPA hierarchy. The NPA leadership had developed a series of courses with standardized scripts, and each consecutive course indicated a higher degree of commitment to the movement. The first of the series, the General Mass Course for all workers, helped to create sympathizers willing to contribute in small ways. It presented an analysis of the hacienda system and of Philippine society and history at large within the exploitation-and-liberation frame. Attending this first seminar pulled workers over the threshold of illegality (they were aware the seminar was "illegal"), which one of the instructors marked by stating at the end, "now we are all NPA." The series

---

[65] Some authors argue that people tend to support a revolutionary movement when they cease to view the government as legitimate, in particular when the government fails to provide the basic services expected: e.g. Timothy P. Wickham-Crowley, "The Rise (and Sometimes Fall) of Guerrilla Governments in Latin America," *Sociological Forum* 2 (1987): 473–99. The case of Milagros suggests that movement mobilizers may actively encourage such delegitimization.

[66] Kerkvliet similarly argues, regarding poor people's claims to land ownership in Central Luzon, that under favorable conditions that include "the inability of those at the top to maintain control," lower-class people "might indeed go further in both thought and action." Benedict Kerkvliet, *Everyday Politics in the Philippines: Class and Status Relations in a Central Luzon Village* (Berkeley: University of California Press, 1990), pp. 264–65. The more far-reaching notions of rights to land that may then become prominent he views as "otherwise latent." Kerkvliet, *Every Politics in the Philippines*, p. 265. Here, I argue that such notions may be newly acquired.

proceeded with so-called "deeper" courses for selected interested workers, including one based on Mao's "Five Golden Rays,"[67] which made them eligible for positions in the organization. It culminated with the Basic Party Course for a select few, capped by a secret oath-taking ceremony for candidate party-members. Almost all workers in Hda. Milagros followed the first course, and a large number also participated in the consecutive courses as they began to take up tasks in the organization.

Many workers, having little formal education, were interested in the seminars, eager to learn more about Philippine society and their place in it, and to make sense of it all in terms of the new image presented. The first seminar appealed directly to their own condition and problems in the hacienda. "It helped me to understand the *real* situation, and the oppression of the people by the landlord, and I became interested to join the movement," as a worker recounted. The positive value that the Philippine poor attach to education as a means to self-advancement certainly added to the attraction of the seminars. "The explanations of the instructors encouraged us to learn more, to become knowledgeable," as one worker said. Most important, they felt this knowledge empowered them to change their condition.[68]

Reluctant participants, on the other hand, included women and men who were illiterate and therefore suspicious and slightly afraid of anything having to do with pen and paper. Some elderly who felt a personal loyalty towards the planter (for instance, because the planter's father had brought them from one of his haciendas to Milagros) condemned all NPA activities as anti-planter and tried to persuade their children not to attend the seminars. Others had never liked going to school and were bored by the classroom-like atmosphere of the seminars. As one of them said about the seminar she attended, "it simply didn't enter into my head." They would not advance beyond the first seminar.

Some workers resisted the early teachings because they feared planter and military reprisals: "what if I lose my job, can the *hublag* (the movement) support my family?" An old male worker said, "we'll all get killed because of you!" A female worker doubted the activists' faith in the power of worker unity "because the rich have the money," and she feared concerted action would provoke conflict and battle. Such objections died down as repressive measures were not imposed on the hacienda in the early years of mobilization.

The new understandings did not become fully shared in the hacienda community. The extent to which workers adopted NPA ideology was, apparently, roughly related to the level of seminars they had followed and the degree of their incorporation in the NPA apparatus. Many workers easily grasped the notions of planter and government oppression, given their own life experiences and their endless need to haggle with the planter to cover their family's subsistence needs, and given the entwining of political and planter elites. Apparently, many also accepted the need to organize and to support the NPA in its struggle against this oppression. Among those who held positions in the local NPA organization, the need to change

---

[67] The text, mimeographed in the local language Ilonggo, was widely used in Negros Occidental. Mao Zedong, "Lima Ka Bulawanon nga Silak" [Five Golden Rays], n.p., Pangrehiyon nga Departamento sa Edukasyon, 1976. Mimeographed.

[68] Cf. Ruth T. McVey, "The Enchantment of the Revolution: History and Action in an Indonesian Communist Text," *Perceptions of the Past in Southeast Asia*, Anthony Reid and David Marr, eds. (Singapore: Heinemann Educational Books, ASAA Southeast Asia Publications Series, no. 4, 1979), on ideological work among (potential) cadres of Indonesia's PKI [Partai Komunis Indonesia] in the 1950s–1960s.

the system of government and remove the planters as a class appeared widely accepted.

CREATING COMMITMENT TO THE ORGANIZATION

Studies of institutionalized revolutionary movements argue that a revolutionary organization needs to provide individual benefits first, before villagers are willing to contribute to collective goals and eventually to sacrifice for the organization's broader aims. Providing such benefits produces among villagers "a political commitment to the survival of that organization and to the actualization of its goals."[69] Writing about the revolutionary movement in Vietnam, Race notes that people were offered "contingent incentives,"[70] i.e. access to benefits such as land, protection, or positions of power, which they could only benefit from as long as they supported the organization, and as long as the organization had a strong local presence to guarantee these benefits. Individual interests were thereby aligned with the interests of the organization.

The mobilization process in Hda. Milagros suggests a more complex development of commitment, though the gradual creation of an organizational structure of incentives in the hacienda has certainly been crucial. The first stage in commitment formation concerned the "mass organizations" in the hacienda, which dealt with immediate individual and family interests, provided short-term material benefits as well as a sense of empowerment, and helped forge a more solidary community. Activists organized the hacienda population into groups of "mothers" (*nanay*), "fathers" (*tatay*), "youth" (*pamatan-on*), and later of local management and other salaried employees as well. These community-based organizations were all in the "legal" sphere; the threshold for joining was relatively low. Established by union activists in Milagros who had shifted to the NPA, these organizations were under NPA influence.

The second stage concerned participation in the hacienda-based institutional structure of the NPA, which demanded resources while providing few immediate benefits in return, except social rewards. The third step was made by workers who became full-timers in the organization, which involved severe personal sacrifices and required a large degree of personal identification with the interests of the NPA. Though most people in the hacienda passed through the first stage, a minority experienced the second, and a smaller number still (some fifteen persons) moved on through the third.

This was by no means a smooth process. The appeals of the *hublag* crosscut loyalties to planter and family. Some *empleados* and old workers initially strongly resisted the confrontational mobilization against the planter. Later, intra-family conflicts ensued when women, men, and teenagers started to take up tasks in the local organizations of the *hublag*: some husbands protested that their activist wives spent too much time away from home, and many parents tried to forbid their teenaged children from joining the *hublag*. Moreover, as some workers became powerful NPA officials in the hacienda, frictions developed with fellow workers who criticized their performance.

---

[69] Migdal, *Peasants, Politics, and Revolution*, p. 250.

[70] Race, *War Comes to Long An*, pp. 174–75.

In the following, I deal with the process of commitment formation and concentrate on those who participated in the movement and eventually became more deeply involved.

APPEALING TO WORKERS' FAMILY INTERESTS: CHANGING THE POWER BALANCE BETWEEN WORKERS AND PLANTER

Primary concerns of married women and men (organized as "mothers" and "fathers") were wage income and family subsistence, and these were the interests that activists initially addressed. The groups of "mothers" and "fathers," whose membership overlapped with union membership, dealt with labor conditions, wages, and protests against the planter. The women's group was as concerned with these issues as the men's. Whether they worked in the canefields or not, women were particularly motivated by their responsibility to make ends meet as keepers of household finances, a responsibility of married women in the Philippines that may provide fertile ground for militancy.[71]

Workers highly appreciated the activists' concern for their labor problems as well as their careful advice on how to bargain with the planter and make collective claims. A core of interested workers seized the opportunity and collectively presented demands, piecemeal, at the planter's house in the city or in the hacienda itself. These workers had some previous experience in collective action: in 1974–75, they had contacted a moderate labor union (the National Union of Sugar Industries, NUSI) to press the planter to pay legislated benefits, no doubt encouraged by the mobilizing work of the progressive clergy at that time. Responding to the union's radio program, they had signed up at the provincial office of the NUSI, filed a labor case against the planter with the assistance of the union, but then experienced planter repression in the form of lock-outs, decreased work assignments, and long delays in the court case that drained them of funds. Though they finally won the case, they were discouraged from filing cases in court that left them vulnerable to planter repression—all the more so since only a part of the workers in the hacienda had joined.

In contrast, the strategy suggested by the left-wing union NFSW, in the late 1970s, appealed to these workers, because it avoided costly court cases and concentrated instead on informal collective demands that were more effective. This mobilization effort coincided with the sugar crisis of the 1970s, whose effects were felt in the hacienda by 1977–78: the planter economized on work and subsistence credit and tried to lower piece rates, all of which formed acute reasons for collective protests. The planter found it difficult to refuse the persistent face-to-face demands by a growing number of workers, which dealt with concrete subsistence issues. As the planter gave in, "the other workers saw that we won, that we got what we asked

---

[71] cf. Rosanne Rutten, *Women Workers of Hacienda Milagros: Wage Labor and Household Subsistence on a Philippine Sugarcane Plantation*, Publikatieserie Zuid-en Zuidoost-Azië, no. 30 (Amsterdam: Anthropologisch-Sociologisch Centrum, Universitiet van Amsterdam, 1982). The issue of gender relations was treated as a secondary problem in the women's group, possibly to avoid discord in the workers' ranks. Cadres spoke of women's subordination, but blamed the social system rather than local men, and gender relations hardly formed a rallying point for local collective actions. However, the movement's professed goal of gender equality did eventually induce several women to report cases of wife-beating, in particular, to the local party branch, which helped to pressure these husbands to mend their ways.

for" (as one active member recounted), "and eventually they all became members." The union won a certification election in 1981, and the planter finally signed the first collective bargaining agreement in 1983. As the planter's bookkeeper explained, "he probably got tired of the persistent protests by his workers, and hoped the union would discipline the workers."

Pre-existing networks of relatives, friends, neighbors, and members of work-teams, were instrumental in this process of union mobilization. Such networks can cut both ways. When Rafael was still the overseer, most of his relatives were anti-union, as they feared losing the few privileges they received compared to others in the hacienda. His kin group only gravitated towards the union when Rafael lost his management position in the late 1970s and turned union organizer, which facilitated the full unionization of the hacienda by the early 1980s.[72]

In retrospect, workers mark this period as one of gradual empowerment with support of the union as well as the NPA. "Before, the people were afraid of the planter, now the planter is afraid of the people." They note they are "wise" now, can no longer be fooled by the planter or other authorities. They say they learned to face the planter without fear, state their demands with confidence and defend these tenaciously—all to the initial astonishment of the planter and his wife. The planter's bookkeeper recounted: "Before, everything was fine. Now the workers talk and argue, and the planter cannot answer!" The planter started to address some of the most tenacious (female) spokespersons of the workers with the term *atorniya* (attorney), partly jokingly, partly in exasperation. A crucial change had occurred in workers' behavior: feelings of embarrassment (*huya*, shame) in the face of the powerful, common among the Philippine poor in their dealings with employers and authorities and inhibiting assertive protest,[73] eased as workers enhanced their sense of self-worth and efficacy through seminars on workers' dignity and rights, learned to overcome feelings of shame in the course of collective actions, and experienced an increasing bargaining power.

The CBA (collective bargaining agreement) marked a significant change in the power balance; from relatively powerless dependents, workers had developed into recognized partners of the planter in institutionalized bargaining. Eventually, activists guided workers to present so-called "tactical" demands aimed at small non-legislated benefits whose acceptance signified that "whatever our demands, we can successfully face the planter," as a confident member explained.

Conditions that facilitated these successes included the increasing membership and influence of the left-wing union provincewide, the growing morale of workers as they were convinced of their (legislated) rights, the personalized form of collective claim-making, and the need for the planter to maintain a minimum of goodwill in his contacts with the workers, if only to enable him to visit the hacienda without trouble.

The coercive power of the NPA contributed to these small victories as well. As NPA influence in the area expanded, the NPA started to back worker demands by burning canefields and hacienda trucks of planters who were unwilling to give in.

---

[72] Rosanne Rutten, "Class and Kin: Conflicting Loyalties on a Philippine Hacienda," *Cognation and Social Organization in Southeast Asia*, Frans Husken and Jeremy Kemp, eds. (Leiden: KITLV Press, 1991).

[73] Michael Pinches, "The Working Class Experience of Shame, Inequality, and People Power in Tatalon, Manila," *From Marcos to Aquino: Local Perspectives on Political Transition in the Philippines*, Benedict J. Kerkvliet and Resil B. Mojares, eds. (Quezon City: Ateneo de Manila University Press, 1991).

Reluctantly, planters began to yield to wage demands. In the case of Milagros, former overseer Rafael, as member of the NPA section (and later, district) committee, formed a mediating link between planter and NPA. He exhorted the planter (by letter) to treat the workers well, advice the planter heeded, and during the sugar crisis of the mid-1980s he requested the planter to yield several hectares of hacienda land to the workers as subsistence lots, which the planter did. In return, Rafael exempted the planter from forced NPA taxation and protected his property from destruction when the planter was late in giving in to demands.

Workers tended to credit the NPA, in part, for these collective short-term benefits. This enabled activists in the hacienda to present the NPA as the true "army of the people": "the NPA will defend us when we have problems with the planter," and, "without the NPA, we will lose our gains and the planter will become despotic again." The short-term gains began to function as "contingent incentives" that induced continued support of the movement. Workers were willing to provide the regular contributions to the NPA expected of "organized masses" (*masa*), in particular a monthly contribution of a small can of rice and two pesos (about one-tenth of the daily wage in the mid-1980s).

THE YOUTH GROUP: CULTURAL ACTIVISM

Young, unmarried people are, as a category, least interested in mundane problems of family subsistence but are the most "biographically available" for full-time activism, having fewer family responsibilities than married persons.[74] The activist youth group in the hacienda (called *kultural*, the cultural group) did not bother the hacienda teenagers with actions for better wages and benefits, but appealed to their longing for entertainment, adventure, friendship, and purpose in life. It functioned, in a way, as an extended peer group for girls and boys of fifteen years and older from Hda. Milagros and two neighboring haciendas. Former overseer Rafael started the group as a serenading circle, which serenaded at the homes of people celebrating their birthdays, and at the houses of wayward youths to persuade them to join. As a former hacienda leader of the conservative Catholic Barangay Sang Virgen movement—a province-wide movement that was short-lived in the hacienda after its introduction by the planter in the early 1970s—Rafael used its songs and serenading practice but gave them a left-wing twist.

An outside activist who came to live in the hacienda for a year in the early 1980s reshaped the group into an *agit-prop* theater group, training the youths in songs and sketches every evening after work in the fields. They would perform at rallies throughout the area, which gave them a vivid sensation of being part of a larger movement. A professional *drama* instructor further developed the group in the mid-1980s, when Milagros had become one of the best organized haciendas in the area.

The youths became bearers of the movement's ideology. The *drama* and songs they staged—also in the hacienda during special occasions—vividly depicted landlord and government oppression and the need for a liberating struggle, and were meant to "enlighten people who do not yet understand," as a former youth-group member explained. They also suggested the need to bear sacrifices, and included heartbreaking presentations about women whose husband or son was

---

[74]cf. Doug McAdam, "Recruitment to High-Risk Activism: The Case of Freedom Summer," *American Journal of Sociology* 92 (1986): 70.

killed by the military. These songs and plays attached social value to sacrifice, expressed collective sympathy and support for the bereaved relatives, emotionally prepared workers for the possible loss of loved ones, showed that personal sacrifice would be acknowledged by the movement and valued by the community, and thereby eased the way toward high-risk, full-time involvement in the movement.

Consciousness of oppression, among some of these youths, came about in the course of their activist work, even though they had labored in the canefields since they were ten, twelve years old. One young man recounted that he joined the group "for fun," but as he acted out the stories of injustice and oppression, "I started to reflect on them." A woman explained that even when she performed in the cultural shows, as a teenager, "I was only reading the script, I didn't really understand it yet." Only when she became an organizer herself, and had to analyze and explain to others, the message about systemic oppression, of hacienda workers in particular, "really came from my brain."

Intended to draw teenagers into the movement, the youth group eventually formed the main recruiting ground for full-time cadres. Once part of the group, youths tended to be more open to participation in ideological seminars, more moved by the activists' message about injustice and abuses in the province, more interested to do tasks for the movement, and more motivated to take part in the struggle. Peer-group feelings were strong: "we were very close." Several became part-time youth organizers in Milagros and neighboring haciendas under the guidance of older workers, and learned to be activists by trial and error. "We were snubbed at first," as one recounted, because "we were not yet able to explain well." Most of the fifteen young women and men of the hacienda who eventually became full-time cadres (most of them single) had started their movement-career in the youth group. Only few of the youths who did not participate in the group would take up tasks in the movement.

However, the disciplining authorities of *hublag* and parents sometimes clashed with the teenagers' drive to liberate themselves from social fetters. Some youths resisted the NPA's ban (intended for youthful activists) to attend dances at fiestas and other occasions, and were not impressed by the cadres' warning that, at dances, women were treated as a commodity. One girl recounted, "I wanted to be in the *hublag*, but I also wanted to have fun—after all, I was a *dalaga* (adolescent girl)!" She loved going to dances, broke the rule together with other members of the group, had to sweep the hacienda's basketball court as punishment, and eventually she and her friends quit the group, which then was moribund for a while. When the theater instructor settled in Milagros in an empty house and brought along teenagers of other haciendas for training, the niche of sexual freedom they established there brought married hacienda women up in arms, until one of the local female activists (Rafael's wife) began to chaperon the place.

On the whole, however, many teenagers developed commitment to the *hublag* through this youth group which familiarized them with the organization's ideology and aims and embedded them in a network that was tightly linked to the organization.

THE ORGANIZATION OF LOCAL MANAGEMENT

Local management (overseer and foremen), as well as truck drivers, tended to be hostile to the movement. They feared losing their position and partly identified with the interests of the planter.[75] In order to win over and "neutralize" them, Rafael and other activists in the area proposed to organize them into an association of their own. They made a creative reinterpretation of the position of local management to suit the purpose: overseers are not, they argued, "the auxiliary class of the landlord" as official doctrine has it, but exploited wage earners essentially similar to hacienda workers, and their grievances should be taken seriously. The aim was "to use the overseer to mediate between workers and landlord and to convince the landlord that the organization of his workers was not a threat to his interests," as one of the activists recounted. It called for a non-confrontational approach: overseers would be persuaded to negotiate with the planter to solve workers' practical problems.

This *rapprochement* to local management, which included a temporary shift away from confrontation with individual planters, took place in the mid-1980s in the context of two broad developments. One was the sugar crisis of 1984–85, which left planters in dire financial straits and lowered workers' chances of obtaining better wages and financial benefits. Second, it was the time of the broad anti-Marcos alliance, in which the political left in the province allied with members of the middle classes and planter elite. Expecting a revolutionary victory soon on the wave of this concerted anti-government drive, movement cadres in the province were convinced that "the main goal now is to topple the Marcos dictatorship," as one of them said. Anti-planter militancy was toned down in that period.

Educated activists of middle-class background were tasked to address overseers on an equal footing, discuss the financial problems of their respective planters, and stress that planters, too, were exploited, by sugar mill owners, the government sugar trade monopoly, and the United States. They evoked the image of interdependence rather than antagonism between planter, overseer, and workers, and called for a concerted effort to solve the problems of the country. Implemented at least in the north-central part of the province, this strategy was successful in facilitating and expanding worker organization by coopting local management.

In Hda. Milagros, local management was organized at a time when NPA control was already fully established in the hacienda. The overseer, foremen, and drivers who had kept aloof of the *hublag* had been socially and politically marginalized. The association of local management in the hacienda lessened worker-management frictions and helped reinsert the *empleados* into hacienda social life. Though the *empleados* considered their association part of the *hublag*, they were not too reluctant to join. Some pointed at the increasing respectability of the movement at that time, as they interpreted the growing support by members of the middle-class and elite for the province-wide left-wing campaign against Marcos as support for the *hublag*. One foreman said, "if even planters and lawyers are joining, then why shouldn't I?" But activists in the hacienda also exerted pressure, and one foreman said he joined to avoid being ostracized.

---

[75] After Rafael's demotion, the position of overseer was occupied by several outsiders and local workers in succession. The high turnover was partly due to the effective organization of the workers, whose collective complaints about various overseers were heeded by the planter. As a result, the successive overseers had a rather weak power base in the hacienda. Both locals and outsiders, moreover, lacked a (large) local kinship network.

BECOMING PART OF THE NPA ORGANIZATION: TASKS AND TARGETS

As an increasing number of workers of Milagros participated in the political institution of the NPA, they became part of a top-down command structure, responsible for executing party directives and collecting local contributions for the movement. This subjected them to a wholly new incentive and sanctioning structure and produced new short-term interests. Besides other considerations and convictions, the incentives provided by the NPA organization itself became important in motivating their participation. Moreover, as these workers acquired responsibilities within the organization, their commitment to the movement increased. A key word here is "tasks/obligations" (*hilikoton*), which people in the hacienda used over and over when talking about their involvement in the movement.

The process of institutionalization took place as the leaders of the hacienda-based mass organizations were brought together in an organizing committee and later into a party branch, which had a direct link to the regionwide CPP-NPA organization. When the party branch was in place, the following part-time positions were held by workers in the hacienda: secretary of the party branch; chairpersons of the organizations of mothers, fathers, and youth; officials responsible for ideological work, simple medical services, collecting the monthly contributions in cash and rice as well as emergency contributions, gathering intelligence information, and providing security. Each of these officials had his or her own personnel, for instance, people who went house to house to collect the taxes in cash and rice, eavesdroppers, paramedics, unarmed militiamen, and couriers. Women did work having to do with finances, medical services, and information gathering; men were local militia-members and couriers; both women and men did organizing work. In many households in the hacienda, at least one member had some task or another, from trivial to time-consuming and influential. All the while, most of these part-timers still worked as laborers in the canefields.

Two things struck me when I talked with workers who held responsible positions in the hacienda-based NPA apparatus. First, their language was thoroughly institutional. Their work evolved around "tasks," "targets," "activity plans," "assessments" (they used the English terms). Their daily worries were those of any member of an institution: doing their tasks well and avoiding a bad record. Second, they tended to speak in the passive voice. They often used expressions such as, "I was called by higher officials," "I was given the task of . . . " They spoke as agents of an institution, executing directives handed down from above.

And indeed they were. They were now doing tasks that were not (only) in the immediate interest of themselves and their fellow workers in the hacienda, but in the interest of the wider institution. They were asked to secure the contributions expected of each hacienda household: a small can of rice and two pesos a month for the full-time cadres and guerrilla fighters, participation in at least the first basic seminar of the NPA, participation in workers' collective actions in the hacienda, and regular participation in rallies in Bacolod City by at least one member of the household, in particular the rally at Labor Day. Besides, they helped provide courier services, intelligence information, food and shelter for mobile activists and guerrillas, and other services.

They usually did not volunteer for these positions, but were asked by higher-ups within the hacienda, or by outside activists, often at the closing of a seminar they attended. Some were very interested, others were ashamed to refuse, still others thought they might be considered anti-movement if they turned down the request. They tended to identify with the interests of the organization once they were made responsible for a task, however small, as is common in any organization. Party-branch members would even ask some reluctant supporters to carry out tasks in order to weaken their resistance.

Once given a task, what motivated workers to carry it out, to "move" so to speak, was not only their conviction that the NPA defended their interests and, in many cases, a belief in the wider aims of the movement. They were also prompted by the activity plans and assessments. All people in the organization, down to the members of the party branch, operated on the basis of activity plans—transmitted by higher-ups and elaborated by the responsible collectives at each level—that stated the tasks and targets of each activist within a certain period of time. The head of the party branch would receive, for instance, the target to mobilize thirty workers for the Labor Day rally in the city, and his activity plan included house-to-house visits to request people to attend.

Everyone was accountable to his or her direct superiors. Members of the party branch had to attend weekly or monthly assessment meetings in which a member of the section party committee checked targets against actual performance. People who fell short of their target needed to explain at length why they did so, which pinpointed obstacles to mobilization but also pressured the particular activist to do a better job next time. Many activists I talked to found the assessments a nuisance, in particular the lengthy questionings when they fell short of their targets, which certainly served as a powerful sanction. A good performance, on the other hand, led to a good record, personal satisfaction, and opportunities for upward mobility within the organization.

Workers were interested to hold responsible positions and learn new skills, something their life as hacienda workers rarely offered. What they valued most was gaining a sense of effective agency, of being able to change their lives through systematic analysis and planned action. This carried over into their daily lives: much more than during my first stay in the hacienda, I heard people tackle a problem head-on once it was mentioned, analyze it point by point, and weigh various types of solutions.

This sense of personal achievement and collective efficacy was fostered by a training in self-restraint, foresight, cooperation, and the making of short-term sacrifices for future benefits. Through "criticism and self-criticism" sessions (referred to by its acronym, CSC), party-branch members were trained to increase their ability to control their impulses and analyze objectively. These sessions were only gradually introduced in the hacienda because, as a mobilizer said, the workers were rather "emotional": some were "arrogant," others got angry when people did not accept their point. A premium was placed on the individual learning process ("the person who does not want to be taught, does not want to progress") in the service of the larger struggle. Though the local activists hardly reached the ideal behavior propagated, they certainly made an effort to move in that direction. Also in their personal and family lives workers showed a greater interest in planning ahead and making sacrifices for future benefits. Some pointed to the high rate of family planning in the hacienda and to the many worker families that sacrifice to send one or two children through high school, and compared this situation favorably with that in a neighboring hacienda where workers had been mobilized less intensively and where workers, in their view, "just make babies, drink and gamble, without thinking about the future."

GOING UNDERGROUND

The step towards full-time work in the movement as a mobile activist was a major step towards, what McAdam calls, "high-risk activism."[76] It involved a high threshold. It yielded no (material) benefits to the people involved nor to their families, but instead demanded severe sacrifices. Then why did people move in and stay in? Race notes, for the revolutionary movement in Vietnam, that the opportunity to gain access to positions of status and power provided a strong incentive to poor village youths.[77] Others argue, concerning the NPA, that the personal experience of a severe injustice, such as landgrabbing or military abuse, convinced people to take this ultimate step.[78] In the case of Milagros other incentives were relevant as well, which may be uncovered by a more sequential analysis, with an eye for the small-group settings in which recruitment took place.

Some thirteen teenagers and two married men left the hacienda to become full-timers, each carrying a knapsack with some clothes and a blanket, and stepped into lives of fully illegal work. This group included young single women who were asked to become organizers, financial officers, and medical cadres linked to guerrilla squads, and young men who were recruited as organizers, guerrilla fighters, members of assassination squads, and operators of radio handsets, deployed throughout the province. Engaged in illegal work, they were given an alias and were assigned outside their home area to avoid being recognized.

What moved them in? "I saw that the system was rotten and that even with hard work we remain poor, and I wanted to change it," a former cadre said when asked why he became a full-timer. Others mentioned "to change the social system in the Philippines," or "to serve the people." Though sounding like exemplary answers expected of cadres, the youths' belief in the righteousness and aims of the struggle, and in their own sense of mission, appeared sincere enough. These convictions were, in many cases, not the direct result of an injustice they or their families had suffered, but were developed in the course of their participation in the mobilizing organizations in the hacienda, in which other incentives were at work as well. [79]

First, they had already followed a "career" in the movement as part-time activists, which eased the way. Most had started in the cultural group, then worked as part-time youth organizers and finance officers (young women) and organizers and local militia members (young men), which created a first identification with the movement and a genuine interest in its goals. Taking up these tasks, they became part of the network of local hacienda-based activists and developed new loyalties towards this group. On a practical level, they developed familiarity with their tasks,

---

[76] Doug McAdam, "Recruitment to High-Risk Activism, pp. 64–90.

[77] Race, *War Comes to Long An*, 174.

[78] Porter, "The Politics of Counterinsurgency," p. 15.

[79] In contrast to people from Milagros, two married men who lived elsewhere when they became full-timers (but who presently live in Milagros) mentioned repression as an important reason. One was a union organizer suspected by the military of NPA activities, the other had done part-time work for the NPA which had been exposed to the authorities. They went underground to avoid being "salvaged" (summarily killed) by the military.

and most continued in the same line of work when they became full-timers: for instance, part-time organizers became full-time members of mobile Propaganda Organizing Teams, militia members became guerrilla fighters,.

Second, they were pulled in through persistent requests by their superiors, who were themselves driven by activity plans that called for more recruits. These superiors were, for instance, party-branch members or former overseer Rafael— relatives or otherwise thoroughly familiar figures in the hacienda, whose NPA-backed authority the recruits had come to respect. They were always on the look-out for new recruits, supervising youths who were doing part-time tasks, assessing them for their willingness and capability to become full-timers. A valued quality was the ability to explain and persuade well, crucial for any activist, and youths who had "a slow brain" or "a limitation of the brain" (*limitasyon sa otok*), as locals called it, were not selected. Nor were young men who suffered from a "gunpowder brain" (*otok pulbura*), that is, who were only interested in battle and not in the political work that carried the armed struggle.

Third, recruitment took place in a web of peer group and kinship ties that produced added incentives and pressures. For instance, three childhood friends entered the cultural group together, became local militia-members, and jointly decided to become full-timers after they had been invited to do so. In several families, two or three children became full-timers, one convincing the other. Party-branch members (female and male), as well as cadre Rafael, often concentrated on close relatives in their recruitment work, and former cadres would recount, for instance, that they were "recruited by my aunt" or by their relative Rafael.

Attracted, too, by adventure, some appeared hardly aware of the personal risks involved when they decided to go full-time; this was particularly true of the most youthful activists.

Those who were fully aware of the risks were their parents. And parents had much to lose—a child and a breadwinner—whereas the NPA had little to offer in return—no salary and only an occasional small allowance for the full-timers themselves. Worker families depended heavily on the wage income of teenaged daughters and sons just to make ends meet or to cover the schooling costs of younger children. Some teenagers (girls and boys) had followed several years of high school thanks to the financial sacrifice of their families, and the parents had high hopes their child would obtain a better paid job and help his or her siblings in turn. Fearing for the safety of their son or daughter, anxious about the loss of a breadwinner, and seeing their hopes for family improvement along the educational route dashed, many parents were adamantly opposed to yielding their children to the *hublag*, even those parents who were themselves active in the movement. A teenager's decision to become a full-timer, then, usually entailed struggle and conflict within the family.

The NPA dealt with parent opposition by seriously and solemnly asking parents permission, and focusing on the moral value of the sacrifice. High-placed activists were responsible for this task, and it was former overseer Rafael, in his position as section-committee secretary, who persuaded many parents of Milagros to let their children go. He would ask them: "Do you accept that your child, in the course of his life, will be oppressed by the rich, just like you have been?" He argued that the only way to give their children and grandchildren a truly brighter future (a prime cultural value) was to let the activist child join the struggle, thus recasting familial sacrifice and loss as contributions to future family improvement.

Parents who asked about death benefits or allowances in case their child would perish were answered that the organization had no material assistance to offer since "it is the movement of the poor and the oppressed," but "if he dies, the most important is that he has served the people: he will be like a hero," and the *masa* in the hacienda would stand by the bereaved family. Some parents were not convinced, but the face-to-face encounter with Rafael or other authoritative activists pressured them to tone down their opposition. Whatever their sentiments, they could not force their children to stay. Many youths left against their parents' will.

Once they were in, these new full-timers faced serious disincentives: hardships, poverty, feelings of shame because they had to depend on the meager food supply of hacienda workers and poor villagers in their areas of operation. The few who were married and had a wife and children in the hacienda had a particularly hard time. When I asked one of them what his positive experiences were as an organizer in the extremely poor uplands of the municipality, he said, "none; my head was always reeling from anxiety—whether I was in my area, or taking part in the assessments, or home for a visit and confronted with my family's lack of income."

What kept them "moving" despite these disincentives was, for one, their identification with the movement and its wider goals. Since they lived apart from their families, their daily sense of self-worth was closely linked to the success of the movement and their own efforts to contribute to it. Some women who had been full-time organizers elsewhere, for instance, told me how happy and proud they were when they were able to mobilize large numbers of people for a rally in the city or when they had successfully guided workers in staging collective actions against planters. Activity plans and assessments provided added incentives, as did supervision by superiors, and opportunities to rise in the hierarchy. Moreover, the full-timers established new ties of loyalty that mediated their loyalty to the movement. All full-timers were part of a "collective," a group of some five to eight people who shared the same work (e.g. organizing) within a designated area. They came together for task assignments, assessments, and criticism/self-criticism sessions, as well as for informal gatherings. This collective became the activists' new peer group. Within this group, social pressures were at work to perform well as an activist; bad performance reflected on the other members of the group. If one member would quit, the other members would be "ashamed towards the masses that one of them was no longer serving the people," as one said. As they were redeployed and visited other areas for seminars and assessments, their network of contacts within the movement expanded, and their sense of loyalty to the larger movement increased. "We share a bloodline with the organization," some former full-timers said, expressing a sense of connectedness and loyalty.

Eventually, many gained a new, activist identity geared to "service to the people," helped along by criticism/self-criticism sessions that condemned *personal enteres* (personal interests) and that emphasized service to the *masa* and contribution to the "struggle" (*paghimakas*) as their main purpose in life. There were temptations, as life in the movement provided opportunities, despite controls, for embezzlement of funds and illicit love affairs, in particular among members of the same collective. Such transgressions were not uncommon in the movement; those responsible would either flee the area or succumb to "disciplinary actions," mainly demotion or ouster from the movement.[80] A full-time organizer from Milagros, for instance, with a family in another hacienda, ran off to Mindanao with a female comrade.

The cost of "exit"[81] was a disincentive to drop out, but was not so high as to force full-timers to stay in. Those who moved out lost their claims to their achieved positions and, upon re-entering, would have to start at a much lower rank. Dropping out could also be dangerous: returning to one's home area could lead to arrest or worse. But the organization did not severely condemn those who moved out, just lay low, and returned to their families or moved to the city. This type of moving out was called "to rest" (*magpahuway*), a euphemism that signaled that the people in question had not lost their loyalty to the movement and might re-enter anytime. A main worry of the organization was, of course, that people who moved out would leak information to the authorities, but it dealt with this problem not by severely sanctioning those who had left active duty, but by monitoring them.

MONITORING AND CONTROL: THE USE OF COERCION

A small-scale community is a favorable setting for the monitoring and sanctioning of individual behavior (through gossip, community meetings, and public sanctions, for instance), and thus for inducing the participation of all in collective action.[82] Community sanctioning, then, may serve as a powerful tool for activists to gain support or compliance. I concentrate on negative sanctions here.

In pre-NPA times, local management and the overseer's kin, backed by the planter, formed the main sanctioning force in the hacienda. They used, for instance, malicious gossip, veiled threats, and an occasional anonymous letter with warnings to discourage workers from associating with the progressive nuns in town. As the balance of power in the hacienda changed, a core of local NPA activists formed the new community sanctioning force, backed up by the coercive powers of the NPA.

The mobilization strategy of the NPA calls for the support or compliance of all members of a community, partly inspired by the illegality of the enterprise. Once there is a core of active NPA supporters and a large group of interested-to-neutral supporters, NPA activists start to pressure unwilling community members into compliance. Coercion was used late in the mobilization process in Hda. Milagros, possibly because NPA influence in the area was still weak at the time mobilization started.

NPA activists institutionalized a system of monitoring and sanctioning in Milagros that encouraged workers to police their own ranks, but whose effectiveness ultimately depended on the NPA's punitive powers. The rules were simple. What made a person suspect was his unwillingness to contribute to the movement. Relevant here were the basic contributions expected of all hacienda members (or their households): the monthly portion of rice and cash for the guerrillas,

---

[80] Similar frictions regarding a movement's code of conduct have been discussed, for Huk guerrillas in Central Luzon in the 1950s, by Jeff Goodwin. See Jeff Goodwin, "The Libidinal Constitution of Social Movements: The Case of the Huk Rebellion," Paper presented at the 1992 Annual Meetings of the American Sociological Association, Pittsburgh, PA, August 1992.

[81] Albert O. Hirschman, *Exit, Voice, and Loyalty: Response to Decline in Firms, Organizations, and States* (Cambridge: Harvard University Press, 1970).

[82] Cf. Taylor, "Rationality and Revolutionary Collective Action," p. 67, and Michael Hechter, "The Attainment of Solidarity in Intentional Communities," *Rationality and Society* 2 (1990): 142–155.

participation in at least the first seminar of the NPA, and participation in city rallies and in hacienda-based labor actions. Another "contribution" expected of everyone was silence about the NPA vis-à-vis outsiders. These contributions, most of which could be easily checked, functioned as yardsticks of people's loyalty to the movement. As the NPA established control, unwillingness to give in to requests to attend a rally or participate in a seminar was considered an act of resistance.

Several families in the hacienda, or one of the spouses in certain families, were publicly known to be unwilling supporters. They were old-timers in the hacienda, workers and a driver. Personal loyalty to the planter, fear of the risks of collective action and NPA support, lack of confidence in the NPA, social isolation, and an unwillingness to go along with the rest, were among the reasons for their reluctance. Some openly resisted the activities of organizers in the early period of mobilization. An old widowed worker, for instance, used to argue with activists, refused to accept their message, and was tagged by local activists as someone who "always thinks he knows better." As the NPA established institutional control, vocal resistance was curtailed and reluctant supporters tried, instead, to disengage from their institutionalized obligations.[83]

People unwilling to contribute were branded *backward* by activists (using the English term). Considered potential informers for the authorities, they were socially marginalized, isolated from the NPA core group, and not informed, for instance, about impending military operations in the area. They were monitored by fellow workers who were tasked to "collect data" (*kuha datus*), not only about trespassing outsiders such as military men, police, and itinerant vendors, but also about locals. The hacienda monitoring force consisted of some fifteen people, primarily women and girls operating under the party branch, who were simply alert while going about their daily chores. They also tried to check whether "very talkative" people (mainly women) provided information to outsiders, and suspected culprits were subjected to thorough interrogations by party-branch members and an outside activist.

When persuasive talks by activists did not induce compliance, threats followed. The threats were not made by local or outside activists (tasked to persuade), but by mobile teams of guerrillas or snipers with whom the activists coordinated. The 'suspects' were given several so-called *warnings* through intimidating home visits by these heavily armed men, and knew they might be killed after the third time if they failed to heed the message. "There are no prisons in the NPA," as one activist said. The threats were effective: people of Milagros were well aware of NPA liquidations of suspected informers or abusive overseers in the area, though none of their own rank fell victim.

How people experienced the punitive power of the NPA depended, quite obviously, on their position vis-à-vis the organization. As part of the apparatus, responsible for tasks in the hacienda-based organization, local activists approved of coercion to make everyone contribute his or her share: the rules were clear and contributions not too burdensome, so people who received a *warning* were themselves to blame. Unwilling supporters, in contrast, felt threatened. They participated in city rallies in order to "avoid a bad record," as one of them explained. They were cautious in what they said when local activists were around. Coercion prompted many of their contributions. To the large category of more or less

---

[83] Cf. F. G. Bailey, *The Kingdom of Individuals: An Essay on Self-Respect and Social Obligation* (Ithaca: Cornell University Press, 1993), pp. 7–17, about disengagement within collectivities.

sympathetic supporters, the possibility of coercion was probably always at the back of their minds when they received requests for contributions once the NPA began to exert control, but this was combined with other considerations and incentives.

With monitoring in the hands of community members, as well as the ability to request punitive action, one might expect petty jealousies and animosities—the nastier side of community life—to play a role in these sanctioning activities. To avoid this, the NPA had made the section committee, and not the local party branch, responsible for decisions about punitive actions, and required local checks on incriminating information. In Milagros, for instance, several workers had tagged personal enemies as informers but activists dismissed the accusations. A woman whose younger brother was a guerrilla did succeed occasionally in threatening her personal opponents with *warning* visits by members of her brother's squad.

NPA HEGEMONY IN THE HACIENDA

By the mid-1980s, a new power group had emerged in the hacienda: the workers (women and men) who had made active use of the opportunities offered them in the course of their mobilization. They eventually formed the party branch, backed by the organizational and coercive powers of the wider NPA organization. Social boundaries in the community were redrawn as the balance of power changed. The members of the party branch formed the center of local power and the center of social life. Linked to them were the workers who had some tasks in the local organization. Further to the margins were the families who only provided the basic contributions, the *masa*. At the margins were unwilling supporters, the *backward* people. Local management was marginalized as well, up to the time when they were organized into their own association. The hacienda was, in appearance, still fully controlled by the planter, with laborers drudging in the fields and collecting their wages on weekly pay-days. In reality, worker-activists regulated community life to a large extent, and controlled the allocation of hacienda work among the laborers, which was formally still the responsibility of the overseer.

Eventually, the party branch headed an institutional structure (extracting contributions for the NPA) that appeared to be self-perpetuating: local personnel carried out the state-like functions of taxation, policing, intelligence, and justice (settling local quarrels). Unwilling supporters were coerced into compliance. The youth group formed a pool of interested recruits for full-time activism. Commitment to the organization was perpetuated by, among others, regular gains in workers' bargaining power and benefits vis-à-vis the planter, and by workers' responsibilities within the local institutional structure. Regular "cultural shows" by the youth group, participation in rallies and occasional seminars, informal singing of revolutionary songs, and "mass meetings" attended by most workers each Sunday, provided ideological reminders and made the ideology of the movement into a part of local commonsense. Activists were successful in neutralizing competing mobilizers: they monopolized workers' contacts with the planter and shielded the workers off from patronage politicians by enforcing a boycott of the 1984 congressional elections and the 1986 presidential elections (with the argument, for instance, that "whoever wins, it won't make any difference to our situation"). Such conditions are crucial to the ongoing support for any social movement. They involve the establishment of a "routine flow of resources into the organization" and an "ongoing production and maintenance of meaning and ideology" that keeps members committed to the movement's collective action frame.[84]

A conducive environment, by the mid-1980s, made this ongoing support for the NPA possible. First, risks were relatively low at that time, since planters opted for accommodation with the NPA, and the military concentrated on NPA bases in the uplands. Though the authorities did resort to killings and torture in the lowlands, people in Hda. Milagros were, at that time, not yet personally affected.

Second, benefits were relatively high, in particular in the form of gains vis-à-vis the planter. Workers reached a strong bargaining position; their protests helped to prevent mechanization of cultivation tasks in the early 1980s, and during the sugar crisis of the mid-1980s they obtained from the planter access to farmlots that somewhat cushioned the drop in family income. Partly responsible for these gains were the province-wide expansion of union influence and the growing coercive powers of the NPA. Moreover, the NPA was "rich" at that time, as some people said, thanks to income from taxes and support from members of the middle and upper classes in the province, and so it could temporarily provide some allowances to the families of married cadres.[85]

There was, moreover, a strong link between the local party branch and the higher levels of the organization, in particular through former overseer and high-ranking cadre Rafael. Finally, workers thought the NPA was on the winning side. As the broad anti-Marcos alliance, which had a strong left-wing component, staged ever larger demonstrations in the provincial capital, workers experienced this as a sign of increasing support for the *hublag*. The NPA persistently expanded its provincial mass base in this period. When I visited the hacienda briefly in 1985, there was a slightly euphoric feeling among the workers that "liberation" was soon to come.

DECLINE AND SPLIT IN LOYALTIES

The installment of a democratic regime in 1986 under President Corazon Aquino did not, in itself, weaken support for the NPA in the hacienda region. In 1986–88, support among hacienda workers even peaked in the whole north-central part of the province, according to several activists. Since activists presented left-wing electoral candidates as supportive of the *hublag*, people of Milagros perceived electoral politics as potentially supportive of, rather than opposed to, the NPA struggle. But support for the NPA did start to decline in Milagros in 1988. Apparently, the immediate causes were (1) the intensification of counterinsurgency activities that started in 1987 and hit Milagros hard in 1988, disrupting the mobilization routine, increasing risks of NPA support, and weakening the links with the NPA apparatus; (2) the split among regional NPA leaders in 1987, with "moderates" resigning from the movement and turning against the NPA; former overseer and NPA district secretary Rafael shared the viewpoints of the moderates and, after his capture in 1988, became a

---

[84] McAdam et al., "Social Movements," pp. 724–25.

[85] Other benefits to workers of Milagros included funds for livelihood projects, in particular inputs for workers' farmlots and a poultry project. These funds were part of the flow of international aid to Negros Occidental set in motion by the sugar crisis of the mid-1980s and the subsequent international media focus on the plight of Negros sugar workers, in the context of the broader international attention for the political and economic crisis under the Marcos government. The union and newly created left-wing NGOs channeled part of this flow to left-wing constituencies.

countermobilizer in the service of the military; (3) retention of benefits gained by the union, at least in Hda. Milagros, which convinced some *masa* that they could do without the NPA[86]; and (4) some negative experiences of workers with continued NPA control. The nationwide split of the CPP-NPA in 1992–93 further reduced people's willingness to provide support.

Context of the first two developments was the expanded maneuvering space provided by the Aquino administration to elites, military, and initially to the political left as well. Planters and military in Negros Occidental joined in a concerted drive to counter the expanding influence and violent operations of the NPA that included hacienda raids, raids of small army camps, attacks of police precincts and town halls, and assassinations of chiefs of police. On the side of the NPA, the widened democratic space under President Aquino led to strategy debates, with so-called "moderates" in the Negros regional party leadership propagating more participation in the legal political sphere. When after the collapse of the cease-fire agreement in February 1987, the national NPA leadership apparently opted for a break with politically moderate allies and an intensification of military actions and urban assassination campaigns, moderates in the Negros leadership resigned, were granted amnesty by the government, and became vocal countermobilizers when one among their ranks was killed by the NPA.[87] A prominent member of this so-called "splittist group" was Nemesio Demafelis, former secretary of the regional executive committee of the Negros Regional Party Committee. Former overseer Rafael had been a close subordinate of Demafelis, and Rafael's capture and surrender came in the wake of the resignation of his former superior.

By Rafael's own account, the NPA's policy shift in 1987 signaled that the immediate interests of the lower classes were sacrificed to the interests of the armed struggle. As district secretary, he was ordered to cut ties with non-government organizations (NGOs) that were not sympathetic to the NPA (but whose assistance he had helped to broker for livelihood projects of hacienda workers) and was told to disband the organization of local hacienda management (which had gained concessions from planters through peaceful negotiations). He protested that "food" was sacrificed for "arms," but his protests were overruled. In 1988, his resentment against NPA leadership further increased as he was denied financial aid to cure his severe tuberculosis. He was captured while in Bacolod City for medical help. In military custody, cut off from NPA contacts, Rafael was confronted with several military men with nationalist reformist leanings, and he saw common ground in their populism, nationalism, and anti-landlord attitude. Out of conviction or force of circumstance, he came to believe that the government (generous with livelihood funds for the rural poor at that time, partly in the context of counterinsurgency) offered the better solution to rural poverty. In 1989 he became a countermobilizer within one of the army's Special Operations Teams (SOT) stationed close to Hda. Milagros, and a regular speaker at mass surrenders staged by the SOT throughout the area.

---

[86] Unlike developments elsewhere, the union chapter in Milagros preserved its influence and the planter continued to honor the CBA. In neighboring haciendas, planters used the "mass surrenders" in 1990 to force their workers to switch from the alleged NPA-friendly union to a company union.

[87] *The Visayan Daily Star* (Bacolod City), March 17, 1988. Also Benjamin Pimentel, Jr., "The Outlaws of Negros," report in three parts: *Midweek*, July 27, 1988, August 24, 1988, September 14, 1988.

In Milagros, the intensification of counterinsurgency increased the risks of supporting the NPA, in particular when the Philippine Constabulary (PC) and its paramilitary PC Forward Command were responsible for counterinsurgency in the area in 1987–88 and used terror against suspected NPA cadres. Four men of Hda. Milagros were killed by military or paramilitary groups. Three were guerrillas or snipers, one was a courier. One of them, a young man, was mercilessly killed right inside the hacienda in 1988 (before Rafael's capture), and his torture and murder in public view terrified the population. The victims' families received emotional and material help through a large support network in the hacienda, embedded within the *hublag*. But the hacienda killing signified to the people of Milagros that the military were well-informed, and people were fearful who would be next. This traumatic event had far-reaching effects.

For instance, links with the NPA hierarchy weakened as outside activists avoided the hacienda because of the risks, and as non-activist workers (who belonged to *masa*) became less willing to support the organization and its cadres out of fear. For safety reasons, ideological seminars in the hacienda ceased, and the youth group was disbanded when it came under police surveillance. Workers' participation in rallies in Bacolod City declined as the police and PC began to pick up suspected NPAs at rallies, some of whom (from other haciendas) were tortured and killed. Thus, the "routine flow" of contributions to the NPA was disrupted, as well as the regular ideological work through seminars, rallies, and cultural shows. Disrupted, too, was the routine of activity plans, meetings, and assessments of the hacienda party branch and supporting activists—hitherto enforced by higher NPA cadres—which had helped to encourage local activists to keep on "moving."

Countermobilizers subsequently entered the community. An army Special Operations Team that settled in the detachment near Milagros in 1989 took over counterinsurgency work from the PC in the area and introduced a persuasive, relatively non-violent community-based approach. Activists in Milagros were made to participate in a mass surrender of suspected NPA activists and supporters in the municipality, which included a three-day, live-in "seminar" in town on "the evils of communism" and the alleged good intentions of the government, and a collective pledge of loyalty to the Philippine Republic. Though some later said they were not impressed by this effort at re-legitimization of state authority and remained committed to the *hublag*, the accommodating behavior of these military, and the government's offer of livelihood funds, created some openings towards military and government. Moreover, after the "surrender," patronage politicians re-entered the place during election campaigns.[88] Even though most people of Milagros saw no contradiction between supporting the *hublag* and participating in electoral politics, some links with prominent local patronage politicians were (re)established which may have demobilizing effects in the long run. Furthermore, the Roman Catholic Church in town (in conservative hands since the departure of the left-wing priest and nuns in the late 1970s and early 1980s) was led since the late 1980s by a priest who made strong appeals to his parishioners to return to the old faith by means of taped prayers and religious songs broadcast from a loudspeaker attached to the church's belfry, which carried far and wide over the canefields. From Hda. Milagros, the

---

[88] Rosanne Rutten, "Courting the Workers' Vote in a Hacienda Region: Rhetoric and Response in the 1992 Philippine Elections," *Pilipinas* 22 (1994): 1–34.

Church attracted in particular women who sought solace for personal worries and distress, including wives and mothers of local activists and full-timers.

Most influential as a demobilizer was Rafael. Though people feared he might inform on them (which he himself denied), they valued the protection he provided against military violence by mediating between Milagros residents and the army's SOT, and by guaranteeing proper treatment of captured cadres from Milagros. Close relatives of Rafael quit their positions as local activists. Demotivated by Rafael, they were also distrusted by fellow activists as potential informers for the military. Several anxious parents of full-time NPA cadres moved closer to Rafael; he could have their children's names removed from the military order of battle if they would persuade them to leave the movement. Members of the *masa*, who were not part of the NPA apparatus, valued "peace" above all, abhorred "trouble" (*gamo*, violence from both sides), and appreciated accommodation with the military through Rafael. Several reluctant NPA supporters, pressured into support in the days of NPA control, eventually felt they had enough backing to distance themselves from the NPA. Though Rafael helped form a paramilitary group (CAFGU) of former comrades who had followed him out of the movement, sentiment and organization in Milagros was still such that no-one else from the hacienda joined his or any other paramilitary group, unlike several former NPA cadres in nearby haciendas. Based at the military detachment near Milagros, Rafael's group was linked to the army's SOT and was generally considered decent and non-abusive.

By 1992, the army's SOT had moved out (and so had Rafael, who settled in a detachment some ten kilometers distant), and a more aggressive military battalion and paramilitary team had taken its place. Meanwhile, NPA cadres had reestablished links with Milagros and mobile NPA guerrilla teams again frequented the place (under cover of the tall sugarcane) as part of a provincewide effort to recapture lost areas. NPA presence backed up the power of local activists, but also increased people's fear of armed encounters.

Loyalties in the hacienda fragmented along the following lines: First, a core of full-timers and local activists remained committed to the *hublag* and its wider goals; but part of the *masa* began to credit only the union for the benefits of their improved labor conditions and bargaining power, and started to define the NPA as a potential source of "trouble," fearing military encounters in particular. One female worker muttered when referring to mobile guerrillas, "people who only roam around and ask others for food," and said she feared they would spend the night in her ramshackle house. Local activists worried that these workers were taking the union gains for granted and had lost sight of the need for the NPA's countervailing power. Rafael's close relatives formed a separate category among the *masa*, suspected by activists of having been "brainwashed" by Rafael.

Second, organizational problems common to any institution divided local activists. Workers who held positions of power in the hacienda "collective" (formed by local officials in the NPA apparatus) were suspected by fellow workers of favoritism and furthering personal interests. They left their posts with a grudge, tended to retreat from the NPA network, and, together with other workers, considered the new local officials unfit and not credible as local leaders. Few competent full-time organizers were available in 1992 who could mend such divisions; as experienced cadres were surrendering or simply laying low, the gap was filled with hastily trained newcomers who, in Milagros, commanded little respect and were unable to unite local activists and beef up the collective.

Most full-time cadres from Hda. Milagros left the movement when counterinsurgency intensified. They moved to Manila or Mindanao to escape capture, decided to lay low, or surrendered through mediation by Rafael. According to their own account, the increased risks, the decline of the movement province-wide, the unending hardships and receding prospect of victory, and the resignation of superiors of the "splittist group," lowered morale and commitment, whereas the pull of their families was strong. The amnesty program of the government indicated the opportunity of a safe exit. An added disincentive to carry on was demographic in nature: those who had entered the *hublag* as teenagers, had married in the movement, and had placed their children under the care of others ("since the hublag takes precedence over the family"), yearned finally to live with their spouses and children and lead normal family lives.

Finally, some negative experiences of workers with NPA control diminished their trust in the *hublag*. Besides alleged mismanagement by local activists, these included the conflict-ridden experiment with communal farming. The collective had successfully claimed from the planter not only several hectares of hacienda land for family subsistence lots, but also some irrigated land for communal rice cultivation to be managed by the collective. Conflicts soon broke out about work remuneration. The system of an equal share for all was swiftly changed into remuneration by work points to solve the free-rider problem, but even then there were numerous protests about alleged unfair computations. This experience did not endear workers to collective production.

Though the NPA did not specify to the *masa* that it aimed for collective land ownership, it did profess in a general manner that everything would become *komun* (collective property), in the sense that everyone would share equally in the use of resources. The term *komun*, meant to capture the social equality the NPA stood for, and closely related to the term *komunismo*, thus got a negative connotation among Milagros workers when they gained some practical experience with it. As one female worker said in 1992: "Communism is bad because then everything is *komun*. Like with the farmlots that are *komunal*, that's already communist. When everything is *komun*, there's trouble (*gamo*). I don't agree with it." Another said with some amusement that the communal farmlot was meant to draw the community together but it had only torn it apart. Workers, including some local activists, told me that the land reform they hoped for was a distribution of land into family-owned plots, not communal property. Some expected collective land ownership under NPA rule, others said they were assured family lots. Both may have been right. Cadres envisioned first a distribution into family lots, and later communal ownership when people's "consciousness" would be ready for it.

The nationwide split of the CPP-NPA in 1992-93 did little to boost workers' confidence in the NPA. The split into the faction of CPP leader Jose Maria Sison (the "reaffirmists") and the faction against the line of Sison (the "rejectionists") materialized in Negros in 1993, when the Negros Regional Party Committee sided with rejectionists, and all people connected to the movement, down to village and hacienda level, were expected to take sides.[89] Mass meetings were organized, by

---

[89] For cadres in Negros Occidental whom I talked with early in 1995, the "controversy" concerned explanations for the decline of the NPA and policies to remedy it, and the leadership style of Sison. Reaffirmists blamed the decline in Negros in large part on the past policy (1987–92) of aggressive actions, including confiscations of hacienda property (rice provisions, livestock, fertilizer, radio handsets), hold-up of payroll clerks, and killing of

district, for full-time cadres and local part-time activists, in which the so-called "controversy" was explained, hefty position papers from both sides were discussed, and the participants asked to make their own decisions. The anti-Sison faction in Negros claimed a majority following in Negros, in particular among guerrilla forces, but it was weakened as its top leaders were captured in January 1994.[90]The two factions staked out their own territories on the island. The split was carried over to legal mass organizations, which became visible with separate demonstrations in Bacolod City on Human Rights Day and Labor Day, and during the *Welga ng Bayan* (people's strike) on February 9, 1994 against the oil price hike.[91]The left-wing union NFSW sympathized with the pro-Sison faction, but part of its staff split off and founded a rival union more sympathetic to the anti-Sison side, apparently taking a number of organizers and organized haciendas with them in the north and south of the province. Realignments were such that NFSW organizers were sometimes barred from their unionized areas by NPA guerrillas who belonged to the anti-Sison faction.

In Hda. Milagros, the split further alienated workers from the NPA. It confused the *masa*, who knew little of the inner-party conflict. Faced with a split in the union and some efforts at organization by its rival, most workers emphatically sided with the union that had supported them for more than ten years: "that's where our heart is," "it's through them that we got benefits." Local activists and former full-timers, on their part, were thoroughly discouraged, and even disgusted, by the split. They blamed top leaders and began to doubt the leadership and organization as such. A female activist said: "it's a problem of the higher-ups, I don't understand it," and added, "so I stopped doing tasks for the movement." A former high-ranking cadre deplored the split as "a controversy over theory and interpretation at the national level," and recounted with regret that after the long seminar on the conflict, the members of his collective of NPA fighters "began to distrust one other, and I feared I might be shot by one of my comrades," which prompted his exit from the movement. Though (former) activists of Milagros did take the controversial issues of strategy and leadership seriously, the organizational fragmentation of the *hublag* left them "unhitched" from the NPA organization, as one said.

---

policemen, which had invited planter repression and militarization in the countryside, though they admitted they had appreciated those actions at the time. They also deplored the rapid expansion of guerrilla forces at the expense of mass organizing and economic uplift, and agreed with Sison's call to return to the original strategy of a rural protracted people's war; after all, they said, Negros was still a "semi-feudal" society. Rejectionists argued that this original strategy was outdated because rural militarization had considerably narrowed the NPA's room for maneuver in the countryside, and because Negros had developed, they said, into a "semi-capitalist" society which required other forms of action. They called either for more emphasis on (urban) legal mass organizing, or, apparently, for a more insurrectionist stand. Moreover, they assailed Sison for having stifled broad policy discussions, and supported the call for a second Party Congress to discuss the differences. Cf. also Jaime Espina, "Inside the Negros Rectification Movement: Special Report," *Today News-Views* (Bacolod City), April 19, 20, 21, 25, 27, 1994 and May 3, 7–8, 14–15, 1994. For an analysis of the decline of the NPA nationwide, see Walden Bello, "The Crisis of the Philippine Progressive Movement: A Preliminary Investigation," *Debate: Philippine Left Review* 4 (September 1992): 44–55.

[90]*AFP-Negros News and Features*, October 8, 1993, January 12, 1994, February 9, 1994. AFP is published by the 602CRT, 6CRG, CRSAFP, Headquarters, Armed Forces of the Philippines, Bacolod City, weekly from July 1987 to April 1994. Mimeographed.

[91] *Today News-Views* (Bacolod City), May 2, 1994.

Nevertheless, activists and former activists in the hacienda still expressed commitment to the aims of the *hublag*—changing the social system and government, and empowering the poor—even as they distanced themselves from NPA leadership and organization. They sustained this commitment through involvement in union and NGO networks (that also kept them informed on national issues that were rallying points of the political left) and informal contacts within and beyond the hacienda. Some former cadres envisaged an active role for themselves in the newly established Rebel Returnees Association in the municipality (an association formed in the context of the government's amnesty program), "to keep it on the right track of mass struggle," as one said. Several activists have taken steps to seek coverage of the hacienda by the government's Comprehensive Agrarian Reform Law, even though chances of success are limited. As their link with the NPA organization weakened, as the armed struggle became less and less viable, and as unions, NGOs, and local government agencies had gained some influence vis-à-vis local power holders, (former) activists in the hacienda have become all the more interested in legal forms of action.

A NOTE ON REPRESSION AND SUPPORT FOR THE NPA

Some studies on the NPA suggest a direct relation between repression (including repression of legal forms of claim-making), militarization, and military abuse on the one hand, and popular support for the revolutionary movement on the other, and argue that repression and abuse provoke support for the NPA.[92] Some assume a linear relationship, with popular support rising and falling depending on the intensity of repression and abuse.

The experience of Milagros shows a more complex relationship. It indicates variations in people's response to repression depending on the place, timing, targeting, and type of repression, as well as on people's involvement in supportive organizations that recast repression and military abuse as rallying points for activism.[93]

Repression did induce Church and union activists from Milagros—in the late 1970s when they were thwarted in their union activities in haciendas near Milagros—to support the armed struggle, helped along by NPA proselytizing that

---

[92] For instance, Kessler speaks of a "historical pattern of repression-rebellion-suppression" in the Philippines. See Richard J. Kessler, *Rebellion and Repression in the Philippines* (New Haven: Yale University Press, 1989), p. 140. Rosenberg says, "the rebels will continue to attract recruits as long as the poor rural majority are victimized by . . . military abuses," among other factors." See also David Rosenberg, "The Philippines," *Revolution and Political Change in the Third World*, Barry M. Schutz and Robert O. Slater, eds. (Boulder and London: Lynne Riener Publishers, 1990), p. 187. Hawes states, "the landless laborer or tenant who seeks piecemeal or peaceful reforms is almost immediately brought face-to-face with the repressive machinery of the state. Often, the average peasant or rural worker faces the choice of accepting his or her fate in an unequal and unjust situation or offering support to an armed revolutionary movement." Gary Hawes, "Theories of Peasant Revolution: A Critique and Contribution from the Philippines," *World Politics* 42 (1989–90): 297. See also Porter, "The Politics of Counterinsurgency," p. 22, and David Wurfel, *Filipino Politics: Development and Decay* (Quezon City: Ateneo de Manila University Press, 1988), p. 268.

[93] For a discussion of relevant literature on repression and protest along similar lines, with a case study on developments in Guatemala, see Charles D. Brockett, "A Protest Cycle Resolution of the Repression/Popular-Protest Paradox," *Repertoires and Cycles of Collective Action,* Mark Traugott, ed. (Durham, NC: Duke University Press, 1995).

presented armed struggle as a viable alternative. Not themselves victims of military abuse, they were deeply affected by the Church's protest campaigns against military abuses elsewhere in the province, campaigns that created empathy for distant victims and outrage against the government.

But when repression abated and opportunities for legal collective action expanded in the Milagros area around 1980–87, support for the NPA did not decline but, on the contrary, increased and peaked. A main reason was that opportunities for NPA mobilization were favorable: while repression remained a rallying point (repression elsewhere in the province, and the potential of repression locally), cadres could easily operate in the hacienda, workers' risks of supporting the NPA were low, benefits were high in the form of successful union actions backed by the NPA, and workers' confidence in NPA strength increased since a military backlash did not occur for some time. Moreover, workers viewed legal and NPA activities as mutually reinforcing.

Support in Milagros declined when militarization and military abuses intensified and hit the community itself. The first victims from Milagros were NPA activists, mostly full-timers, who were killed in places *outside* the hacienda when the hacienda was already fully organized by the NPA. Considered casualties of war, their killings confirmed anti-government feelings and did activate involvement in established NPA networks as workers provided emotional and financial support to the victims' families. But when a worker's son and cadre was killed *within* the hacienda, when workers harboring guerrillas risked "strafing" of their houses by military patrols, and as military surveillance in the hacienda increased—in short, as the community itself was targeted—the risks to family safety proved a strong disincentive for supporting the NPA. Moreover, the risks of detection deterred cadres from operating in the area.

Repression, then, may prompt activists and victims to support the NPA, and activists may learn, in turn, to accept the personal risks involved in NPA activism. But repression may also narrow the opportunities of mobilizers to solicit support, and may weaken people's willingness to provide such support when they fear retaliations against their own community and family.

CONCLUSION

With this sequential analysis of the rise and decline of support for the NPA in a hacienda community, I argue that workers' motives for supporting the NPA were affected by the mobilization process itself, and that their motives and aspirations changed in the process. Their support came about in the course of their interaction with mobilizers within a wider structure of political opportunities that allowed mobilizers room for maneuver and enabled mobilized workers to acquire new perspectives and gain some tangible social and economic improvements.

The image of rural communities making an alliance with a revolutionary movement to defend traditional rights, relying on indigenous solidarities and remaining relatively autonomous of the revolutionary organization, does not fit the experience of Hda. Milagros. Movement and community became intertwined: workers of Milagros became NPA activists themselves and thus part of the revolutionary organization. They began to claim new rights as defined by the NPA. Their mobilization produced (if only temporarily) new solidarities in the community. Worker-activists started to identify with the wider aims of the NPA, in particular, capturing state power and removing the landlord class. Moreover, the institutionalization of the NPA in the community changed the balance of power in favor of worker-activists who replaced local management as the new power group in the hacienda. I elaborate some of these developments below.

First, NPA activists did not just try to address the immediate problems and grievances of the workers. Rather, they redefined workers' interests, shifted the object of workers' grievances from the individual planter to an encompassing exploitative system, and outlined a course of action to end their exploitation. Moreover, they expanded the definition of workers' rights, moving from traditional rights to family subsistence (which had motivated earlier collective demands by workers) to rights to land and a life without oppression. In presenting this collective action frame, the activists could connect to previous ideological work by progressive clergy and a left-wing union in the hacienda. By linking the problems of workers to an exploitative system that they were helping to overthrow, activists could solicit from workers considerable contributions for the wider struggle of the NPA. Despite initial resistance by supervisory personnel and worker-relatives of the overseer, most workers eventually accepted the basic premises of the new frame, not in the least because it appeared to be true—collective actions against the planter, inspired by the exploitation frame, were successful—and widely shared, as shown by the large demonstrations in the provincial capital that people of Milagros joined.

Thus we cannot assume a clear-cut distinction between indigenous, self-generated views on justice and rights among poor rural populations and external, mainly urban views propagated by movement leadership, as some of the peasant-movement literature suggests. Instead, the case of Milagros shows that notions of rights among the rural poor may change as movement leaders inform local populations of new rights whose enforcement appears plausible, and as movement activism helps improve opportunities for making successful claims. External notions of rights may thus become "indigenized."

Second, the movement was gradually institutionalized in the hacienda through local "mass organizations" and eventually a party branch. Through these channels, workers began to connect their individual and family interests to the interests of the NPA—which mitigated the potential conflict between the two—and developed commitment to the movement in the process. Cadres and worker-activists promoted labor organization and labor actions whose successes the workers credited, in part, to the coercive powers of the NPA. In return, workers were willing (some more than others) to make the basic contributions to the NPA in rice and cash expected of "organized masses" (*masa*). Many hacienda teenagers were less concerned with problems of family subsistence and developed, instead, an initial commitment to the organization through the "cultural" youth group that appealed to their longing for peer-group company, entertainment, and purpose in life, and eventually to their ideal—generated in the process—of helping to create a just society for all.

Those workers who were incorporated in the NPA party branch and related committees (the local activists) began to operate, to a varying extent, in the interest of the wider organization and with wider aims in mind. Exposed to a system of incentives and sanctions common to any institution, with activity plans and assessments, they gradually identified with the NPA organization and operated as its local agents. Some eventually became full-time cadres. Because full-time activism demanded severe sacrifices, only a strong identification with the interests and aims of the organization, combined with institutional incentives and support by the cadres' peer groups, kept these activists motivated. Personal ties of kinship and friendship with mobilizers (often fellow workers) and the small-group settings in which each mobilizing act took place, contributed to workers' individual decisions to increase their involvement in the movement.

Finally, the balance of power in the hacienda profoundly changed as active NPA supporters and officials became the new local power group. Backed by the NPA organization and by fellow workers, they helped to pressure the planter into accommodation, neutralize local management, and coerce unwilling residents of the hacienda into compliance.

The recent decline of support for the NPA in Milagros can be seen in terms of a lessening of interactions between cadres and workers. The intensification of counterinsurgency since the late 1980s disrupted the mobilization routine, increased the risks for NPA supporters, weakened the community's links with the NPA apparatus, decreased the power of local activists, and diminished ideological work in the hacienda. The surrender and amnesty policy of the government as well as the successive splits in the regional leadership of the movement, led to an increase in surrenders and captures. Former NPA cadre Rafael became a countermobilizer in the service of the military and helped to undermine NPA hegemony in the hacienda. Some negative experiences with continued NPA control in the hacienda also weakened workers' confidence in the movement's leadership and policies. As NPA strength declined in the province and country as a whole (exacerbated by the party's split of 1993) and prospects of an NPA victory looked ever more dim, workers of Milagros lowered their aspirations. A core group of worker-activists who remained committed to the aims of the movement and involved in activist networks turned, more than before, to legal forms of action.

WHEN A REVOLUTION DEVOURS ITS CHILDREN BEFORE VICTORY: OPERASYON KAMPANYANG AHOS AND THE TRAGEDY OF MINDANAO COMMUNISM[1]

Patricio N. Abinales

INTRODUCTION

In July 1985, while top leaders of the Communist Party of the Philippines' (CPP) Mindanao Commission (Mindacom) were in Manila attending a Central Committee plenum to decide the next phase of the revolution, a caretaker group that remained in Mindanao was startled to receive reports from territorial committees that military agents had successfully infiltrated certain levels of the Party, its armed group, the New People's Army (NPA), and its united front organization, the National Democratic Front (NDF).[2] Deeply concerned that this would have serious repercussions on the Party, the group did not wait for Mindacom leaders to return. Instead, it ordered a prompt investigation and hunt for the spies inside these organizations.

The investigation was code-named Operasyon Kampanyang Ahos (Kahos), a metaphor inspired by the potency of garlic (*ahos* in Cebuano) in repelling evil spirits and *demonyos* (demons), which in Party parlance was how the military was commonly described.[3] Kahos began in the provinces of Misamis Oriental and Bukidnon but

---

[1] I wish to thank Donna Amoroso, Benedict Anderson, Coeli Barry, Vince Boudreau, Dominique Caouette, Anne Foster, Ben Kerklviet, Shawn McHale, Jose Eliseo Rocamora, Antoinette Raquiza, Saya Shiraishi, Takashi Shiraishi, John Sidel, Peter Zinnoman and two outside readers for their help, comments, criticisms and suggestions. This essay is for Ric Reyes, friend and mentor whose agony I deeply share.

[2] Mindanao is the second largest island in the Philippine archipelago, located south of Manila.

[3] "Pangkalahatang Pagbabalik-Aral sa mga Mahalagang Pangyayari at Pasya (1980 hanggang 1991)," *Rebolusyon: Theoretical Organ of the Communist Party of the Philippines*, January 1993 (Special edition), as translated and reprinted in *Debate: Philippine Left Review* 7 (August 1993): 53. Peasants and guerrillas refer to the military as *demonyo* (devil) or *asuwang* (vampire). The genealogy of the use of these terms dates as far back as World War II, when Japanese troops were alternately called "*Hapon*" or "*demonyo*." In the era of the NPA, cadres popularized the same phrases not only to bring back memories of a dark period, but also to underscore that the Philippine military and the Japanese, both interlopers in peasants' lives, are no different from each other.

quickly spread throughout Mindanao.[4] In its frenzied effort to "contain" and eliminate the problem, the caretaker group sanctioned the use of torture ("hard tactics") to
obtain confessions. It also approved the use of testimonies drawn from at least two
tortured suspects as evidence against other suspects.[5] A third directive was the most
fatal: political officers of basic party cells and of NPA platoons were given the power
to act as judge, jury and executioner. Suspects were not given the right to appeal to a
higher body, and those who "admitted" their "crimes" were promptly executed.[6]

What began then as a systematic investigation turned out to be a brutal affair.
The directives did not only cause panic and hysteria; they promptly transformed
Kahos into an out-of-control bloody Mindanao-wide investigation to ferret out and
eliminate suspected and real spies.[7] Stories of cadres and activists who were ordered
to go to the guerrilla zones "for consultation" and then did not return began to circu-
late within Mindanao. Unable to get a clear explanation from their leaders, many
cadres who received these notices fled from their areas after hearing of such stories;
others simply resigned their posts. The alleged formation of special "investigation
teams" sent from the countryside to as far as Cebu and Manila to pursue and mete
out the "appropriate punishment" to "traitors" and spies only aggravated fears
inside. One cadre painfully recalled what happened in the NPA camps all over
Mindanao where suspected spies were interrogated and eventually killed by their
interrogators:

> The arrested persons were herded into investigation camps, brutalized in a
> Kafkaesque manner by tormentors equally brutalized by their own brutality.
> Many of them perished by torture not by any formal act of a death sentence.
> But to be brought to those camps, stripped of their basic rights as human
> persons, and subjected to torture was already tantamount to a death penalty.[8]

---

[4] These two provinces, according to Arguelles, accounted for 70 percent of the fatalities. Paco
Arguelles, "KAHOS: A Soul Searching," *Human Rights Forum* 4, 1 (1994): 112.

[5] This directive was based on an earlier experience in 1982, when the CPP's Southern Tagalog
committee's proposal to use "the testimonies of at least two persons [as] sufficient to confirm
that one is a suspected military infiltrator" was approved by the Central Committee.
Arguelles, "KAHOS," p. 110.

[6] According to Arguelles this was based on a compromise reached by leaders who favored the
use of torture and outright execution, and others who argued for "the dignity of the human
person, irrespective of class and political differences, no matter how sharp." Mindacom
rejected the use of torture as policy but "allowed exemptions in cases where proof of betrayal
was solid and strong." As Arguelles noted, "Such a compromise was fatally flawed."
Arguelles, "KAHOS," p. 113.

[7] According to George Madlos, chief of the CPP's northeastern Mindanao regional committee
and alternate member of the party's central committee . . . presided over affairs at a time
(*AHOS* was implemented). He seems to have lost control of a number of units under his
command and his own capture suggested the existence of an informer within the ranks of the
Mindanao Military Commission." The panic spread. See Peter Sales, "The Once and Future
Insurgency in Northeastern Mindanao," *Mindanao: Land of Unfulfilled Promise*. Mark Turner, R.
J. May, and Lulu Respall Turner, eds. (Quezon City: New Day Publishers, 1992), p. 215.
Madlos was released in 1992 and promptly returned to the *maquis*. *Philippine Daily Inquirer*,
July 22, 1992, p. 7.

[8] Arguelles, "Kahos," p. 112.

The killings shocked the returning Mindacom leaders who immediately issued an order to discontinue Kahos. This, however, came belatedly—three months after the killings had already taken their toll. The distrust had spread to even include Mindacom itself, making it doubly difficult to implement the order particularly in guerrilla zones where NPA units had become extremely suspicious and closed the zones against outsiders, including even the Party leadership. It took another six months before a task force organized purposely to end Kahos had stopped the killings.[9]

The formal discontinuance of Kahos, however, did not necessarily mean an admission that a serious mistake had been made. While conceding that "excesses" did happen, Mindacom also insisted that the "campaign" was a success and that it did weed out spies among the ranks. With most of its leaders retaining influence, supporters, or control of important positions inside the Party's powerful Politburo, the report was officially accepted. However, as more stories of "mass executions" came to light, admitted even by media people sympathetic to the revolution in Luzon, and began to filter into the public sphere, the Party was forced to alter its position.[10]

In 1989, the Politburo issued a new explanation for Kahos: it called the killings a major mistake brought about by "ideological errors" that warped the investigation and allowed for paranoia to break out within the ranks and cause the unwarranted and uncontrolled killings. Mindacom reluctantly accepted this revisionist assessment, qualifying its acceptance however by asserting that while Kahos decimated the organization, it failed to destroy it completely. It then almost instantaneously announced that the movement was already on the road to recovery, fast reclaiming its presence in Mindanao.[11]

These Party actions—revising an official evaluation, then claiming a crisis was over—did not erase the devastating impact of Kahos. The killing cost the CPP dearly. While it did ferret out military spies, Kahos's victims were mainly loyal cadres, guerrillas, and activists whose only transgression was to be critical of and disagree with Party policies.[12] Within a six-month period, 950 cadres, guerrillas, and activists were executed for being *demonyo* suspects.[13] The dislocation was massive—in nine months party membership declined from nine thousand to a mere three thousand due to resignation, surrender, or AWOL; the NPA was reduced from fifteen or

---

[9] Although the killings did continue well into 1988 and became a nationwide phenomenon by 1989. Arguelles, "Kahos," p. 107. See also Gregg Jones, *Red Revolution: Inside the Philippine Guerrilla Movement* (Boulder: Westview Press, 1989), pp. 266–67.

[10] Right-wing propaganda that portrayed the CPP as the "New Khmer Rouge" stoked the frenzy. See Russ H. Munro, "The New Khmer Rouge," *Commentary* 80 (December 1985): 19-38; see also Romy Chan, "Mass Graves of NPA Death Squads found in Davao," *Manila Bulletin*, February 20, 1987, pp. 1 and 9.

[11] "NPA shows Continuing Vigor in Mindanao," *Ang Bayan*, April 1989, pp. 3-4. "Ang Pagbawi ng Davao," *Ang Bayan*, June 1990, pp. 11-16.

[12] It was obvious that the military was engaged in an intensive effort to penetrate the CPP, and I recognize that Kahos and similar efforts were partly successful in repulsing this attack. One military unit that was exposed was a so-called "Davao Counter-Revolutionary Group," whose leader, a certain Sonny Aragon, was assassinated by NPA armed city partisans. Interview with a Mindanao cadre, December 1985. I am grateful to Jose Eliseo Rocamora for reminding me of the military's culpability in all this. Personal communication, June 11, 1995. The costs, however, for the success of cleansing the movement of spies were catastrophic and tragic.

[13] Jones, *Red Revolution*, p. 268.

sixteen companies to a mere two, supported by seventeen platoons; and the CPP lost over 50 percent of its mass base.[14] Reports of Kahos-like incidents in Southern Luzon, albeit on a minor scale, worsened matters for a CPP already placed on the political defensive after 1986. By the end of the decade, the CPP was experiencing the most serious crisis of its twenty-year history, with Kahos being the most painful of all its misfortunes.

Why did Kahos happen, and why most intensely in Mindanao? Existing explanations within and outside the CPP focus on two themes. One interpretation regards Kahos as the ultimate effect of an internal struggle over revolutionary strategy. Another view suggests that Kahos was the disastrous aftermath of an authoritarian paranoia that grows within Leninist parties in crisis. This essay posits a parallel explanation that looks at Kahos within the structural and historical frames that helped to shape it. It argues that Mindanao, as the Philippine's last land frontier, was "closing" up fast demographically. But even as it was doing so, the social instabilities continued, in part caused by the war that broke out between the military and armed Muslim separatists, but also in part caused by a more intrusive Philippine national state that sought to integrate Mindanao closer into its "developmentalist goals." I am suggesting that "closure" did not normalize Mindanao's demography by calcifying emergent social ties. On the contrary, the closure exacerbated social instabilities and mutated social relations. It was this contextual flux within which the CPP grew. It would reap its benefits, but it would also fall victim to its outcomes.

In returning to the importance of context, I do not claim that this essay's argument fully explains the emergence of Kahos. There may be merit in looking at this disaster as a product of paranoia or as a fallout of failed strategies. However, I do maintain that context and history cannot be ignored as fundamental factors, and in the light of the prevailing explanations for Kahos, this essay hopes to reassert the importance of the larger frame. Kahos, however, remains to be fully explored. A full understanding of the killings warrants in-depth field research to collect and record especially interviews and conversations with the survivors, the victims' kin, the perpetrators, Party leaders, and other actors and actresses involved in it. It also requires conducting a more intensive comparative study of Mindanao and other regions in the Philippines where the CPP is/was active and where Kahos-type killings did and did not happen. Finally, a full contextualization of Kahos inevitably leads us to the "larger phenomenon" of Filipino communism itself—a topic which I am, at this stage, ill-prepared to deal with. This essay must then be seen as one of the many windows opened on the subject. As such, the essay is itself open to criticism and revision by those who decide to investigate much more fully the still uncharted territories of contemporary Filipino communism.

THE KAHOS DEBATE: THE VERSIONS AND THEIR AUTHORS

The 1986 "tactical mistake" of ordering its forces to stay away from the confrontation between Marcos and Aquino was the catalyst that would bring forth long-suppressed but unsettled internal problems inside the CPP. The Party began to unravel, ultimately splintering in 1989 into two factions that disagreed over almost every significant topic: interpretations of the Party's history, the value of its fidelity

[14] *Ang Bayan*, March 1989, p. 6. See also Carolyn Arguellas, "The Antongalon Incident: Are the Rebels Really Killing their Comrades?" *Veritas Newsmagazine*, September 30, 1986, p. 15.

to Maoism, questions about the united front, assessment of the Marcos and post-Marcos periods (especially on how to deal with the popular Aquino), evaluation of the crisis socialism with the breakdown of Eastern Europe, and predictions for the future of the Philippine Left.[15] However, the most divisive issue that, in a way, precipitated the CPP's split was Kahos.[16]

The faction that fired the first salvo was the group identified with Jose Ma. Sison, founding chairman of the CPP who regained control of the party from a younger group of leaders known to be critical of Sison's obstinate devotion to Maoism.[17] In a 1991 document that "re-affirmed" the CPP's return to its Maoist roots, Sison made extensive use of Kahos as proof of his rivals "political opportunism."[18] Pointing to the killings as "a devastation [that] was unprecedented in the entire history of the Philippine revolution," Sison linked Kahos to what he called "the worst kind of dogmatism" inside Mindacom. He argued that Mindacom dogmatism was best illustrated by that group's adoption and imposition of the Sandinista model on Philippine conditions in hopes of creating a "revolutionary situation" that would usher in the final confrontation between dictatorship and revolution. This deviation from the Maoist strategy of people's war induced the "worst kind of disorientation" which in turn, prompted a series of other mistakes leading fatally to Kahos. But the worst thing, according to Sison, was that those responsible for the killings were

---

[15] The public was given an initial preview of these internal debates in *Praktika*, described as a "Theoretical Journal of the Party National Urban Center." See, for example, "Against the Snap Election Boycott," *Pratika* 1, 1 (May 14, 1986); and Marty Villalobos, "Where the Party Faltered," *Praqtika* 1:2 (August 1986). Internal CPP differences and debates have also been analyzed by "outsiders." Some of these writings include: Armando S. Malay, "The 'Legal' vs. the 'Illegal': Problem in CPP-ML Strategy and Tactics," *Asian Studies* 20 (April-August 1982); Armando S. Malay, "Random Reflections on Marxism and Maoism in the Philippines," in *Marxism in the Philippines* (Quezon City: Third World Studies Center, 1984), pp. 45-98; Armando Malay, "On Marxism-Leninism-Mao Tse Tung Thought: An Overview," *Diliman Review* 35, 4 (1987); Gareth Porter, "Philippine Communism after Marcos," *Problems of Communism* 36, 5 (1987): 14-35; Gareth Porter, "The Politics of Counter-Insurgency in the Philippines: Military and Political Options," *Philippine Studies Occasional Paper* 9 (Hawaii: Center for Philippine Studies, 1987); and several of the essays in the collection *Marxism in the Philippines: Second Series* (Quezon City: Third World Studies Center, 1988).

[16] The split spilled over the so-called "legal Left." The *Kilusang Mayo Uno* [May First Movement, or KMU] broke up into two groups, one supporting Sison, the other the declaration of autonomy by the Manila-Rizal leadership. The KMU's peasant counterpart, the Kilusang Magbubukid ng Pilipinas [Peasant's Movement of the Philippines, KMP] expelled its more famous leader, Jaime Tadeo, after he professed support for "reforms" inside the KMP. Tian Chua and Rex Varona, "Fault-lines open in (Philippine) Labour Movement," *Asian Labour Update* 13 (October 1993): 1–5; and Jaime "Ka Jimmy" Tadeo, "A Triumph of Democratic Process," September 7, 1993, statement, mss.

[17] Dario Agnote, "Communist Party disbands the NPA General Command," *Philippine Newsday*, November 28, 1991, pp. 1–2; "CPP Chairman Sison confirms Party Split," *Philippine Daily Inquirer*, December 10, 1992; "Sison steps up attack on Former Followers," *Philippine Daily Inquirer*, December 11, 1992; and "ABB and Manila-Rizal Committee ordered Dissolved," *Philippine Daily Inquirer*, January 1, 1993; *Manila Chronicle*, December 27, 1992; *Philippine Daily Inquirer*. March 2, 1992; and "Sison for Communist Rift: Letter to the Editor by various CPP Cadres," *Manila Chronicle*, December 30, 1993. p. 7.

[18] Patnubay Liwanag (Jose Ma. Sison), "Reaffirm our Basic Principles and Rectify Errors," December 26, 1991, as reprinted in *Kasarinlan: A Philippine Quarterly of Third World Studies* 8, 1 (1992): 83–133.

absolved of their crimes and even managed to circumscribe a full-blown investigation into the tragedy due to their powerful positions in the Party.[19]

With the Party leadership under its firm control, the Sison faction saw its chance to push for a reinterpretation of Kahos among the ranks of disoriented party followers. (The arrest of his rivals during the years 1988–91 facilitated the seizure of power by the Sison faction.) It sanctioned the slogan "wrong line, temporary military success, and urban *pasiklab*, enemy counter-action, and finally Kahos" as the official explanation for the tragedy, even as it initiated a "re-orientation" of loyal Mindanao cadres.[20] Sison, in the meanwhile, ordered the expulsion of those linked to Kahos, calling them "renegades" and promoters of "gangsterism, grave abuse of authority, corruption of partisan units and men [and] criminal neglect" inside the Party.[21]

The ferocity of Sison's attacks stunned his rivals.[22] For a time, most thought naively that the debate could be handled along comradely lines and also by deferring to Sison as Party founder.[23] Some were at a loss to decide how to respond to this

---

[19] "Under conditions of ultra-democracy, those elements responsible for the incomparably far biggest error and disaster in Mindanao were able to ride on the campaign against the boycott error of 1986. They obscured or kept silence on the error and disaster and some of them had the gumption to claim that had it not been for the boycott error of 1986, the people would have been able to seize political power and share it with other forces." Liwanag, "Reaffirm," *Kasarinlan*, p. 127.

[20] "Memorandum to all Central Committee Members, 10th Plenum of the Central Committee," Study, Debate, Discussion, Summing-up: Profound Re-Examination and Revitalization on the Crisis of Socialism, Strategy of Action and Internal Democracy (Manila: n.p., January 1993), p. 335. This clumsily-titled compendium, popularly referred to as the Red Book, contains arguments from the two contending factions. It was published by a group of "concerned cadres" hoping to guide their confused comrades through the ideological mess. The intensity of the arguments by both sides, not to mention their organizational consequences, reflected not only a Party in flux, but also a Party that was apparently quite vibrant in its internal politics— at least for a time. The conflicting narratives found in Red Book showed a CPP that was not a mere replica of the Chinese model. The maze of stories and interpretations suggests a Party that had more affinities with the more boisterous and "divided" groups like the Nicaraguans and ultimately Lenin's Bolsheviks pre-1924, than it had with the more staid Chinese or Vietnamese parties with whom the CPP is normally identified with. More importantly, the exchanges allow us a glimpse into the internal mechanisms of an hitherto inaccessible organization. It was as if the CPP, frustrated by its inability to resolve the crisis within its ranks except through purges and expulsions, decided to bare its soul to the public. Thus, I will cite liberally from this remarkable collection.

[21] Foreign Broadcast Information Service (FBIS), December 20, 1993, pp. 50–51. On the Mindanao "re-orientation," see "Lessons from Mass Work in the Mindanao Countryside," *Ang Bayan*, April 1990, pp. 6–13.

[22] These cadres were principally responsible for the growth of the CPP after the first generation of leaders were either killed or detained (Sison included). Their first political officer was Sison. They proved to be able students, rescuing the CPP from initial fix, and—through pragmatism and resourcefulness—overseeing the growth of the Party, which developed to become the most important opposition to the Marcos dictatorship up until 1986 and the Sison *coup*. These cadres, however, do not form a cohesive group, but are loosely organized around their rejection of Sison's 1991 document of reaffirmation. As such they are referred to as "Rejectionists" [as against those who supported Sison, the "Re-affirmists"]. See Antonio Lopez, "Running a Revolution," *Asiaweek*, March 9, 1994, pp. 28–41.

[23] As one former CPP leader put it, "We practically learned our Marxism at his feet." [Siya yong leader namin. Iyong paradigm namin, siya.] "Interview with Ricardo Reyes," *Manila Chronicle*, January 19, 1993. See also, "Reply to Sison's Charges—December 11, 1992 (by Ricardo Reyes, Romulo Kintanar and Benjamin de Vera)," *Conjuncture* 6:2 (December 1992–

systematic, all-out attack on them, while others warned of a witchhunt and the threat of "a form of one-man rule" inside the Party.[24] As they recovered from initial attacks by the Sison faction, these variously splintered units and individuals began to coalesce into a "Democratic Opposition" inside and outside the CPP.[25] This consolidation also led to a much better response to the attacks from the Sison faction, among which were the cadres whom Sison accused of being responsible for Kahos.[26] Their initial response was to deny that the shift in strategy caused the tragedy. They would also insist that the "excesses" notwithstanding, Kahos was a success, and that the setbacks because of the killings were being systematically remedied.[27]

January 1993), p. 2; and, "Letter of Concerned Comrades in Mindanao to the CC/EC-CC," *Red Book*, p. 151.

[24] Note the pain and anger over Sison's attacks in Nathan Quimpo, "Barrio Utrecht: Coup D'Etat in the NDF," *Sunday Chronicle,* November 21, 1993, p. 4; and Joel Rocamora, "The Crisis of the National Democratic Movement and the Transformation of the Philippine Left," *Debate* 6 (March 1993). Rocamora demanded that the Kahos investigation "must not be manipulated to served (sic) the requirements of Liwanag in the current ideological struggle." He also cited noted Sison's selectiveness on whom to attack in Mindacom; see p. 37. A Ka Barry charged that Sison was leading an "anti-MindaCom campaign (which was) unfair, vindictive and divisive," and demanded that Sison himself be investigated for his role as one of those who decided on the Southern Tagalog purges in 1988, information the CPP chairman had conveniently omitted in his attacks. Ka Barry, "Resist Authoritarian Tendencies within the Party! Let a Thousand Schools of Thought Contend!" *Kasarinlan* 8, 1 (1992): 141.

[25] "Declaration of Autonomy by the Manila-Rizal Regional Committee of the Communist Party of the Philippines," and "NDF-US Vision Statement," July 10, 1993, as reprinted in *Kasarinlan* 9, 1, (1993): 37–43, and 114–122 respectively; "Uphold Marxist-Leninist Principles, Advance the National Democratic Revolution: Declaration of Autonomy by Party Organizations in the Visayas and the Western Mindanao Regional White Area Cadres Conference," *Debate* 9 (November 1993): 60–72; "Sorsogon Communist Unit joins Revisionist Group," FBIS, September 1, 1993, p. 31; "Out of Crisis, Renewal: A Joint Statement of the Democratic Opposition within the Communist Party of the Philippines," mss. December 26, 1993; and "Open Letter of Ricardo Reyes, Convenor, Suriang Sosyalista," May 15, 1993.

[26] The first members to acknowledge that the rupture was real were not those from the original Mindacom, but from the more cohesive Manila-Rizal committee. It declared its "autonomy" from the Sison-controlled Politburo, proclaiming that the Sison faction had become despots. See "Tumindig sa Tama at Totoo, Pawalang Bisa ang Bogus na Plenum," October 10, 1992, *Red Book*, p. 85. The history of the Manila-Rizal committee [KT-MR is acronym for "Komiteng Tagapagpaganap, Manila-Rizal" or Executive Committee, Manila-Rizal] is quite interesting. In 1978, the same lower body defied a Central Committee memorandum to break its alliance with anti-Marcos politicians during the elections for the new "parliament." The difference was resolved by organizational *fiat* instead of allowing for a full-blown ideological debate [the KT-MR was disbanded, and its leaders either resigned or were sent to the countryside for "re-education"]. The issues surrounding the 1978 debate have now resurfaced, with the same KT-MR chairman [who reclaimed his position in 1988 after his full rehabilitation] demanding a reassessment of that brief period of *kaluwagan*. See Armando Malay, "The Dialectics of *Kaluwagan*: Echoes of a 1978 Debate," *Marxism in the Philippines: Second Series*, pp. 1-25. See also the following documents: KT-MR, "Ang Ating Taktikal na Islogan para sa Kasalukuyang Yugto ng Rebolusyon," mss, August 1975; KT-KS [Executive Committee, Central Committee], "Paglalagom ng Karanasan ng Partido sa Maynila-Rizal Kaugnay sa Huwad na Halalang IBP," mss., December 1973.

[27] The National Democratic Front newspaper acknowledged that by 1984 "the NPA was admitting defeats on the battlefield." *Liberation*, April–May 1987, pp. 14-15, as quoted by Peter Sales. See Peter Sales, "The Once and Future Insurgency in Northeastern Mindanao," in Turner et al., ed., *Mindanao*, p. 215.

The "Rejectionists" also took the offensive arguing that the attention focused on the killings had obscured the significance of the Mindanao comeback.[28] Once Sison turned on the heat, however, there was no way his rivals could skirt Kahos. Most preferred to look at Kahos in relation to the debates over strategy. A former Mindacom leader named Ka Taquio agreed that Kahos was a product of an "ideological error" and that a "militarist tendency" inside the Mindacom organization led to "the narrow interpretation of class struggle as violent elimination of the enemies (and a) mechanical interpretation of the Maoist principle 'political power grows out of the barrel of the gun.'" However, he strongly disagreed with Sison's argument tying Kahos to a deviation from Maoism. He notes:

> It is difficult to imagine whether the so-called 'erroneous line of quick military victory' and 'wishful armed insurrection' was one of the root causes of the Kahos debacle because in the first place, it still has to be proven whether such an erroneous line really took shape . . . [It] was more a lack of seeking truth from facts and actual processes and procedures in the Party that caused the Kahos campaign to snowball without the tight control of the Commission. . . . [All this was due to] a limited familiarity with the Marxist tools for assessment and summing up.[29]

Paco Arguelles, the author cited in the introduction of this essay, responded to Sison along the same lines, stating emphatically that Kahos "was the decisive factor in the sharp decline of revolutionary strength on the island" and not an "erroneous line" promoted by Mindacom. He questioned Sison's selective use of evidence, his failure to use "Marxist analysis" and a penchant for "reductionism" in explaining both Kahos and the general condition of the CPP. Arguelles turned Sison's argument on its head by questioning the viability of Maoist strategy itself. He argued that "the limited and low level of capability of the theory of protracted people's war in grasping, throwing light on, and guiding the revolutionary process of the country" was in fact the real culprit that made Kahos possible.[30]

Others, however, insisted that there was something inherently wrong inside the Party's way of life. A "Standing Group" of the Visayas Commission (VISCOM) disputed Sison's assertion that Kahos flowed out of Mindacom's "adventurist"

---

[28] As *Ang Bayan*, then under Rejectionist control argued: "Party discipline has . . . improved. The arrogance and liberalism of some comrades are being corrected. The excesses that had been committed in meting out punishment have been analyzed and rectified. We have accepted responsibility for specific weaknesses and errors. We have learned to be more strict and more selective in recruiting members into the Party. We have been able to restore the atmosphere of trust and faith among cadres." See "Persevere in the Struggle and We Will Surely Win: CPP Mindanao Commission Statement," *Ang Bayan* 2, 1 (April 1989), p. 8.

[29] Comrade Taquio, "Comments on the Current Polemics within the Party," *Red Book*, p. 159.

[30] Paco Arguelles, "*Pagbabalik-Aral*: Aprioprism Reaffirmed," *Debate* (August 1993): 27. Arguelles continued: "The theory of stages of the war is decisively anchored on the balance of armed strength between revolution and counter-revolution. It is clear that this kind of framework is more useful in explaining the development of the war rather than the whole course of the revolution. . . . [Only] a politico-military framework covering the urban-rural combination, basing itself on solid accumulation of strength but prepared to seize opportunities as they emerge, can free the revolutionary movement from the fetters of dogmatism and conservatism which have dominated the old mode of struggle." Arguelles, "*Pagbabalik-Aral*," p. 32.

policies of "insurrectionism," insisting that the killings were the byproduct of excessive paranoia and mistrust inside the Party. They called Kahos a "right error" reflective of a larger problem—that of a failure of strategy to adopt to changing conditions, a failure which allowed sentiments like paranoia to persist.[31]

Walden Bello, however, broadens his argument by claiming that Kahos was the dire outcome of Marxist-Leninist politics itself. He argues:

> An instrumental view of people is a tendency that affects particularly activists in the Marxist-Leninist tradition, making them vulnerable during moments of paranoia at the height of the revolutionary struggle to expedient solutions involving the physical elimination of real or imagined enemies. In normal times, the combination of a tactical view of people, ideological fervor, youth, and the gun already carries a threat potential. Touched off by social paranoia, it can easily become an uncontrollable force, as it did in Mindanao and Southern Tagalog.[32]

Bello, a long-time leader of the American anti-Marcos solidarity network, conducted interviews with survivors of Kahos and came to the conclusion also that "the absence of an institutionalized system of justice and scientific assessment . . . allowed paranoia to spread unchecked."

The efforts of members in the emerging anti-Sison group to respond to the criticisms of "Reaffirm," however, was blunted by one decisive factor: Kahos had weakened their positions in the CPP leadership and undermined their abilities to respond to the Sison group's assaults. Some of their leading spokespersons were accused of being involved in one way or the other in the killings, while others had been displaced from their positions of power and influence due to imprisonment or to the varied organizational ruses employed by their rivals. In the end, therefore, it was the Sison group which gained the upper hand in the Kahos debates, and within Philippine Left circles today, their version has become the "official" story.[33]

(RE)SORTING THE NARRATIVES: THE MISSING CONTEXT

Kahos may very well have been caused by all the reasons cited above. There is enough evidence of paranoia existing inside the CPP, as well as evidence to show that members who were caught up in Kahos challenged the Maoist paradigm, as Sison claimed. Kahos could also be the product of a multiple number of causes, some

---

[31] The VISCOM cadres said, "ang esensyal na kamalian sa *Ahos* ay walang malaking pagkakaiba sa makakanang kamalian ng 'paranoia' at kawalan ng tiwala sa kasama't masa, tulad ng naganap sa Luzon noon 1988."[Ahos' essential mistake is no different from the rightist error of paranoia and the lack of trust and confidence on comrades and the masses that happened in Luzon in 1988]."Magpunyagi sa Wastong Paglalagom sa Magkaisang-Panig ng 'Reaffirm,' Oktubre 25, 1992." *Red Book*, pp. 32–35.

[32] Walden Bello. "The Crisis of the Philippine Progressive Movement: A Preliminary Investigation," *Kasarinlan* 8, 1 (1992): 151.

[33] Rocamora also opined that Kahos undermined the ability of the anti-Sison camp to push for "reforms" inside the CPP as well as for "changes in [revolutionary] strategy that might have changed the history of the movement if implemented." He elaborated: "They [the anti-Sison group] were relatively successful in pushing these ideas at the 1980 CC [Central Committee] plenum and subsequent PB [politburo] meetings, but at the pivotal 1985 CC plenum, they or more their ideas were marginalized." Personal communication, June 11, 1995.

apparently traceable to the CPP's nature as an underground organization, a conspiratorial organization disadvantaged by the deficient "ideological" training of its cadres and activists.

Yet, even within these contrasting positions, certain flaws in the Party are camouflaged and ignored. Most importantly, in their efforts to validate their own visions of the suitable CPP strategy, both sides actually ended up reifying Kahos. Sison and his opponents could be faulted for understating the nature of the tragedy by using it as a mere empirical source to confirm their respective strategic preferences while repudiating the others. Even the Visayas "Standing Group," perhaps the nearest among the CPP cadres to recognize the tragedy of Kahos, unavoidably contextualized it within a discussion of how best to win power in the Philippines. Thus enclosing Kahos inside this conceptual frame, they—like others—depreciated the profound implications of the tragedy.[34]

Neither can arguments about "low ideological training" sufficiently explain the eruption of Kahos. Revolutionaries never attain the perfect ideological state where they and their followers can profess complete devotion to the cause. Multi-layered, complex individuals bring to the organization different levels of perceptions, various levels of commitment to the prevailing doctrine, and different propensities when it comes time to act on those doctrines. Moreover, time and again, communists always encounter "problems" from below, which may arise when "little traditions" resist directives from above, or conversely, when the more elite members of a revolutionary body lack adequate ideological sensitivity to popular sentiments and consciousness.[35]

Only Bello appeared to have taken Kahos seriously. But even he still ended up digressing towards using Kahos as a didactic example to score theoretical points by bringing in his critique of Leninist vanguardist politics in the Philippines via Kahos. His argument that, by being Leninist, the CPP all-but-naturally deteriorated into instrumentalist politics and thus made itself ready for Kahos betrays an ahistorical understanding of the nuanced development of the Party.

Looking back at the biggest crisis of the Party before the tragedy—that of the rift between Manila-Rizal Executive Committee (KT-MR) and the Central Committee in 1978—one is surprised to note that the purge ordered by the latter never led to executions. As the documents of that period show, there were not only considerable democratic exchanges between the two party organizations, the Central Committee was surprisingly tolerant of the Manila regional committee for a while, giving it remarkable leeway to try to prove its point. The decision to purge only came at the last minute when, despite evidence to the contrary, the KT-MR had come to believe its own logic that an anti-Marcos coalition could win in an election stage-managed by the dictatorship. Bello may be correct in expressing his wariness towards Leninist instrumentalism, but he must reconcile his theoretical-psychological argument with

---

[34] Arguelles is drawn to the psychological position of Bello and the Visayas cadres, calling Kahos a "cancer" which began in 1982 and spread throughout the Party in 1988–89, "growing steadily and, during certain periods, rapidly destroying the normal and health cells of the movement." Arguelles, "*Kahos*: A Soul-Searching," p. 1.

[35] See, for example, James C. Scott, "Protest and Profanation: Agrarian Revolt and the Little Tradition," *Theory and Society* 4, 2 (1977); see also his larger opus, *The Moral Economy of the Peasant: Rebellion and Subsistence in Southeast Asia* (New Haven: Yale University Press, 1976).

that of a history showing a CPP acting less as a centralized organization and more like a set of "squabbling sects."[36]

In short, both these sets of explanations—one which describes Kahos as a by-product of errors in strategy (orthodox or otherwise), and the other, which describes Kahos as the fatal outcome of paranoia and Leninist instrumentalism—cannot fully account for the tragedy because they remove it from its historical moorings and ultimately shove it into a minor place of import. The debates thus regressed until they had become nothing more than an ideological version of "who is to blame" while transmuting Kahos into an incident caused by individuals or groups of individuals obsessed by an agenda. The essays in the Red Book and other writings, aside from their revelatory features, are notable for their incessant propensity to quibble over facts, the inclusion and/or exclusion of evidence, and mutual charges of selective data use, all to validate each other's assumptions and ideological presuppositions. Somewhere along the way, Kahos disappeared amidst the brawl over the right evidence. In the din of the rhetoric, the tragedy's meaning and import got lost.

It is not surprising therefore that none of the various antagonists ever considered explaining Kahos as the outcome of the structural features of Mindanao society itself and the manner in which CPP cadres adjusted their organizing to that society. Why, for example, did an organization as schooled in conspiracies as the CPP only respond with such widespread brutality in 1985, and only in Mindanao? Why not in the periods before 1985, and why not as massively as in other areas? Such questions, normally expected to be posed by Marxist analysis, do not appear in any of the internal Party tracts that tried to explain the tragedy. None took into consideration the "instabilities" of Mindanao society nor the more inherent features of the island as a land frontier.

Once removed from its historical context, Kahos was eventually explained away as a psychological malady. The contending factions oddly ended up sharing this conclusion as the litter of terms like "collective paranoia," "over-suspiciousness," "hysteria," and "madness" found in all the writings suggests. If the historical terrain upon which Kahos rested had been reified, so would the social context upon which it stood. In the succeeding pages, I would like to elaborate on this context, without necessarily arguing a direct causality between this context and Kahos but instead suggesting that the structural-historical frame cannot be ignored if one wishes to arrive at a multi-causal explanation of Kahos.

REASSESSING COMMUNISTS AND FRONTIERS

The CPP came to Mindanao at a crucial period in the island's evolution as the Philippines' last large island frontier. While the Party's first attempts to set up guerrilla units and underground cells in Mindanao ended up in failure, it was initially saved by two political developments: the Muslim armed separatist movement and the radicalization of the Mindanao church.[37] The war waged by the Moro National Liberation Front (MNLF) drew over 60 percent of the Armed Forces of the

---

[36] Francisco Nemenzo. "Rectification Process and the Philippine Communist Movement," in Lee Joo Jock and Vani S., eds., *Armed Communist Movements in Southeast Asia* (Singapore: Institute of Southeast Asian Studies, 1984).

[37] Kit Collier, "The Theoretical Problems of Insurgency in Mindanao: Why Theory? Why Mindanao," in Turner et al., ed., *Mindanao*, pp. 197–212.

Philippines (AFP) into the Muslim provinces, thereby creating a "breathing spell" which allowed communists to try again.[38] Party organizing was facilitated when Catholic clergy, nuns and laity began drifting towards a Filipino "theology of struggle" as they sought to protect their flock from an increasingly militarized society. This "religious sector" became the CPP's biggest resource base as well the foundation upon which an island-wide network of legal and underground organizations was created.[39]

In five years (1975–80), Mindanao communists had recovered to become the fastest growing regional organization of the Party. By 1980, conditions had remarkably changed, so much so that in its Eight Plenum, the Central Committee established Mindacom to supervise island-wide revolutionary activities.

Yet it was not only the secessionist war nor a radicalizing religious that gave CPP cadres their new lease of life. The fluidity of Mindanao itself made it ripe for radical expansion. Everything associated with a frontier "filling up" was in evidence by the late 1960s and early 1970s: increased population density, decline of land to people ratio, and, in settler-dominated areas like southeastern Mindanao, the re-emergence of early stages of land concentration, tenancy, and class stratification. The frontier had not only lost its efficacy as a safety valve because it had reached the limits of its absorptive capacity, it also began to mimic land-related problems in more densely-populated areas with highly-skewed land ownership and concentration.[40]

As demographic changes during the period signaled frontier closure, the other side of the coin, capitalist expansion to tap the island's rich resources, also grew. Domestic and foreign corporations had launched a drive to invest in agriculture, notably pineapple and bananas, to expand existing industries like timber, and to make initial moves to open up more of the island's mineral resources.[41] Not unlike the northern Brazilian frontier, demographic saturation and capitalist penetration eventuated into different kinds of tensions, the most serious of which occurred between indigenous and settler communities fighting against each other over land ownership, and against expanding corporate capital seeking freer access to land and

---

[38] On the Muslim rebellion see T. J. S. George, *Revolt in Mindanao: The Rise of Islam in Philippine Politics* (Kuala Lumpur: Oxford University Press, 1980); Aijaz Ahmad, "The War Against the Muslims," *Southeast Asia Chronicle* 82 (February 1982): 15–22; and W. K. Che Man, *Muslim Separatism: The Moros of Southern Philippines and the Malays of Southern Thailand* (Quezon City: Ateneo de Manila University Press, 1990).

[39] Robert Youngblood, *Marcos against the Church: Economic Development and Political Repression in the Philippines* (Ithaca: Cornell University Press, 1990), pp. 96–99, 124–25. See also Warren Kinne, *The Splintered Staff: Structural Deadlock in the Mindanao Church* (Quezon City. New Day Publishers, 1990).

[40] Wilhelm Flieger, "Internal Migration in the Philippines during the 1960s," *Philippine Quarterly of Culture and Society* 5 (1977): 202–04; Albert L. Danielson, "The Effect of Inter-regional Migration on the Philippine Population," *Philippine Economy Bulletin 5,* 2 (November–December 1966); Peter Krinks, "Old Wine in a New Bottle: Land Settlement and Agrarian Problems in the Philippines," *Journal of Southeast Asian Studies* 5 (1974): 6–8; Paul D. Simkins and Frederick L. Wernstedt, *Philippine Migration and the Settlement of the Digos-Padada Valley, Davao Province* (New Haven: Yale University Southeast Asian Studies Monograph Series, no. 16, 1971), pp. 104-106.

[41] Eduardo Tadem, *Mindanao Report: A Preliminary Study on (sic) the Economic Origins of Social Unrest* (Davao City: AFRIM Resource Center, 1990), pp. 22–23; Rad Silva, *Two Hills of the Same Land: Truth Behind the Mindanao Problem* (Mindanao: Mindanao-Sulu Studies and Research Group, 1979), pp. 55–63.

mineral resources.[42] Those with the capacity to fight back, like the Muslims, did so, while others were marginalized. The Muslim resistance began as a land-related conflict but was soon transformed into a religious war which escalated once the Philippine military stepped in to suppress it.[43]

Tensions, however, were not increasing solely in the Muslim areas. Social friction over land ownership, access, and use also began to affect erstwhile "stable" provinces at just about the time the Muslim secessionist war broke out. In the northeast and southeastern portions of Mindanao, reports of land conflict had become regular news fare.[44] Clearly, with very few exceptions, the general consequence of these massive changes was the exclusion, impoverishment and marginalization of indigenous and settler communities in Mindanao.[45]

Martial law was the final qualitative twist to all these changes. *Pace* the arguments of scholars re-examining contemporary Mindanao politics, the intrusion of the national state in 1973 signaled stronger state involvement in Mindanao as compared to earlier periods. Unlike its predecessors, who gave Mindanao only cursory attention, the Marcos dictatorship exerted the strongest and most directed effort at asserting state power in Mindanao to date.[46] Muslim armed secessionism was the initial reason for this unparalleled state intrusion. Over 60 percent of the military was involved in containing a rebellion where undisguised brutality had become the norm. The military war effort—despite an impasse in 1977–78—also became the justification for the national state to maintain its overarching presence in the island, the first time since the US Army administered the Moro Province at the turn of the century. The bulk of the army would stay in Mindanao, although by the 1980s it had a different enemy—the CPP.

The dictatorship not only escalated its presence to contain the Muslim rebellion; it also sought to integrate Mindanao into its "developmentalist agenda." State centralization activated old national agencies as well as creating new ones, and with ample external financing, the dictatorship undertook a massive infrastructure program designed to make Mindanao and its resources more accessible to capital.

One author notes that over twenty-seven billion pesos were poured into Mindanao during the 1970s; eleven major road projects were funded through sixty-eight million dollars external financing and 1.4 billion pesos local counterpart.[47]

---

[42] Krinks, "Old Wine," p. 8.

[43] George, *Revolt in Mindanao*, pp. 143–61, 178–93; Ahmad, "War against the Muslims," pp. 15–22.

[44] "New Land Disputes in Davao," *Manila Times*, October 8, 1970; "Davao Tribal Leaders ask Lopez's for Help (in Land Dispute)," *Manila Times*, July 28, 1970; "1,000 Settlers vow to fight Ejectment; Bloodshed Eyed," *Daily Mirror*, December 30, 1971.

[45] E. Tadem, Susan Magno and Johnny Reyes, *Showcases of Underdevelopment: Fishes, Forests and Fruits* (Davao City: Alternate Resource Center, 1984); and "Outline: Historical Development of Mindanao (sic) Economy," *Mindanao Focus* 18, pp. 30-43.

[46] Turner ahistoricizes when he argues that in Mindanao, "the state is weak but the society is fragmented and shallow rooted." Turner et al., ed., *Mindanao*, p. 1. One of my readers suggested that this may too one-dimensional an approach, noting Anthony Gidden's distinction between *scope* and *intensity* of state presence and sanctions. While I agree with this theoretical reminder (when set in comparative historical settings), the Marcos dictatorship's intrusion into Mindanao in 1973 was unprecedented in scope and intensity as compared to earlier state efforts at controlling the frontier.

[47] Eduardo Tadem, "The Political Economy of Mindanao: An Overview," in Turner et al, ed., *Mindanao*, p. 13. The dictatorship reconstituted Mindanao special agencies like the Mindanao

Specific regions also became prime targets; in southwestern Mindanao, for example, Australian economic assistance totaling $A 50.4 million (with local counterpart of $A 43.1 million) helped establish the Zamboanga del Sur Development Project which undertook the infrastructure development of the area. Its total budget, resources and personnel, observes one author, "exceeded that of the provincial government and the line agencies of the national government in the province."[48] The impact of this massive developmentalist thrust may have benefited some, but it also exposed various communities to the vagaries of economic transformation. Infrastructure opened up inaccessible areas and hastened land re-classification, which, in turn, brought in more dominant economic actors like foreign and local investors, to the detriment of communities in the island.[49]

The 1970s, therefore, was a decade of unusual volatility, and the economic and social instabilities provided the CPP with various sources of potential partisans from within the ranks of these affected communities. It was under these intensely turbulent conditions that the CPP grew remarkably after its 1975 miscues. From the ranks of these marginalized groups, the CPP recruited its first generation of cadres.[50] The MNLF war also presented the Party with a potentially powerful ally who, if handled well, could be convinced to work together with the CPP in eroding the national state in Mindanao.[51] Under new leadership consisting of cadres from Manila as well as those "indigenous" to the place, Mindacom lost no time consolidating Party growth while shaping larger plans for the future.[52] It systematized the available party data base on the difference provinces of the island, introduced some measure of "professionalism" into cadre training, organizational procedures and routines, and established more systematic training for NPA guerrillas.

Mindacom also initiated contacts with potential non-communist "allies," notably anti-Marcos groups like the MNLF, church and human rights groups, and politicians displaced by the declaration of martial law. The aim was to build a broad coalition that would spearhead the anti-dictatorship movement in Mindanao under the direction of the CPP. The administrative talents of Mindacom leaders, not to mention the enthusiasm with which they set themselves to task, immediately showed astounding results. In a year's time, the Mindanao CPP had become the strongest of all the

---

Development Authority by increasing its powers to control and distribute development resources. See Marife B. Clamor, "SPDA: Meeting the Challenges in the South," *Salam* 3:2 (April–September 1976).

[48] Brian Lockwood, "The Zamboanga del Sur Development Project, 1975–83," in Turner et al., ed., *Mindanao*, pp. 78–79.

[49] Eugenio A. Demegillo, "Mindanao: Development and Marginalization," *The Philippines in the Third World Papers* 20 (August 1979): 9–19. A case example of infrastructure, capitalist intrusion, and peasant marginalization is comprehensively examined by Randolf S. David, et al., *Transnational Corporations and the Philippine Banana Export Industry* (Quezon City: University of the Philippines Third World Studies Center, 1908).

[50] Jones, *Red Revolution*, pp. 140-141.

[51] "Ang Mamamayang Moro at and MNLF-BMA: Ang Kanilang mga Suliranin at Pakikibaka," CPP Social Investigation Report on the Muslims, mss, 1980 (?), 27 pp.

[52] Mindacom then was composed of Edgar Jopson (Manila, Jesuit-trained, former head of a reformist social-democratic student association, became radicalized on the eve of martial law), Magtanggol Roque (University of the Philippines graduate, active in the Manila and united front underground before being assigned to Mindanao), Benjamin de Vera, and Romulo Kintanar (another Mindanao "native"). On the biography of Jopson, see Benjamin Pimentel, Jr., *Edjop: The Unusual Journey of Edgar Jopson* (Quezon City: Ken Incorporated, 1989).

regional bodies of the Party, outdistancing Central Luzon and Manila. It had also replaced the MNLF as the strongest threat to the dictatorship.

There are no exact statistical data on the numerical rise of the Party and the NPA in Mindanao, as compared to other regions. Security considerations figured prominently in the blurring of positions, but the lack of very clear data was also due to the actual absence of any effort to distinguish the Party from its "people's army" or its "mass activists." One may be able to draw certain tentative inferences from available information in hand, however. A declassified aerogram from the US consulate in Cebu reported an upsurge in NPA activity in eastern and northern Mindanao in the 1980s as well as Party expansion in provinces hitherto the domain of the MNLF, like the Lanao provinces. In eastern Mindanao (consisting of the provinces of Davao del Norte, Davao Oriental, Agusan and Surigao), the report cited a 30–50 percent increase in the number of NPA personnel, reaching a high 950 guerrilla force with 288 weapons of various types.[53] Based on the figures supplied in Table 1, one can extrapolate that Mindanao communists in 1981 comprised 15.7 percent of the total CPP–NPA force. Assuming that this percentage remained consistent, and using the US embassy figures as a base, one can thus make the inference that Mindanao communists grew from 950 in 1981 to as many as 2,396 on the eve of Kahos. This also meant that those who were killed or resigned roughly comprised 40 percent of the entire Mindanao communist force.

Given the ambiguity of the figures, other indicators of Mindacom's growing importance as the new and vital cog in the revolutionary wheel could be seen in the following areas: the promotion of its leaders and the manner in which Mindacom as a "lower organ" related to the central leadership. In 1980, its top leaders were promoted to important party bodies. The Party center likewise gave Mindacom considerable latitude to experiment with strategy. This was partly in compliance with a policy laid down in the mid-1970s; but it was also partly the center's admission of Mindacom's extraordinary mobilizing capacities.

From here, Mindacom immediately initiated a series of "mass struggles" revolving around issues that ranged from campus reforms to anti-militarization. These were soon supplanted by larger "multi-sectoral" anti-dictatorship mobilizations, some of which involved as many as 150,000 people.[54] The 1983 assassination of Benigno Aquino, Jr., provoked more mobilization as new anti-Marcos groups materialized among the hitherto uninvolved middle class and worked in tandem with if not parallel to CPP-influenced organizations. By the middle of the decade, Mindacom was launching the first of its *welgang bayan*, popular strikes staged to choke key road arteries all over Mindanao, thereby disrupting industrial and commercial activities and keeping the military in constant disequilibrium.[55] These "advances" reinforced the confidence of Mindanao communists to a point where Mindacom cadres proposed to the Party leadership an alteration in the strategy.

---

[53] "Airgram to SecState, WashDC, from AMCONSUL Cebu, Subject: Eastern Mindanao and an Ominous Future, April 13, 1982," pp. 5–7, 9. It also noted that in 1981, the Philippine military had "shifted forces from Western Mindanao and the Sulu archipelago [areas were Muslim secessionists were active] to Eastern Mindanao to offset the increased activity of the [NPA] which had begun in early 1981." "Airgram," p. 1.

[54] Collier, "The Theoretical Problems of Insurgency," p. 208.

[55] And more wary. The army soon deployed twenty battalions in the non-MNLF territories as a way of acknowledging the newfound import of MINCOM. Pimentel, *Edjop: The Unusual Journey*, p. 265.

Using the *welga* as model (and inspiration), Mindacom began lobbying for a modified *ruse de guerre* which would emphasize what they called a "politico-military framework" (pol-mil).

Table 1. CPP/NPA Armed Strength

Year	Regulars	Firearms	Mindanao CPP/NPA (estimate)**
1969	250	300	—
1970	245	240	—
1971	500	700	—
1972	1,320	1,520	—
1973	1,900	1,515	—
1974	1,800	1,600	—
1975	1,800	1,620	—
1976	1,200	1,000	—
1977	2,300	1,700	—
1978	2,760	1,900	—
1979	4,908	1,960	—
1980	5,621	2,843	—
1981	6,013	2,546	950
1982	7,000	2,500	1,050
1983	8,900	4,620	1,335
1984	10,570	8,351	1,585
1985	15,978	10,125	2,396
1986	16,018	11,179	2,402
1987**	25,000	15,000	3,750***

Sources: Felipe B. Miranda and Ruben F. Ciron, "The Philippines: Defence Expenditures, Threat Perceptions and the Role of the United States," in Chin Kin Wah, ed., *Defence Spending in Southeast Asia* (Singapore: Institute for Southeast Asian Studies, 1987), p. 138.

** *Asiaweek Magazine*, Nov. 2, 1994 and from extrapolation of data provided by US Embassy; assuming that Mindanao CPP consistently make up 15 percent of the total CPP-NPA force.

*** The calculation is based on the assumption that Kahos casualties had not been taken into account yet.

Using the 1981 Central Committee declaration that the "last sub-stage of the strategic defensive" was soon to give way to a "strategic counter-offensive" (SCO) phase, Mindacom proposed that the Party replace Maoist strategy with "pol-mil." Adopting the latter would require the CPP to do away with Maoism's "constrictive dichotomy" of defining arenas of resistance, a stubborn partiality to countryside resistance over urban political and armed mobilization, and an image of the revolution as "advancing in waves" from the countryside to the cities with the decisive confrontation between state and revolution still decades ahead. The alternative pol-mil framework would exercise a fair amount of flexibility, combining "all forms of struggle," with the final confrontation not to be decided by just the rural guerrilla army's tempo of development.[56]

The apparent effectiveness of the strikes in paralyzing Mindanao from late 1983 throughout 1984 became the justification for Mindacom leaders to continue pushing for a new strategy, and in fact they experimented with pol-mil without apparent sanction from the center. The *welgang bayan* were broadened into mini-uprisings which combined strikes with the increased use of NPA "armed city partisans" in urban and town centers.[57] NPA guerrilla units were also reorganized into "larger mobile formations" and ordered to engage the military in set battles aside from the usual "war of the flea" types of confrontations. As NPA attacks, strikes, and urban assassinations increased in tempo and intensity all over Mindanao, so too did the confidence of Mindacom that it would soon enough pressure the Party to adopt the new strategy. And as long as the *welgang bayan* appeared to be working, leaders in the Party center—although expressing discomfort at the deviation—could not do anything.

The excitement also suggested a more fundamental evolution within Mindacom. The series of "autonomous actions" that its cadres initiated not only signified inventive improvisation; more importantly, it evinced the power of a regional body to pursue its own goals independent of its superior's original intentions. In the 1980s, therefore, the surprising expansion of Mindanao communism had two notably contradictory features. On the one hand, a rapid escalation of the revolution occurred both organizationally and in terms of political influence.[58] On the other hand, a growing tension between Mindacom and its superiors developed as the former continued to proceed with its own plans.[59] These fairly common, and perhaps predictable, tensions between the "small tradition" (Mindanao communism) and the super-ordinate and "bigger" counterpart produced a recurring sideshow to accompany the overall drama of a CPP coping with rapid changes after 1983. The calling of a plenum in early 1985 was regarded as an effort to ease the tension while preparing the Party for what was thought of as the final confrontation with the dictatorship by the end of the decade. Kahos changed all this; an aggravating factor was to be the CPP's fatal mistake of boycotting the 1986 elections.[60]

---

[56] In the words of one cadre, the new framework "opened the way for the development of higher forms in the cities, such as the *welgang bayan* . . . coordinated workers' strikes, or a combination of both, up to the preparations for a possible uprising, including local uprisings in the countryside. *All forms of struggle can be creatively combined wherever they can take place, whether countryside, city, town, etc.*"Roberto Sibunga, "Rejoinder to the Theorizing of Armando Liwanag and the CPP Executive Committee on the Mindanao Experience (1983-84)," *Debate* 8 (November 1993): 49.

[57] The "armed city partisans" were essentially urban guerrillas who were to be subordinated to the "urban mass movement." Their responsibilities included selective assassination and collection of arms and other paraphernalia for the larger NPA rural force's use. Jones, *Red Revolution*, p. 137.

[58] See "Ang Ating Walong Taong Pakikibaka sa Mindanaw, 1971-1979," mss [draft written by Mindacom leaders]. Despite the official rhetoric, the divergent impulses were clear in this document.

[59] "Interview with Ricardo Reyes," *Manila Chronicle*, January 19, 1993, p. 5.

[60] See "Politico-Military Struggles in the Main Urban Center," *Debate* 6 (March 1991): 65–71.

THE BREAKDOWN OF MINDANAO COMMUNISM

If demographic changes, active national state intervention, a "neighboring" secessionist war, and an imaginative corps of cadres catapulted Mindanao communism to political prominence (and notoriety), the very same factors would become its bane. For out of these processes emerged conditions which, while allowing Mindanao communists to expand swiftly, also made that growth unsteady and quite brittle.

The resurrection of social and class stratification in settler communities, for example, had as one of its effects the creation of rural underclasses, particularly new tenants and landless peasants. These new groups would be the main sources of mass activist and NPA guerrilla recruits as well as sympathizers of the revolution.

Yet, the appearance of these underclasses also indicate that as settler communities sink their roots into new settings, so also do social relations also become rooted and begin to define how people and groups relate to each other. Simply put, class relations may be unjust, but they also function as a stabilizing agent for communities, especially in settler areas. In Mindanao, this "normalization" of frontier life was derailed at its early stage and thus was not able to set itself upon more enduring foundations.

Table 2. Estimates of Net Migration Exchange for Provinces of
Mindanao and Sulu, 1960-1970 and 1970-1975

Provinces	1960-70	1970-75
Agusan	+60,291	-18,201
Bukidnon	+106,100	+33,808
Cotabato	+127,533	-89,163
Davao	+191,080	+91,586
Lanao del Norte	-21,899	-28,802
Lanao del Sur	-80,128	-15,720
Misamis Occidental	-13,178	-5,705
Misamis Oriental	-6,814	+765
Sulu	-16,098	-76,407
Surigao	-188	+22,310
Zamboanga del Norte	+9,739	+11,597
Zamboanga del Sur	+2,009	-40,341

Source: Michael Costello, "Social Change in Mindanao: A Review of the Research of the Decade," *Kinaadman: A Journal of the Southern Philippines* 6 (1984): 5.

Demographic and migratory patterns were disrupted by the massive population shifts *within Mindanao itself*; these were caused in part by the Muslim secessionist war, but also aggravated by the initial impact of the dictatorship's developmentalist agenda. "Christian" and "Muslim" provinces that adjoined each other experienced constant population changes as the conflict forced people to flee to ethnically congenial areas.[61] In fact, between 1970 and 1975, despite an aggregate population

---

[61] Notes a sociologist: "Large scale migrations occurred after widespread violent clashes broke out between Muslim and Christian groups. [From 1970-75], Muslims appear to have out-migrated heavily from the Christian-dominated provinces of South Cotabato, Davao del Sur

growth due to increased migration, the distribution of migrants was fairly uneven, with the more turbulent areas experiencing out-migration and more stable ones suddenly facing a deluge of new "home-seekers." Table 2 above gives us a sense of the demographic commotion going on during the period.

From the figures one can trace the frequent shifting of people who had very little time to establish themselves at a place of their choice. Social ties, including class relations, had no time to root themselves as people moved from one place to the other. The war with the MNLF in particular created "internal refugees" from out of the affected provinces. Instead, new instabilities began to materialize, partly as a result of renewed competition over land and resources between newcomers and those who preceded them. The tensions would disrupt not only nascent social ties but also social rhythms and routines necessary to steady a community's life.

It is especially worthy to note that in the provinces where the most extensive Kahos killings were said to have been committed—northern Davao, Surigao, Zamboanga del Sur and the Misamis-Bukidnon boundary—population pressure had increased significantly, not so much due to an influx of incoming settlers from northern and central Philippines, but to an incursion of Mindanao residents who had settled on the island but, menaced by war and also seeking better land opportunities, chose to migrate to new provinces. Social ties therefore remained unstable in these areas; the rapid capitalist transformation of the Mindanao countryside would merely exacerbate these instabilities, as settler communities felt the impact of the intrusion of corporate agriculture into their lives.[62]

The changes were not exclusive to the settled countryside. Increased state and capital penetration likewise animated placid urban and town centers, turning them, almost overnight, into "growth points" for economic expansion.[63] These areas began to attract migrants although they were structurally unprepared to absorb them. One immediate effect was an urban version of rural tensions; as one sociologist notes , the "rapid rates of urban growth [became] a two-edged sword [with the] probability that the supply of in-migrating to the cities may exceed the number of viable opportunities found there."[64]

The inability of the urban areas to absorb immigration and the unpreparedness of local officials to anticipate the transformation of their cities into "growth points" resulted in the enlargement of their "slum communities" and uncontrolled urban expansion. In turn social problems arising from constricted urban space, intense competition over available employment, and the emergence of underground economies began to intensify, leading to an increase in criminality, constant violence,

---

and Bukidnon. About half of the Christians living in Muslim-dominated Lanao del Sur departed (also) to other residencies." Michael Costello, "The Demography of Mindanao," in Turner et al., ed. *Mindanao*, p. 54.

[62] Collier eloquently remarked that capitalist transformation was so intense over so short a time that "land and labour [became] alienable commodities rather than socially embedded, [and] traditional institutions [were] destroyed or . . . [had] never been established." See Collier, "The Theoretical Problems of Insurgency," p. 205.

[63] National Economic and Development Authority (NEDA), *Regional Development Projects; Mindanao* (Manila: NEDA, 1974). The identified "strategic leading growth points" included the "cities" of Davao, General Santos, Jolo, Cotabato, Iligan, Cagayan de Oro and Zamboanga. Davao City was supposed to become the regional economic capital of southern Mindanao; Cagayan de Oro for the northeast; and Jolo for the West.

[64] Costello, "The Demography," p. 54.

brutal and brutalized lives, and the prevalent notion that authority and order were either inadequate or non-existent.[65]

What I am suggesting therefore is that the social ties and group identifications necessary to bind communities and individuals together and to stabilize social life in Mindanao were unable to thrive in such an environment. Instead mutable relations continued to predominate in a lot of urban and rural communities and the "normalization of frontier life" never completely transpired even as late as the 1980s. While one may argue that language- or religion-based loyalties did compensate for the frailty of other social and class ties, scholars who advance this argument ignore the fact that these two general buttresses of fidelity were themselves weakened by internal "sub-rifts."

Tensions between Muslims and Christians, for example, were quite pervasive, but so too were rivalries within these two major ethnic and religious categories. Among Christian settlers, endemic divisions based on provinces or regions of origin, as well as language/dialect differences, created constant friction; among Muslims, "age-old tribal differences" among the major groups and between Muslim "elites" and their followings also persisted. These smaller rifts were hidden from outside observers because of the inordinate attention given the generalized religious basis of the conflict as a way of explaining Mindanao's violent landscape. A closer examination within each group, however, will reveal a more nuanced picture that belies the capacity of religion and ethnicity to function as social adhesives.[66]

The Mindanao war, however, did not only displace people, unsettle demographic patterns, and exacerbate rural and urban problems. It also gave an already turbulent frontier society a more violent edge by preserving a continuous state of war which by the 1980s had advanced into the erstwhile peaceful provinces by virtue of the expansion of the CPP. It has been argued that the centralization attempts of the Marcos dictatorship were facilitated by the massive militarization of Philippine society.

Tables 3–5 show that it was Mindanao which bore much of the brunt of state violence compared with other areas. In three important categories of human rights violations, the human cost of state coercion in Mindanao soared rapidly upwards by the 1980s, coincidentally the same period when the CPP underwent its most dramatic growth. Yet, there was more happening here than a magnified exercise of State coercion. The war also created an opportunity for the violence to be spread horizontally. With the MNLF amply supplied by Libya, and the Philippine army benefiting from increased American assistance after Vietnam, the secessionist war gave rise to a proliferation of arms easily obtainable from both sides.

By the late 1970s, the government ban on weapons had become an impotent policy in Mindanao as cheap arms proliferated everywhere, with military men

---

[65] In the case of Davao, for example, see the following: Robert A. Hackenberg, "The Poverty Explosion: Population Growth and Income Decline in Davao City, 1972," (Boulder, CO: Institute of Behavioral Science, University of Colorado, no. 152); Robert A. Hackenberg, "Fallout from the Poverty Explosion: Economic and Demographic Trends in Davao City, 1972–1974," (Davao City: Davao Action Information Center, no. 2). On Mindanao underground economies, see Jonathan R. Asunto et al., "The Makings in (sic) the Underground Economy: A Study," *Mindanao Focus* 26 (1990): 5–26.

[66] None of the Mindanao scholars has taken this issue into consideration. I base my observation on experience as a Mindanao "native" and on observations gathered during my field research in 1991 and 1993.

peddling these weapons of war themselves and even selling them to their new nemesis, the NPA.[67] With "democratized" access to arms, it became easier for people to justify arming themselves as a way of coping with the uncertainties of the times. With arms, one could defend oneself against rivals or seek to eliminate them before they became a threat. Various "armed groups" became conspicuous all over Mindanao, especially in areas where army and guerrilla fighters were involved in intense conflict with one another.

Having weapons facilitated the creation of Mafia-type associations and alliances operating outside of both state and the revolutionary networks which offered services and "protection" to an insecure population, while playing both the military and NPA against each other.[68] The splits within the Muslim armed movement, and active military support for "civilian" anti-communist groups (organized either as militias or "private armies" of politicians), escalated this process. In the 1980s, Mindanao had become a complex landscape where different armed groups competed for space, resources, and attention with communist revolutionaries, army units, and armed secessionists.

Violence was thus gaining acceptance as a "normal way of life" in this frontier zone. Immersed in this condition, the CPP had no problems attracting a steady supply of recruits, supporters, and sympathizers. This beneficial situation, however, was double-edged. It also meant that the types of solidarities and fidelity that the Party hoped to ingrain and strengthen in its mass base would be ultimately as fragile as the other social ties and identifications found in unstable frontiers.

More importantly, the constant state of war, accompanied by widespread availability of coercive resources and blended with the shifting demographics, exacerbated the general state of flux, giving the CPP very little time to consolidate and stabilize its influence over the areas it "controlled." A condition existed wherein the speed of people's attachment to the revolution was equaled by the speed of their subsequent abandonment. This partly explains, for example, why the same "slum" community that was in the early 1980s the stronghold of communist urban guerrillas in Davao, became, after 1986, the stronghold of the anti-communist vigilante group Alsa Masa (People Rise).[69] This brings us to the final issue of Mindanao communism itself. The contextual determination of the remarkable growth of the CPP in Mindanao contradicts the argument that internal "structural" problems determined the expansion and shrinking of the Party. One should note that the Party was already growing at an amazing rate prior to and even despite the "professionalization" of its

---

[67] See the fascinating account of purchasing arrangements set up by Muslim secessionists, NPA guerrillas, and soldiers of the Armed Forces of the Philippines in Mindanao that date as far back as the 1970s in Cynthia de Leon, "Communist Rebels Reveal Arms Sales," *Philippine Daily Inquirer*, February 27, 1992.

[68] R. J. May, "The Wild West in the South: A Recent Political History of Mindanao," in Turner et al., ed., *Mindanao*, pp. 131–133. See also Ronald Edgerton, "Social Disintegration on a Contemporary Philippine Frontier: The Case of Bukidnon, Mindanao," *Journal of Contemporary Asia* 13 (1983): 151–75.

[69] Sheila Coronel, "Davao Diary: Vigilantes hold the City in Thrall," *Manila Chronicle*, April 5, 1987; and, Yazmin Arquiza. "'Alsa Masa' Anti-Communists Growing," *Agence France Press*, February 15, 1987. See also Ronald J. May, "Vigilantes in the Philippines: From Fanatical Cults to Citizens' Organizations," Philippine Studies Occasional Paper 12 (Manoa: Center for Philippine Studies, University of Hawaii at Manoa).

Table 3. Disappearances likely due to Military Arrests or Executions

Year	Manila	Luzon	Visayas	Mindanao	Total
1977	2	11	1	3	17
1978	1	3	4	2	10
1979	2	12	-	34	48
1980	2	17	-	-	19
1981	-	8	-	45	53
1982	-	16	2	24	42
1983	2	13	15	115	145
1984	7	34	24	93	158
1985	11	28	43	129	211
Total	27	142	89	445	703

Table 4. Extra-Judicial Killings Attributed to the Military

Year	Manila	Luzon	Visayas	Mindanao	Total
1977	-	24	21	6	51
1978	1	25	44	16	86
1979	-	56	38	102	196
1980	-	45	36	137	218
1981	-	65	28	228	321
1982	-	46	28	136	210
1983	1	62	41	265	369
1984	2	114	61	361	538
1985	8	53	74	260	395
Total	12	490	371	1,511	2,384

Table 5. Number of Arrests by the Military

Year	Manila	Luzon	Visayas	Mindanao	Total
1977	414	345	214	378	1,351
1978	320	202	193	905	1,620
1979	265	183	111	1,402	1,961
1980	170	125	141	526	962
1981	52	304	255	766	1,377
1982	226	795	76	814	1,911
1983	185	152	108	1,643	2,088
1984	599	375	403	2,725	4,102
1985	737	132	227	3,729	4,825
Total	2,968	2,613	1,728	12,888	19,197

Source: Leonard Davis, *The Philippines: People, Poverty and Politics* (New York: St. Martins Press, 1987), p. 149 (for Tables 3 and 4) and p. 156 (for Table 5)

leadership, and that beneath the revolutionary surge was a delicate foundation that would break down with Kahos.

The pre-1980 expansion of the CPP leading to the eventual formation of Mindacom is not simply attributable to a refined and experienced corps of cadres. Mindanao communist leaders were running the Mindanao section of the CPP like an informal *barkada*, seeing no reason to professionalize the organization. It was only upon the transfer of Manila cadres led by Edgar Jopson, Benjamin De Vera and Magtanggol Roque that the Mindanao leadership began to take the form of a well-organized machine.[70] Thus, the source of the CPP's growth between 1975 and 1980 came not from its cadres' organizing skills but from the social context of Mindanao itself. The CPP's lack of experience was more than made up by a readily available mass of "warm bodies" stirred up by the turbulence of the land frontier. The tragic human and social consequences of Mindanao's transformation and militarization ultimately profited the CPP when it came time to recruit new members—it was an opportunity the CPP could ill-afford to pass up as the recruits, so to speak, were there for the picking.[71]

It was in the dynamic between organizational opportunity and inadequate capacities, however, that institutional weaknesses within the Party would come to light. Foremost among these was the decline in the "quality" of people joining the revolution. In the pre-Mindacom period, the slow pace of Party development may have had disadvantages, but it also had merits. At that time, the process of recruitment and training of cadres into the Party and the NPA could be carefully handled, offsetting the pervasive inexperience and inefficiency among cadre ranks. Stringent security requirements and the slow process of "political education" assured that a reliable core of cadres was being developed, "reliable" in the sense that these new members were familiar with and dedicated to the CPP's cause.

In the Mindacom era, this almost conservative approach to revolutionary growth was replaced by more relaxed recruitment and organizational criteria in response to the deluge of recruits. As Party membership grew, Mindacom leaders applauded the vigor and valor they were witnessing. However, reports from the field increasingly alarmed the leadership, especially when they saw pervasive "ideological problems" within the organization. The Party was turning out exceptionally good protest organizers and guerrilla fighters, but all this was being counteracted by inadequate ideological training, a generally low level of political education, and a simplistic and crude approach to solving problems. A 1980 Mindanao evaluation report admitted that despite the escalation of the revolution, organizational and ideological problems had worsened. The cadre Taquio noted that Mindanao communism's "party-building" phase was notably weak. The absence of a "systematic educational campaign" was paralleled by cadres' "limited familiarity with Marxist tools for assessment and summing up."[72]

---

[70] Pimentel's informants noted that the leadership did not appreciate the need to write reports, conduct regular evaluations of the progress of both legal and underground networks, formulate future plans, and even develop their writing skills! Pimentel, *Edjop*, p. 251.

[71] See Jones's description of an urban poor family whose hatred of the military was matched by its economic deprivation, making its members instant recruits of the revolution. Jones, *Red Revolution*, pp. 140–41.

[72] Taquio cites a 1990 Mindanao report which listed: "problems as to how to systematize and make functional the [political officer's] system, to improve [Party] building and to raise the level of [Marxist-Leninist] military theory [sic] among [its] cadres and forces. [The Mindanao

In the 1980s, these "weaknesses" had worsened as Mindacom began to notice more evidence of "militarist tendencies" in the organization. Often observed was the increasing propensity of the NPA to resort to coercion when attempting to settle land disputes and to dispense with the judicial "people's hearing" before condemning and executing "bad elements" in rural communities. In the towns, executions of "class enemies" and "fascist troops" quickened, opening up occasions for indiscriminate killing.[73] Mindacom had also become aware of the changing credentials of some of the fresh revolutionary recruits; it was increasingly alarmed at the number of activists and guerrillas "with a lumpen background" who were joining the party and who had positioned themselves in the vanguard of its mass mobilizations and military campaigns.[74] The inclusion of these "Robin Hood-types" further burdened a Mindacom facing "difficulty in combining ideological consolidation with other activities." Mindacom tried to put a stop to this alarming development by instituting counter-measures like stepped-up educational training and "ideological consolidation" to complement increased political mobilization. It also issued an order to study other "models" of revolution deemed more appropriate to Mindanao.

In the whirl of the rapidly changing political climate after 1983, however, these counter-measures were never fully implemented; problems of communication between urban and rural areas, as well as between Mindacom and its subordinate units, worsened the predicament. The momentum hastened by the strikes excited and preoccupied Mindacom, which became increasingly absorbed by the upsurge of mass mobilization and an apparent retreat by the state. Growing fascination with the mini-uprisings and hopes that these uprising might act as launching pads for a possible general insurrection prompted calls for consolidation and unity among members. The dictatorship was dying, the revolution was "advancing," and those who called for a slowdown were regarded as conservative, even reactionary.[75] Then Kahos erupted and changed everything.

CONCLUSION

The two remaining questions to ask are these: why was Kahos not replicated in other areas where the CPP had a presence and to what extent was it unique to the Philippine experience?

Given the limitations of this essay already stated in the introduction, here I can only venture some tentative explanations. There were indeed similar cases reported between 1988–91 in Southern Tagalog and Central Luzon, two regions located just outside of Manila.[76] Apart from the killings, however, there were also significant

---

party] also had problems in developing other forms of mass struggles, especially in the areas where there were imperialist extractive industries and comprador plantations. [It] also had problems since 1973 with the liquidation of so-called *demonios* [sic] because there was [sic] no safeguards and regular processes." *Red Book*, p. 154.

[73] "Davao City White Area Preliminary Summing-up: April 1986," in *Red Book*, pp. 171–73.

[74] See, for example, the anxieties of the Davao "White Area Committee" which noted that these types of people were now becoming a substantial force inside the organization. *Red Book*, pp. 171–73.

[75] "1984 Mindanao Commission Summing-up," *Red Book*, p. 157.

[76] In 1982 the anti-infiltration campaign waged in Southern Tagalog led to over one hundred killed and about two hundred arrested and tortured. Like Kahos, the full story of the 1982 executions has not been told, though there are indications that this may come out soon. One

differences between the situations in these regions compared to Mindanao. These were smaller in scale and were immediately checked by a CPP leadership that had learned a painful lesson from Kahos. The structural features in these areas were also different from Mindanao. These two regions had been settled regions, experiencing no social breakdown of the same breadth and intensity as Mindanao's in the postwar period.

Southern Tagalog and Central Luzon were no longer the frontiers that they had been when the CPP re-established its presence in those regions and labored to build on some of its pre-existing social ties while introducing a revolutionary/class element to them. Moreover, the war between dictatorship and revolution may also have been intense in these areas, but it could not compare with the breadth and severity of the violence in Mindanao.[77]

Kahos also distinguishes Philippine communism and the CPP from other Southeast Asian communist parties.[78] First, executions do not normally happen while communists are still fighting for power; they tend occur after the seizure of power.[79] Kahos happened when mechanisms for internal repression that "normally" become central once a party is in power were not even set up yet. Moreover, while most communist parties tend not to admit bloody episodes in their histories, the CPP not only involved itself in this ruthless enterprise, but also discussed it openly.[80] he CPP was still far from the point of needing a Cheka for internal policing. Instead, it relied on and used extensively its own army, whose assumed function at that point in time was to do battle with the state in a much more intense and regular manner. The metamorphosis of the NPA into an internal policing force merely abetted the breakdown leading to the killings.

Mindanao communism thus appeared powerful only on the outside. Internally, its foundations were brittle. Thus, its attempts to position itself among the challeng-

---

problem, as Arguelles admits, is that this precedent "was never fully assessed and summed up, both by the regional leadership or by the central leadership of the party which was certainly well-informed about the campaign." Arguelles, "Kahos," p. 109.

[77] One former Mindacom cadre noted that Mindanao was always on a "war situation" while in other areas the confrontation ebbed and flowed.

[78] Scholars who have studied the Indonesian, Vietnamese, and Malayan communist movements could not recall episodes analogous to the Mindanao tragedy when asked by the author. Even the Khmer Rouge, the most likely to resemble MINCOM, appeared not to have undertaken extensive bloody purges like Kahos before they seized power. See Ben Kiernan, *How Pol Pot Came to Power: A History of Communism in Kampuchea, 1930-1975* (London: Verso, 1985), pp. 308–93. The nearest comparable case, ironically but perhaps not unexpectedly, is the CPP's model—the Chinese communist party. As one China scholar noted: "Chinese communists numbering as many as ten thousand and including 'many excellent, independent-minded people' were accused of being 'Trotskyites' or 'Nationalist agents' and 'eliminated by drowning, burying alive, or death in squalid prisons.'" Perry Link, *Evening Chats in Beijing* (New York: Norton, 1991), p. 145. See also Dai Qing, *Wang Shiwei and 'Wild Lilies': Rectification and Purges in the Chinese Communist Party, 1942–1944* (New York: M. E. Sharpe, 1994), and Frederic Wakeman, Jr., *Policing Shanghai, 1927–1937* (Berkeley: University of California Press, 1994), pp. 158–59.

[79] As Bello puts it: " . . . whereas in other revolutionary movements, similar purges on such a scale took place after the seizure of power, in the Philippines it occurred *before the seizure of power, something which is rare in revolutionary history.*" Bello, "The Crisis," p. 147.

[80] Again the uncanny dissimilarities are clear here: Stalin, Mao, and the Khmer Rouge never really admitted to their deadly enterprises. It was outsiders, academics, the conservative and radical opponents of these regimes, and exiles who exposed these tragedies to the world.

ing forces and pressures of divisive national politics were bound to lead to disaster; Mindacom was primed for a situation like Kahos to happen. With no stable under-pinnings, it was only a matter of time before the organization would crack. As Kahos spread, Mindacom began to lose its political stature; there was little to distinguish its deadly bands of cadres from the rest of the "armed groups" that roamed Mindanao. The CPP's post-1986 general crisis would only exacerbate this particular condition.

ACRONYMS

ACSPPA: Ateneo Center for Social Policy and Public Affairs
ACT: Alliance of Concerned Teachers
AFP: Armed Forces of the Philippines
AKBAYAN: Kaakbay ng Sambayanan (Companion of the People)
ANP: Alliance for New Politics
BARC: Barangay Agrarian Reform Council
BAYAN-MMR: Bagong Alyansang Makabayan—Metro Manila-Rizal
BAYAN: Bagong Alyansang Makabayan (New Nationalist Alliance)
BCC: Basic Christian Communities
BISIG: Bukluran sa Ikauunlad ng Sosyalistang Isip at Gawa (Alliance for the Advancement of Socialist Thought and Action)
CAFGU: Civilian Armed Forces Geographic Units
CARP: Comprehensive Agrarian Reform Program
CBA: Collective bargaining agreement
CHDF: Civilian Home Defense Forces (government militia)
CNEA: Citizen National Electoral Assembly
CODE-NGO: Caucus for Development—Non-government organization
COG: cause-oriented groups
COMELEC: Commission on Elections
COMPEL: Citizens for Meaningful and Peaceful Elections
CPAR: Congress for People's Agrarian Reform
CPD: Council for People's Development
CPP-ML: Communist Party of the Philippines–Marxist-Leninist
CPP: Communist Party of the Philippines
DA: Democratic Alliance
DND: Department of National Defense
DPA: deep penetration agent
EDSA: Epifanio de los Santos Avenue; street where people converged on February 23, 1986 to spark the "People Power" Revolt
FDSM: Federation of Democratic Socialist Movements
FFF: Federation of Free Farmers
FLAG: Free Legal Assistance Group
GABRIELA: women's organization named after a woman rebel who fought the Spanish
GAD: Grand Alliance for Democracy
GO: government organization
IPD: Institute for Popular Democracy
IBP: Interim Batasang Pambansa (national parliament)
IMO: International Mission of Observers

IPER: Institute for Political and Electoral Reforms
JAJA: Justice for Aquino, Justice for All
KAPATIRAN: Kilusan ng Alternatibong Pulitika para sa Inang Bayan
KASAPI: Kapulungan ng mga Sandigan ng Pilipinas (Council of Philippine Forces
KBL: Kilusang Bagong Lipunan (New Society Movement)
KKD: Kilusan para sa Kalayaan at Demokrasya (Movement for Freedom and
    Democracy)
KMP: Kilusang Magbubukid ng Pilipinas (Peasant Movement of the Philippines)
KMU: Kilusang Mayo Uno (May First Movement)
KT-KS: Executive Committee of the Central Committee
KT-MR: Komiteng Tagapagpaganap, Manila-Rizal (Executive Committee,
    Manila-Rizal)
LACC: Labor Alliance Consultative Committee
LFS: League of Filipino Students
LIC: Low-intensity conflict
LP: Liberal Party
MIND: Movement for Independence and National Democracy
MNLF: Moro National Liberation Front
MPD: Movement for Popular Democracy
MPM: Magsaysay for President Movement
MR-KR: Manila-Rizal Regional Party Committee
NACFAR: National Advocacy Committee for Fisheries and Aquatic Resources
NAFP: New Armed Forces of the Philippines
NAJFD: Nationalist Alliance for Justice, Freedom and Democracy
NAJFD: Nationalist Alliance for Justice, Freedom, and Democracy
NAMFREL: National Movement for Free Elections (1950s); National Citizens
    Movement for Free Elections (1980s)
ND: national democratic, National Democrats
NDF: National Democratic Front
NEDA: National Economic Development Authority
NFSW: National Federation of Sugar Workers
NGO: non-government organization
NMCL: National Movement for Civil Liberties
NPA: New People's Army
NPC: Nationalist People's Coalition
NUSI: National Union of Sugar Industries
ODA: Official Development Assistance
OIC: Officer-in-charge
PAHRA: Institute for Political and Electoral Reform
Pandayan: Pandayan para sa Sosyalistang Pilipinas (Forgers for a Socialist
    Philippines)
PBSP: Philippine Business for Social Progress
PC: Philippine Constabulary
PCFC: Philippine Constabulary Forward Command
PCHRD: Philippines-Canada Human Resource Development Program
PDP-LABAN: Partido Demokratiko Pilipino–Lakas ng Bayan (Philippine
    Democratic Party–Strength of the People)
PDSP: Philippine Democratic Socialist Party

PHILDHRRA: Partnership for the Development of Human Resources in the Rural
    Areas
PKP: Partido Komunista ng Pilipinas
PMA: Philippine Military Academy
PnB: Partido ng Bayan (People's Party)
PNP: Philippine National Police
PO: people's organization
PPCRV-MCQC: Parish Pastoral Council for Responsible Voting–Media Citizens
    Quick Count
PPP: Philippine Progressive Party
PRRM: Philippine Rural Reconstruction Movement
RAM: Reform the Armed Forces Movement
SD: social democratic, social Democrats
SMO: Social movement organization
SOT: Special Operations Teams
SPP: Solidarity for People's Power
TriPARRD: Tripartite Program for Agrarian Reform and Rural Development
VISCOM: Visayas Commission

CONTRIBUTORS

Patricio N. Abinales is visiting assistant professor at the Department of Political Science, Ohio University (Athens). He is finishing his dissertation on State Formation and the Development of Local Power in Mindanao, Southern Philippines, and commencing work on a documentary history of the Community Party of the Philippines.

Vincent Boudreau is assistant professor of Political Science and Director of the Masters' Program in International Relations at City College of New York. His research interests include Southeast Asian social movements and popular culture, and he has written most extensively on social protest in the Philippines. He is currently undertaking research on the relationship between the process of state formation and the rise and development of movements in Southeast Asia.

Eva-Lotta Hedman is a PhD candidate in the Department of Government, Cornell University. She is finishing her dissertation on Participatory Crises and Critical Elections in the Postwar Philippines. Her research focuses on questions of modernity—mass mobilization and social engineering; political hegemony and public culture—in the twentieth-century Philippines.

Benedict Tria Kerkvliet is professor at the Department of Political and Social Change, Australian National University, and author of *The Huk Rebellion: A Study of Peasant Revolt in the Philippines* (1977) and *Everyday Politics in the Philippines: Class and State Relations in a Central Luzon Village* (1990), both published by the University of California Press. He also co-edited the book, *Everyday Forms of Peasant Resistance in Southeast Asia* (1986).

Rosanne Rutten is lecturer at the Anthropological-Sociological Center of the University of Amsterdam. She is the author of *Women Workers of Hacienda Milagros: Wage Labor and Household Subsistence on a Philippine Sugarcane Plantation* (1982), and *Artisans and Entrepreneurs in the Rural Philippines: Making a Living and Gaining Wealth in Two Commercialized Crafts* (1990).

Kathleen Weekley is a PhD candidate at the Department of Government and Public Administration, University of Sydney. She is finishing her dissertation on the strategy debates within the Communist Party of the Philippines.

SOUTHEAST ASIA PROGRAM PUBLICATIONS
Cornell University

Studies on Southeast Asia

Number 35   *Nationalism and Revolution in Indonesia,* George McTurnan Kahin, intro. Benedict R. O'G. Anderson (reprinted from 1952 edition, Cornell University Press, with permission). 2003. 530 pp. ISBN 0-87727-734-6.

Number 34   *Golddiggers, Farmers, and Traders in the "Chinese Districts" of West Kalimantan, Indonesia,* Mary Somers Heidhues. 2003. 316 pp. ISBN 0-87727-733-8

Number 33   *Opusculum de Sectis apud Sinenses et Tunkinenses (A Small Treatise on the Sects among the Chinese and Tonkinese): A Study of Religion in China and North Vietnam in the Eighteenth Century,* Father Adriano de St. Thecla, trans. Olga Dror, with Mariya Berezovska. 2002. 363 pp. ISBN 0-87727-732-X.

Number 32   *Fear and Sanctuary: Burmese Refugees in Thailand,* Hazel J. Lang. 2002. 204 pp. ISBN 0-87727-731-1.

Number 31   *Modern Dreams: An Inquiry into Power, Cultural Production, and the Cityscape in Contemporary Urban Penang, Malaysia,* Beng-Lan Goh. 2002. 225 pp. ISBN 0-87727-730-3.

Number 30   *Violence and the State in Suharto's Indonesia,* ed. Benedict R. O'G. Anderson. 2001. Second printing, 2002. 247 pp. ISBN 0-87727-729-X.

Number 29   *Studies in Southeast Asian Art: Essays in Honor of Stanley J. O'Connor,* ed. Nora A. Taylor. 2000. 243 pp. Illustrations. ISBN 0-87727-728-1.

Number 28   *The Hadrami Awakening: Community and Identity in the Netherlands East Indies, 1900-1942,* Natalie Mobini-Kesheh. 1999. 174 pp. ISBN 0-87727-727-3.

Number 27   *Tales from Djakarta: Caricatures of Circumstances and their Human Beings,* Pramoedya Ananta Toer. 1999. 145 pp. ISBN 0-87727-726-5.

Number 26   *History, Culture, and Region in Southeast Asian Perspectives,* rev. ed., O. W. Wolters. 1999. 275 pp. ISBN 0-87727-725-7.

Number 25   *Figures of Criminality in Indonesia, the Philippines, and Colonial Vietnam,* ed. Vicente L. Rafael. 1999. 259 pp. ISBN 0-87727-724-9.

Number 24   *Paths to Conflagration: Fifty Years of Diplomacy and Warfare in Laos, Thailand, and Vietnam, 1778-1828,* Mayoury Ngaosyvathn and Pheuiphanh Ngaosyvathn. 1998. 268 pp. ISBN 0-87727-723-0.

Number 23   *Nguyễn Cochinchina: Southern Vietnam in the Seventeenth and Eighteenth Centuries,* Li Tana. 1998. Second printing, 2002. 194 pp. ISBN 0-87727-722-2.

Number 22   *Young Heroes: The Indonesian Family in Politics,* Saya S. Shiraishi. 1997. 183 pp. ISBN 0-87727-721-4.

Number 21   *Interpreting Development: Capitalism, Democracy, and the Middle Class in Thailand,* John Girling. 1996. 95 pp. ISBN 0-87727-720-6.

Number 20   *Making Indonesia,* ed. Daniel S. Lev, Ruth McVey. 1996. 201 pp. ISBN 0-87727-719-2.

Number 19   *Essays into Vietnamese Pasts,* ed. K. W. Taylor, John K. Whitmore. 1995. 288 pp. ISBN 0-87727-718-4.

Number 18   *In the Land of Lady White Blood: Southern Thailand and the Meaning of History*, Lorraine M. Gesick. 1995. 106 pp. ISBN 0-87727-717-6.

Number 17   *The Vernacular Press and the Emergence of Modern Indonesian Consciousness*, Ahmat Adam. 1995. 220 pp. ISBN 0-87727-716-8.

Number 16   *The Nan Chronicle*, trans., ed. David K. Wyatt. 1994. 158 pp. ISBN 0-87727-715-X.

Number 15   *Selective Judicial Competence: The Cirebon-Priangan Legal Administration, 1680–1792*, Mason C. Hoadley. 1994. 185 pp. ISBN 0-87727-714-1.

Number 14   *Sjahrir: Politics and Exile in Indonesia*, Rudolf Mrázek. 1994. 536 pp. ISBN 0-87727-713-3.

Number 13   *Fair Land Sarawak: Some Recollections of an Expatriate Officer*, Alastair Morrison. 1993. 196 pp. ISBN 0-87727-712-5.

Number 12   *Fields from the Sea: Chinese Junk Trade with Siam during the Late Eighteenth and Early Nineteenth Centuries*, Jennifer Cushman. 1993. 206 pp. ISBN 0-87727-711-7.

Number 11   *Money, Markets, and Trade in Early Southeast Asia: The Development of Indigenous Monetary Systems to AD 1400*, Robert S. Wicks. 1992. 2nd printing 1996. 354 pp., 78 tables, illus., maps. ISBN 0-87727-710-9.

Number 10   *Tai Ahoms and the Stars: Three Ritual Texts to Ward Off Danger*, trans., ed. B. J. Terwiel, Ranoo Wichasin. 1992. 170 pp. ISBN 0-87727-709-5.

Number 9   *Southeast Asian Capitalists*, ed. Ruth McVey. 1992. 2nd printing 1993. 220 pp. ISBN 0-87727-708-7.

Number 8   *The Politics of Colonial Exploitation: Java, the Dutch, and the Cultivation System*, Cornelis Fasseur, ed. R. E. Elson, trans. R. E. Elson, Ary Kraal. 1992. 2nd printing 1994. 266 pp. ISBN 0-87727-707-9.

Number 7   *A Malay Frontier: Unity and Duality in a Sumatran Kingdom*, Jane Drakard. 1990. 215 pp. ISBN 0-87727-706-0.

Number 6   *Trends in Khmer Art*, Jean Boisselier, ed. Natasha Eilenberg, trans. Natasha Eilenberg, Melvin Elliott. 1989. 124 pp., 24 plates. ISBN 0-87727-705-2.

Number 5   *Southeast Asian Ephemeris: Solar and Planetary Positions, A.D. 638–2000*, J. C. Eade. 1989. 175 pp. ISBN 0-87727-704-4.

Number 3   *Thai Radical Discourse: The Real Face of Thai Feudalism Today*, Craig J. Reynolds. 1987. 2nd printing 1994. 186 pp. ISBN 0-87727-702-8.

Number 1   *The Symbolism of the Stupa*, Adrian Snodgrass. 1985. Revised with index, 1988. 3rd printing 1998. 469 pp. ISBN 0-87727-700-1.

SEAP Series

Number 19   *Gender, Household, State: Đổi Mới in Việt Nam*, ed. Jayne Werner and Danièle Bélanger. 2002. 151 pp. ISBN 0-87727-137-2.

Number 18   *Culture and Power in Traditional Siamese Government*, Neil A. Englehart. 2001. 130 pp. ISBN 0-87727-135-6.

Number 17   *Gangsters, Democracy, and the State*, ed. Carl A. Trocki. 1998. Second printing, 2002. 94 pp. ISBN 0-87727-134-8.

Number 16   *Cutting across the Lands: An Annotated Bibliography on Natural Resource Management and Community Development in Indonesia, the Philippines, and Malaysia*, ed. Eveline Ferretti. 1997. 329 pp. ISBN 0-87727-133-X.

Number 15   *The Revolution Falters: The Left in Philippine Politics after 1986*, ed. Patricio N. Abinales. 1996. Second printing, 2002. 182 pp. ISBN 0-87727-132-1.

Number 14   *Being Kammu: My Village, My Life*, Damrong Tayanin. 1994. 138 pp., 22 tables, illus., maps. ISBN 0-87727-130-5.

Number 13   *The American War in Vietnam*, ed. Jayne Werner, David Hunt. 1993. 132 pp. ISBN 0-87727-131-3.

Number 12   *The Political Legacy of Aung San*, ed. Josef Silverstein. Revised edition 1993. 169 pp. ISBN 0-87727-128-3.

Number 10   *Studies on Vietnamese Language and Literature: A Preliminary Bibliography*, Nguyen Dinh Tham. 1992. 227 pp. ISBN 0-87727-127-5.

Number 9   *A Secret Past*, Dokmaisot, trans. Ted Strehlow. 1992. 2nd printing 1997. 72 pp. ISBN 0-87727-126-7.

Number 8   *From PKI to the Comintern, 1924–1941: The Apprenticeship of the Malayan Communist Party*, Cheah Boon Kheng. 1992. 147 pp. ISBN 0-87727-125-9.

Number 7   *Intellectual Property and US Relations with Indonesia, Malaysia, Singapore, and Thailand*, Elisabeth Uphoff. 1991. 67 pp. ISBN 0-87727-124-0.

Number 6   *The Rise and Fall of the Communist Party of Burma (CPB)*, Bertil Lintner. 1990. 124 pp. 26 illus., 14 maps. ISBN 0-87727-123-2.

Number 5   *Japanese Relations with Vietnam: 1951–1987*, Masaya Shiraishi. 1990. 174 pp. ISBN 0-87727-122-4.

Number 3   *Postwar Vietnam: Dilemmas in Socialist Development*, ed. Christine White, David Marr. 1988. 2nd printing 1993. 260 pp. ISBN 0-87727-120-8.

Number 2   *The Dobama Movement in Burma (1930–1938)*, Khin Yi. 1988. 160 pp. ISBN 0-87727-118-6.

Cornell Modern Indonesia Project Publications

Number 75   *A Tour of Duty: Changing Patterns of Military Politics in Indonesia in the 1990s*. Douglas Kammen and Siddharth Chandra. 1999. 99 pp. ISBN 0-87763-049-6.

Number 74   *The Roots of Acehnese Rebellion 1989–1992*, Tim Kell. 1995. 103 pp. ISBN 0-87763-040-2.

Number 73   *"White Book" on the 1992 General Election in Indonesia*, trans. Dwight King. 1994. 72 pp. ISBN 0-87763-039-9.

Number 72   *Popular Indonesian Literature of the Qur'an*, Howard M. Federspiel. 1994. 170 pp. ISBN 0-87763-038-0.

Number 71   *A Javanese Memoir of Sumatra, 1945–1946: Love and Hatred in the Liberation War*, Takao Fusayama. 1993. 150 pp. ISBN 0-87763-037-2.

Number 70   *East Kalimantan: The Decline of a Commercial Aristocracy*, Burhan Magenda. 1991. 120 pp. ISBN 0-87763-036-4.

Number 69   *The Road to Madiun: The Indonesian Communist Uprising of 1948,*
Elizabeth Ann Swift. 1989. 120 pp. ISBN 0-87763-035-6.

Number 68   *Intellectuals and Nationalism in Indonesia: A Study of the Following
Recruited by Sutan Sjahrir in Occupation Jakarta,* J. D. Legge. 1988.
159 pp. ISBN 0-87763-034-8.

Number 67   *Indonesia Free: A Biography of Mohammad Hatta,* Mavis Rose. 1987.
252 pp. ISBN 0-87763-033-X.

Number 66   *Prisoners at Kota Cane,* Leon Salim, trans. Audrey Kahin. 1986. 112 pp.
ISBN 0-87763-032-1.

Number 65   *The Kenpeitai in Java and Sumatra,* trans. Barbara G. Shimer, Guy Hobbs,
intro. Theodore Friend. 1986. 80 pp. ISBN 0-87763-031-3.

Number 64   *Suharto and His Generals: Indonesia's Military Politics, 1975–1983,* David
Jenkins. 1984. 4th printing 1997. 300 pp. ISBN 0-87763-030-5.

Number 62   *Interpreting Indonesian Politics: Thirteen Contributions to the Debate,
1964–1981,* ed. Benedict Anderson, Audrey Kahin, intro. Daniel S. Lev.
1982. 3rd printing 1991. 172 pp. ISBN 0-87763-028-3.

Number 60   *The Minangkabau Response to Dutch Colonial Rule in the Nineteenth
Century,* Elizabeth E. Graves. 1981. 157 pp. ISBN 0-87763-000-3.

Number 59   *Breaking the Chains of Oppression of the Indonesian People: Defense
Statement at His Trial on Charges of Insulting the Head of State, Bandung,
June 7–10, 1979,* Heri Akhmadi. 1981. 201 pp. ISBN 0-87763-001-1.

Number 57   *Permesta: Half a Rebellion,* Barbara S. Harvey. 1977. 174 pp.
ISBN 0-87763-003-8.

Number 55   *Report from Banaran: The Story of the Experiences of a Soldier during the
War of Independence,* Maj. Gen. T. B. Simatupang. 1972. 186 pp.
ISBN 0-87763-005-4.

Number 52   *A Preliminary Analysis of the October 1 1965, Coup in Indonesia (Prepared
in January 1966),* Benedict R. Anderson, Ruth T. McVey, assist.
Frederick P. Bunnell. 1971. 3rd printing 1990. 174 pp.
ISBN 0-87763-008-9.

Number 51   *The Putera Reports: Problems in Indonesian-Japanese War-Time Cooperation,*
Mohammad Hatta, trans., intro. William H. Frederick. 1971. 114 pp.
ISBN 0-87763-009-7.

Number 50   *Schools and Politics: The Kaum Muda Movement in West Sumatra
(1927–1933),* Taufik Abdullah. 1971. 257 pp. ISBN 0-87763-010-0.

Number 49   *The Foundation of the Partai Muslimin Indonesia,* K. E. Ward. 1970. 75 pp.
ISBN 0-87763-011-9.

Number 48   *Nationalism, Islam and Marxism,* Soekarno, intro. Ruth T. McVey. 1970.
2nd printing 1984. 62 pp. ISBN 0-87763-012-7.

Number 43   *State and Statecraft in Old Java: A Study of the Later Mataram Period, 16th
to 19th Century,* Soemarsaid Moertono. Revised edition 1981. 180 pp.
ISBN 0-87763-017-8.

Number 39   Preliminary Checklist of Indonesian Imprints (1945-1949), John M.
Echols. 186 pp. ISBN 0-87763-025-9.

Number 37   *Mythology and the Tolerance of the Javanese,* Benedict R. O'G. Anderson.
2nd edition 1997. 104 pp., 65 illus. ISBN 0-87763-041-0.

Number 25   *The Communist Uprisings of 1926–1927 in Indonesia: Key Documents,* ed.,
            intro. Harry J. Benda, Ruth T. McVey. 1960. 2nd printing 1969. 177 pp.
            ISBN 0-87763-024-0.

Number 7   *The Soviet View of the Indonesian Revolution,* Ruth T. McVey. 1957. 3rd
            printing 1969. 90 pp. ISBN 0-87763-018-6.

Number 6   *The Indonesian Elections of 1955,* Herbert Feith. 1957. 2nd printing 1971.
            91 pp. ISBN 0-87763-020-8.

Translation Series

Volume 4   *Approaching Suharto's Indonesia from the Margins,* ed. Takashi Shiraishi.
            1994. 153 pp. ISBN 0-87727-403-7.

Volume 3   *The Japanese in Colonial Southeast Asia,* ed. Saya Shiraishi, Takashi
            Shiraishi. 1993. 172 pp. ISBN 0-87727-402-9.

Volume 2   *Indochina in the 1940s and 1950s,* ed. Takashi Shiraishi, Motoo Furuta.
            1992. 196 pp. ISBN 0-87727-401-0.

Volume 1   *Reading Southeast Asia,* ed. Takashi Shiraishi. 1990. 188 pp.
            ISBN 0-87727-400-2.

Language Texts

INDONESIAN

Beginning Indonesian through Self-Instruction, John U. Wolff, Dédé Oetomo, Daniel
    Fietkiewicz. 3rd revised edition 1992. Vol. 1. 115 pp. ISBN 0-87727-529-7. Vol.
    2. 434 pp. ISBN 0-87727-530-0. Vol. 3. 473 pp. ISBN 0-87727-531-9.

Indonesian Readings, John U. Wolff. 1978. 4th printing 1992. 480 pp.
    ISBN 0-87727-517-3

Indonesian Conversations, John U. Wolff. 1978. 3rd printing 1991. 297 pp.
    ISBN 0-87727-516-5

Formal Indonesian, John U. Wolff. 2nd revised edition 1986. 446 pp.
    ISBN 0-87727-515-7

TAGALOG

Pilipino through Self-Instruction, John U. Wolff, Maria Theresa C. Centeno, Der-Hwa
    V. Rau. 1991. Vol. 1. 342 pp. ISBN 0-87727—525-4. Vol. 2. 378 pp. ISBN 0-87727-
    526-2. Vol 3. 431 pp. ISBN 0-87727-527-0. Vol. 4. 306 pp. ISBN 0-87727-528-9.

THAI

A. U. A. Language Center Thai Course, J. Marvin Brown. Originally published by the
    American University Alumni Association Language Center, 1974. Reissued by
    Cornell Southeast Asia Program, 1991, 1992. Book 1. 267 pp. ISBN 0-87727-506-
    8. Book 2. 288 pp. ISBN 0-87727-507-6. Book 3. 247 pp. ISBN 0-87727-508-4.

A. U. A. Language Center Thai Course, Reading and Writing Text (mostly reading), 1979.
    Reissued 1997. 164 pp. ISBN 0-87727-511-4.

A. U. A. Language Center Thai Course, Reading and Writing Workbook (mostly writing),
    1979. Reissued 1997. 99 pp. ISBN 0-87727-512-2.

KHMER

Cambodian System of Writing and Beginning Reader, Franklin E. Huffman. Originally published by Yale University Press, 1970. Reissued by Cornell Southeast Asia Program, 4th printing 2002. 365 pp. ISBN 0-300-01314-0.

Modern Spoken Cambodian, Franklin E. Huffman, assist. Charan Promchan, Chhom-Rak Thong Lambert. Originally published by Yale University Press, 1970. Reissued by Cornell Southeast Asia Program, 3rd printing 1991. 451 pp. ISBN 0-300-01316-7.

Intermediate Cambodian Reader, ed. Franklin E. Huffman, assist. Im Proum. Originally published by Yale University Press, 1972. Reissued by Cornell Southeast Asia Program, 1988. 499 pp. ISBN 0-300-01552-6.

Cambodian Literary Reader and Glossary, Franklin E. Huffman, Im Proum. Originally published by Yale University Press, 1977. Reissued by Cornell Southeast Asia Program, 1988. 494 pp. ISBN 0-300-02069-4.

HMONG

White Hmong-English Dictionary, Ernest E. Heimbach. 1969. 8th printing, 2002. 523 pp. ISBN 0-87727-075-9.

VIETNAMESE

Intermediate Spoken Vietnamese, Franklin E. Huffman, Tran Trong Hai. 1980. 3rd printing 1994. ISBN 0-87727-500-9.

* * *

Southeast Asian Studies: Reorientations. Craig J. Reynolds and Ruth McVey. Frank H. Golay Lectures 2 & 3. 70 pp. ISBN 0-87727-301-4.

Javanese Literature in Surakarta Manuscripts, Nancy K. Florida. Vol. 1, *Introduction and Manuscripts of the Karaton Surakarta*. 1993. 410 pp. Frontispiece, illustrations. Hard cover, ISBN 0-87727-602-1, Paperback, ISBN 0-87727-603-X. Vol. 2, *Manuscripts of the Mangkunagaran Palace*. 2000. 576 pp. Frontispiece, illustrations. Paperback, ISBN 0-87727-604-8.

Sbek Thom: Khmer Shadow Theater. Pech Tum Kravel, trans. Sos Kem, ed. Thavro Phim, Sos Kem, Martin Hatch. 1996. 363 pp., 153 photographs. ISBN 0-87727-620-X.

In the Mirror: Literature and Politics in Siam in the American Era, ed. Benedict R. O'G. Anderson, trans. Benedict R. O'G. Anderson, Ruchira Mendiones. 1985. 2nd printing 1991. 303 pp. Paperback. ISBN 974-210-380-1.

To order, please contact:

Cornell University
SEAP Distribution Center
369 Pine Tree Rd.
Ithaca, NY 14850-2819 USA

Online: http://www.einaudi.cornell.edu/southeastasia/publications
Tel: 1-877-865-2432 (Toll free – U.S.)
Fax: (607) 255-7534

E-mail: SEAP-Pubs@cornell.edu
Orders must be prepaid by check or credit card (VISA, MasterCard, Discover).

Lightning Source UK Ltd.
Milton Keynes UK
UKHW030700080221
378223UK00017B/247